The Raiser's Edge

Tournament-Poker Strategies for Today's Aggressive Game

The Raiser's Edge

Tournament-Poker Strategies for Today's Aggressive Game

Bertrand "ElkY" Grospellier,
Lee Nelson, Tysen Streib, and Tony Dunst

Huntington Press
Las Vegas, Nevada

THE RAISER'S EDGE

Tournament-Poker Strategies for Today's Aggresive Game

Published by
> Huntington Press
> 3665 Procyon St.
> Las Vegas, NV 89103
> Phone (702) 252-0655
> e-mail: books@huntingtonpress.com

ISBN: 978-1-935396-48-2
Library of Congress Control Number: 2011930170
$34.95US

Front Cover Photo: Copyright Neil Stoddart
Back Cover Photo: Copyright 2011 WPT Enterprises, Inc.
ElkY Author Photo: Copyright PokerStars (photo by Neil Stoddart)
Front Cover Design: OLO, Laurie Cabot
Book Design & Production: Laurie Cabot

Dedication

We would like to dedicate this book to
tournament poker players all over the world and
to express the pleasure it gives us to play with all of you.

Acknowledgments

From Bertrand "ElkY" Gropsellier:

I would like to thank Jacques Zaicik for his tireless help and encouragement, which have made my poker career possible and successful. Stephane Matheu not only helped in the creation of this book, but assisted me in uncovering my true potential. Likewise, my mother's continuous support and love have given me the confidence to achieve anything I want. Finally, I acknowledge PokerStars for believing in my potential from the start and giving me the chance to excel at the highest level at the game I love.

From Lee Nelson:

I would like to acknowledge and thank Huntington Press for their dedication to poker publications, both domestically and internationally, and Deke Castleman, the best editor in the business.

From Tysen Streib:

I would like to thank my wife Allison and my son Matthew for their love and dedication during my long working hours.

From Tony Dunst:

I'd like to acknowledge those who along the way saw opportunity and potential in my eccentricity and provided encouragement, including Kyle Kirkland, Lee Nelson, and the WPT.

The Raiser's Edge has been published in French
under the title *Kill ElkY* by MA-Editions.
To order the French version, go to
www.ma-editions.com.

Contents

Preface

"Poker mirrors life. Successful poker players, and those successful in life, are able to effectively utilize incomplete information, incorporating probabilistic thinking to evaluate risk-reward ratios of
various undertakings (or hands), read the people with whom they're
interacting, and make determinations that, over the long run, are
likely to be profitable.

—Lee Nelson

How This Book Came About

Kill Everyone, a collaboration among Lee Nelson, Tysen Streib, and Steven Heston, introduced a number of advanced concepts for new-school tournament play. Characterized by increased aggression and playing a wider range of hands than the old-school tight-aggressive strategy, new-school players are more unpredictable than those of the old-school. In *Kill Everyone,* concepts such as hand selection, fold equity, fear equity, equilibrium strategies for short-stack play far from the money, bubble factors, tournament odds, and an equilibrium push/fold strategy for heads-up play were discussed in detail.

Lee and "ElkY" (the PokerStars screen name of French poker pro Bertrand Grospellier) met on the tournament trail. It turned out that ElkY had read *Kill Everyone* and was impressed with its content. He agreed not only to spearhead *Kill Everyone's* translation into French, but also to comment on the places in the text where he agreed, and where his approach differed from that of the authors. The resulting book was called *Kill ElkY,* and when a new English edition of *Kill Everyone* was published, ElkY's comments were included.

Tournament poker, both live and online, is constantly evolving. The clear trend is toward looser and more aggressive (LAG) play. In online play, this "laggy" style has become widespread, with players moving chips around at dizzying speeds. As more and more of these talented young online players find their way into live tournaments around the globe, these contests are becoming accordingly more aggressive.

ElkY, Lee, Tysen, and their associates have had numerous discussions regarding this trend and its implications. Now more than ever, identifying player types and tendencies and making appropriate adjustments is critical to tournament success.

In this book, we bring you up to speed with the current state of tournament play. We provide details for all stages of tournament play, and illustrate how and why the loose-aggressive style works and how to defend against it. We analyze 3-bet and 4-bet strategies and reveal an equilibrium strategy based on ranges. We closely scrutinize a number of new-school techniques that have changed the way the game is played. In light of the suspension of the biggest online poker sites in the United States, we've added a bonus Appendix at the end of the book on reading tells to enhance and perfect your live play.

Some readers, even those who have played for decades, may not be familiar with some of the terms and abbreviations used in the modern-day game. Thus, we have provided a complete Glossary, starting on page 359, for all the terms and abbreviations used in this book. It might be beneficial for some readers to peruse this Glossary prior to reading the rest of the book.

All authors contributed to all chapters, but each chapter has a "main author," who sometimes writes in the first person. The main author for the following chapters is:

> Chapter 2, ElkY
> Chapter 3, Tony Dunst
> Chapter 9, ElkY
> Chapter 10, Tony Dunst
> Chapter 12, Tysen Streib
> Chapter 16, Tysen Streib
> Appendix I, Steve van Aperen,
>   with comments from Lee Nelson
> Appendix II, Tysen Streib

This is not a book for beginners. Our target audience is intermediate and advanced tournament players, both online and live. If you fit this bill and want to improve your tournament play, then this book is for you.

Part One
General Concepts

1

Evolution of the Game

Poker is an evolving game. Part of the beauty of poker is that because there are so many game strategies and personal styles, there's no perfect way to play that results in a win every time. Certain styles are effective against some players, but make you a perfect victim for others. Players tend to establish trends, creating a herding effect as they gravitate toward the same strategies. The herd has moved over the last decade, and strategies and styles have shifted.

Overall, the general trend is that tournament poker styles of play have become more loose and aggressive over the last few years. Actually, online play may already be *too* loose. A few years back, the game was too tight, and aggressive players were able to exploit that by opening up their range. Today, the trend may be starting to go the other way around, as tighter ranges seem to be the way to counter the current loose patterns. Online play tends to lead the way in setting new trends, with live play lagging behind a bit. This is generally because online players are playing a vastly greater number of hands and have a multitude of tools that break down the math of the game instantly over a large sample size, from which they can more easily study patterns.

Since today's game probably won't be tomorrow's, no book can prepare you fully for the way things will change between when it's written and when you read it. Therefore, the best thing we can do is teach you how to think. If we can teach you how to think about situations in general—how to rationalize in all situations rather than copying a formula—then you can survive no matter how quickly the playing climate changes.

In the next couple of sections, we take a quick look at adjustments and counter-adjustments that have occurred with some popular plays, such as the squeeze play, 3-betting, and 4-betting. We review these in more depth later in the book.

Raising and Calling

New strategies evolve because players find them to be more effective against the current norm. Poker isn't solitaire; your best response depends on how your opponents play. The subtleties go beyond this, obviously, but let's take a look at the evolution of the overall strategies of raising, 3-betting, 4-betting, etc. and calling.

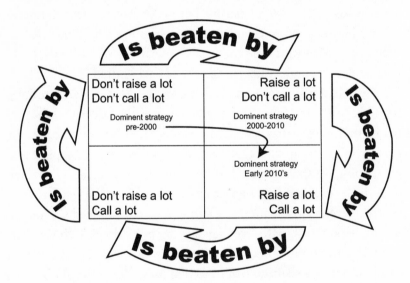

The current trend in poker is moving toward hyper-LAG play and huge raising wars with wide ranges. People's natural response to this in the short term has been to get even more laggy than before. In chart form it looks something like the following:

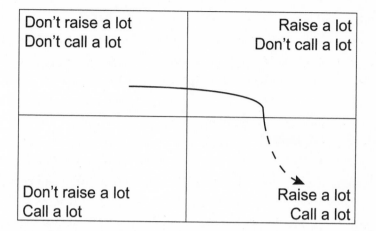

Because this trend can't sustain itself, it will eventually implode. A much more likely scenario is that the good players will eventually curve back and hang around the middle of the chart, which is sort of an equilibrium spot. Since poker is all about exploiting your opponents' strategies while not allowing them to exploit you, that equilibrium spot will be the default starting strategy until the advanced player understands who he's dealing with. At that point, he can leap out in any appropriate direction to take advantage of any situation that presents itself.

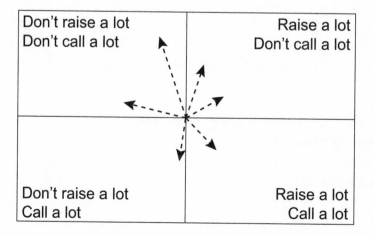

Online Evolution

Nowhere is the LAG style more evident than online, which seems to undergo a serious evolution and major metagame adjustments every six months. Co-author Tony Dunst often alternates between periods of heavy online play and heavy travel for live poker and had the following thoughts on the matter:

"I find that if I go traveling for even just a few months at a time, when I get home, things online have changed to a noticeable degree. Optimal shoving and calling ranges have been adjusted and people's flop aggression has normally increased. Some guys who used to be regulars are hardly playing and guys I've never heard of are suddenly smashing it. Players have accumulated an increased number of statistics displayed by their tracking software, and are increasingly understanding how to use them. Having done this kind of cycle a few times now, I've come to understand that every time I go away, I should anticipate spending my first month back focusing on study as much as play, just to make sure I don't fall behind the trends. From what I can tell, the best way to learn what the current metagame online is like is to read up on poker-strategy forums, as people will often discuss what they believe to be the standard play in given situations. Too bad what's standard keeps changing!"

Live tournaments, though increasingly filled with players coming from an online background, are still evolving at a much slower pace. So by practicing online a lot and staying up on all the new patterns, we can stay way ahead of what will normally happen next live.

Squeezing, Smooth-Calling, Three-Betting, Four-Betting, and More

Here are a few examples of recent poker evolution. In 2008, the squeeze play was a very popular move, especially online. After a while, a counter-move appeared: smooth-calling a pre-flop raise with a big hand, in order to disguise the strength of the holding. Before the squeeze-bet era, it was a much more standard move simply to re-raise with a big pair, such as KK or AA.

Another evolution is that former "squeezers" now tend to smooth-call more often with hands that have good post-flop value in order to preserve potential equity. For example, let's say you and your opponent both have medium-sized stacks. There's a raise from middle position and a call on the cutoff. If you're on the button holding 55 and squeeze by 3-betting, you might have to give up on all the equity if one of your opponents 4-bets you, because you would have to fold most of the time. On the other hand, if you flat-call, you're giving yourself a chance to flop a set and win a huge pot for a much cheaper price—for example, if the flop comes something like A-5-J and your opponent holds AJ-AK, or a chance to outplay your opponent post-flop. In our opinion, most new-school players tend to squeeze more frequently with hands that have no post-flop value, such as K5o or 92o, and with these types of holdings, they'll either fold or re-raise in position when they find a good squeeze spot. As a result, squeezing ranges nowadays are very polarized—that is, either premium holdings that players are ready to play for all their chips, or hands that have practically zero post-flop value.

Four-bets pre-flop, especially heads up, are usually quite polarized too, at least when it involves two competent players with big stacks, especially online. Therefore, 4-betting hands such as JTs or 99 in those spots, considering there isn't some crazy history and your opponent isn't likely to 5-bet shove light, will have you relinquishing all equity in the pot if your opponent has the goods and 5-bets it. So, by 4-betting those hands, we win the pot vs. 3-bet bluffs. However, we could have probably sensed weakness somewhere along the way, and if the 3-bettor has trash and isn't that crazy, he'll give up on the turn anyway. But when he does have a monster, we give him the opportunity to come over the top for a bet large enough so that we have insufficient odds to call.

There was also a time when late-position raising became very popular in order to steal the blinds and antes. The counter that evolved was to 3-bet with air from the blinds, and a counter to the counter was introduced with the light pre-flop 4-bet. Today, we're at a point where players are even starting to 5-bet semi-light! In some spots now, because 4-betting is so popular, when you 3-bet very aggressive players in certain spots, especially in a late-position raising war (also known as a "leveling war"), you have to be ready to 5-bet if you have a hand with decent equity; otherwise, you're just asking to get owned by the new breed of hyper-LAG adepts.

Plays such as this require an understanding of your opponent's style and the courage to go with your read and pull the trigger with the full knowledge that if you're wrong, your odds of avoiding elimination are slim. Taking risks like this against certain players, especially online, is necessary for success in today's game.

Thin Value Bets

Another pattern that has recently evolved is thinner value bets. The good thing about thin value bets is that they allow you to mix up your range much more effectively. For example, if you bet the river with 2nd pair or top pair on a 4-card straight, you'll keep your opponents guessing. When executing a value bet this thin, make sure that your opponent is either a calling station, or a thinking player who's either unaware how thin you bet (and believes you have a polarized range), or who thinks you have a very high bluffing frequency.

However, some players will exclusively bet either as a bluff or with the nuts on such boards. Against these opponents, it's easier to make calls with weaker hands, such as ace-high or bottom pair, because their range is polarized—either they have the straight or flush, or they're bluffing. Additionally, other players at the table who don't have an advanced thought process will see you making what appears to be an incredible call and you'll gain fear equity. Add thin value betting to the mix and it's no longer so easy for others to make such calls.

A counter to thin value bets is to check-raise on the river, either with a strong hand or a missed draw. This strategy also needs to be implemented in a balanced way to be effective. Remember, in order to pull it off as a bluff, your opponents must also know that you might also make the same bet with the nuts. Most players assume that a river check-raise is a monster hand until proven otherwise (e.g., they see you run a river check-raise bluff), so assume that will be their read in all situations when there isn't a serious history between you. With the aggression factor in today's game, by the time you get to the river, the pot is often huge and a river check-raise, except at early levels, would be for a big portion of the stacks. It's definitely an advanced move and takes a lot of guts to spring a river check-raise for your whole stack with complete air. Because you wouldn't usually expect many opponents to do so, this move earns a lot of power.

C-Betting

Here's another example of the changing game. Thanks to Dan Harrington's revelations about continuation betting, players used to c-bet almost 100% of the ace-high boards, especially heads-up and in position against the blinds, but also often in 3-way pots. The counter became to check-raise on the flop more and more frequently.

For example, the initial raiser continuation bet an A-2-2 board almost all the time. Today, due to the increased likelihood of getting check-raised, the initial raiser tends to check behind, even with hands that are likely best in that spot, such as AJ. As a result, delayed c-bets have appeared, where the initial raiser c-bets the turn instead of the flop in order to control the size of the pot and reduce variance. Also, the initial raiser usually gets more credit for a turn bet when he has nothing, since it has become a reasonable move to check behind holding an ace when an ace flops.

Another advantage of the delayed continuation bet is that players usually try to check-raise the flop, but are less likely to do so on the turn. If they have a real hand, they'll more often lead out on the turn instead. As a result, the initial raiser can gather more information and get out of the way relatively cheaply.

An interesting counter to players who've become so check-raise happy on boards with a big card and two rags is to bet every time you have top pair with the intention of calling their check-raise and intending to call them down on later streets. However, if you believe they're completely incapable of "triple-barreling" (continuing to bet on every street) in a spot like that as a bluff, you should call their flop check-raise (and a turn bet), then bet the river for value if they check.

These examples illustrate how important it is for players to be aware of the current trends and patterns at any given time.

Geography and History

One interesting point is that the game actually evolves in different ways in various venues on the planet. For example, tournament poker is noticeably more difficult in the United States than in Australia, because the game is more popular in the U.S. and the quality of information has had a longer period of time to saturate the community. Across Europe, different countries and regions have originated their own styles. The Scandinavians, for example, are most famous for their highly aggressive, tricky, and developed form of the game. In Asia, Korean players have picked up the hyper-LAG style and quite a number of them are using it in live tournaments.

Identifying opponents who have good basics and understanding of tournament poker, as opposed to the ones with limited skills and experience, should determine the way you adjust your game when you play against each category. The earlier you can gauge your opponents' capabilities, the more profitable your strategy will be.

In many cases, you may have a prior history with opponents from previous tournaments, particularly if you play many tournaments in the same region (such as Lee Nelson and Tony Dunst do in Australasia, which has a comparably small player base compared to Europe or North America). If you reach a stage where you become a tournament regular, keep in mind what kind of reputation precedes you to the table. With people you've played with before, keep in mind that dramatic hands will stand out in their memory more so than small ones. You might play fairly tight, but if one of the players on the table has seen you caught out in a couple of large bluffs you've run, he's likely to consider you far more aggressive than you actually are. The adjustment to make there is to play him straightforward and start value betting very thin against him.

Even if you're a total unknown to your table, keep in mind what kind of assumptions people will make based on your age, style of dress, the way you handle your chips, and the other aesthetic details we discuss in Chapter 4 on hand reading. If Lee Nelson (who's in his 60s) and Tony Dunst (who's in his 20s) sit down at a table together where neither of them is known by any players, Lee is able to get away with far more aggression before people adjust than Tony can, because of the assumptions people make about players of Lee's age.

2

The Metagame

The metagame is an increasingly important aspect of the modern game. As conceptually illustrated in Chapter 1, the metagame is the psychological game that exists among players, involving adjustments and counter-adjustments based on how an opponent is likely to interpret a given set of actions. Better players adjust their strategies and styles to those of particular opponents, always analyzing how the opponents are playing in terms of how the opponents *believe* they're playing. Sklansky and Miller sum up the metagame as "trading small mistakes for bigger ones from your opponents."

Maintaining a well-balanced strategy, while deciphering your opponents' strategies, is key to the metagame. If you comprehend the concept of the metagame, accurately perceive the flow of your table and the tournament, and stay alert to and aware of current strategy trends, you'll be able to successfully mix up your play when considering your image and that of your opponents. In return, your game will be highly unpredictable and difficult to read, which should be your ultimate goal.

A Perfect Example

A recent World Championship of Online Poker (WCOOP) tournament provides an excellent look at the metagame.

Lee drew a table that stayed intact for many hours and included Team Pokerstars pros Juan Maceiras on his immediate right and WSOP Main Event winner Joe Cada seated next to Juan. All three had been involved in a number of hands characterized by aggressive play. After about five hours, with blinds and antes of 150/300/40, the following hand came up.

It was passed around to Cada in the hijack; he made his standard raise to 750 off a stack of 22,600. Maceiras 3-bet to 2,100 off a stack of 19,500 from the cutoff, then it was folded around to Cada who 4-bet to 5,700. Juan then 5-bet to 9,300 and Joe insta-6-bet shoved! Maceiras tanked, then called.

Cada held 99. Maceiras had A8o (getting about 3-to-1, Juan was priced in and had to call).

This leveling war typifies the aggression that's becoming common in online tournaments. As Cada said after the hand, "You don't think he was playing me, do you?" Lee commented that Maceiras was obviously playing the player.

Maceiras lost the hand and was eliminated.

About an hour or so later with blinds and antes at 250/500/60, it was passed around to Cada in late position and he raised to 1,350 off a stack of 40,000. Lee 3-bet to 3,000 (from 22,700) and Cada 4-bet to 6,250. Lee 5-bet to 10,000 and Joe 6-bet all-in. Lee called.

Cada held JJ. Lee had AA.

From a metagame perspective, this betting sequence almost exactly paralleled the prior 6-bet hand that Cada had won, which may have made Cada suspicious because it *should* have been indicative of extreme strength, but could easily be the leveling war again, because of this very factor. Since the sequence is meant to indicate extreme strength, and given the earlier precedent, this might be an ideal spot for Lee to 5-bet light. With JJ, Cada decided to shove, this time to his detriment.

Online Versus Live

The metagame is very different live and online. Betting sequences such as these are more common online than live. In most cases live, a sequence such as this would table AA versus KK. This fact also plays directly into the online metagame, where representing AA or KK seems to be happening with ever-increasing frequency.

An example is Joe Cada at the WSOP Main Event final table 2009. The game is 3-handed. Joe Cada, with 39 BB, raises from the SB with 22. Antoine Saout, with 80 BB, 3-bets with QQ from the BB. Cada moves all-in fairly quickly. Regardless of the fact that Cada flopped a set, he later said that he considered his move to be "standard," which to us means that it was "standard" for Joe Cada's online strategy.

Earlier, when play was still 9-handed at the same table, Phil Ivey folded JJ to a re-raise from Antoine Saout (who held 77). Again, this fold probably wouldn't have been "standard" online.

In short, the metagame and table flow are constantly changing and evolving, even throughout any given tournament. It brings to mind a quote I like to think I invented that nicely sums it up: "In poker, there's never an always." And Tysen has a similarly themed statement: "Every poker rule has its exception—even this one."

Styles of Play

Tournaments are played so differently now than they were several years ago that they're almost a different game. The loose-aggressive style and hyper-LAG styles are very effective. Experts in these styles of play also demonstrate good judgment, exercise pot control, stay aware of stack sizes, and alter their play accordingly. They also mix their game up to remain unpredictable. Tough!

Maniacs carry these styles to an extreme, but there's a fine line between the hyper-LAG and the maniac, the difference being a modicum of judgment. While there have always been maniacs in poker, they now seem to be appearing in record numbers, much like a contagious disease. This extremely high-variance style is suboptimal, but one must be careful not to get swept away in the onslaught.

Loose-Aggressive

A loose-aggressive player plays a very wide range of starting hands, which makes him unpredictable. Unpredictability is definitely one of the key strengths of the LAG style, since the player can hold any two cards at any time.

LAG players also have a higher-than-average bluffing frequency. Since they play so many marginal and bad hands that will often miss the flop, they must bluff a lot in order to take down pots without a showdown. Fold equity is a big part of their game.

Hyper-LAG

Hyper-LAG players play even more hands than LAG players, and tend to show even more aggression. Their 3-betting and calling frequencies are extremely high.

Very often hyper-LAG bluffs need to be substantial and on multiple streets, since their image is usually poor and opponents tend not to believe them. However, the fact that they can have any two cards and are capable of putting their opponents under a lot of pressure works in their favor.

Perhaps the best way to illustrate this is to follow a prototypical hyper-LAG, the Dutch player Lex "Raszi" Veldhuis, and his action in the early stages of the 2009 WSOP Main Event. Lex draws a tough table, including Alan Cunningham and Eli Elezra, but immediately goes to work. With blinds at 100/200 and all players deep-stacked, Eli raises to 600 with pocket 4s and Raszi immediately takes control of the hand by 3-betting to 2,300 from the SB with 97o, then leading for 3,300 on a flop of A-6-5 rainbow and getting Eli to fold; he shows the bluff.

Shortly thereafter at the same blind level, Raszi raises to 600 from middle position with KJo; Simon Muenz, a 22-year-old-German player, calls with 7♥6♥ IP. The flop is T♣-7♠-6♣. Muenz bets 1,100 and Veldhuis raises to 5,000! Muenz calls. The turn: Q♣.

This turn card gives Raszi an open-ended straight draw, but puts a possible flush on the board (although neither player has a club).

Raszi bets 6,800; Muenz tanks a bit and calls. The river: 4♣!

With four clubs now on board, Veldhuis leads for 7,000, a bluff designed to look like a value bet with a big flush. Not holding a club, Muenz folds his winning two pair. Again, Veldhuis shows the bluff!

At the next blind level, Veldhuis is after Muenz again. Muenz raises with T♠T♥ and Raszi calls IP with K♠6♠; Cunningham also calls in late position with AJo. The flop is 4♠-3♥-2♥. Muenz checks, Raszi bets 2,300, Cunningham folds, and Muenz calls. The turn: 9♥. Muenz checks, Raszi bets 6,300, Muenz calls. The river: A♠.

Muenz checks again and Raszi announces, "All-in!" He has Muenz well-covered. Muenz tanks and folds. Raszi again shows the bluff!

This sets the stage for an amazing hand. A new arrival raises to 1,050 with blinds still at 150/300. Elezra calls with KTo and Raszi squeezes with K♠4♠, 3-betting to 4,000. Muenz, apparently having enough of Velhuis, moves in over the top for 18,800 with 7♥6♥; it's folded around to Velhuis, who weighs things up. Having plenty of chips and given his history with Muenz, getting 1.7-to-1 and probably not wanting to taint his image by backing down, Raszi makes the call—and wins!

The hyper-LAG style requires extremely high-variance play. It's crucial for players of this style to pick their spots really well.

Maniac

The new breed of young Korean players is truly maniacal. Of course, there are maniacs in every country; Korea, however, seems to spawn them in schools!

Some of these players may 3-bet you with any hand and from any position. It makes it very difficult to play against them, especially when they have a big stack. They're fearless and they don't like folding. They may 5-bet all-in light at an early stage of a tournament.

Players who can 5-bet all-in at the early stages with QT have substantial fear and fold equity and are sometimes able to accumulate mountains of chips early on. However, this strategy can also backfire when they get caught. Usually, if they miss one big bluff early, they get knocked out of the tournament pretty quickly.

The difference between a hyper-LAG and a maniac is often judgment. Playing against them, you need to pick your spots well. Maniacs seldom fold or give up when engaged in bluffs. They're usually the easiest type to trap, as compared to the LAG and hyper-LAG.

Maniacs also tend to be unable to change gears and slow down as the tournament progresses and therefore don't last very long. It's important to note that good hyper-LAG players are, on the other hand, capable of playing the maniac style at times, but can also slow down and go back to more plain LAG play, depending on the tournament phases.

Advantages

Unpredictability. Unpredictability gives the hyper-LAG player credibility for making aggressive plays at any point. Because they play so aggressively, they can take control of the hand on many different boards.

For example, if any 6 or 7 on the river will complete a straight, they'll most often try to represent that they're holding that card. Since it's totally plausible that they indeed hold that card, and since their opponents may be crippled if they call and lose, hyper-LAGs put other players to a high-risk guess. Many players back down and fold, aware that there may be better spots to get their chips in.

Constantly putting opponents to a guess. Opponents are mostly reluctant to play against hyper-LAGs, because they know it'll often be for a big pot and come along with tough decisions.

Before antes. Against old-school players who only play big pots with big hands, the hyper-LAG strategy is extremely exploitive and profitable, especially early on in tournaments.

With antes. Hyper-LAGs accumulate a lot of chips once antes start, due to their high frequency of pre-flop raises, many of which go unchallenged, because other players may try to avoid them. However, as stacks get shallower, hyper-LAGs usually have less and less room to maneuver. Indeed, stacks are better suited for all-in moves on the flop or the turn, and pre-flop, which definitely takes away a part of the ability to bully opponents with a hyper-aggressive style.

How to Use the Hyper-LAG Style

As long as opponents let you steal, keep doing it!

Always be aware that you're walking a fine line, and that any bluff can end up costing you a lot of chips.

It's important to distinguish the line between hyper-LAG and maniac and not fall into the wrong category by being overly aggressive. Maniacs will eventually get trapped and be out of the tournament.

Variance is the key factor in the hyper-LAG style. If you elect to use this style, your play will be high variance. However, there are some things you can do to try to control variance whenever applicable. Bluffs and the ability to use scare cards to your advantage are a critical component of the hyper-LAG style. However, even when you bluff appropriately, there's always a chance your opponent may actually have a hand, so you'll have to risk a lot of chips in almost every hand you play.

Eventually, opponents will play back at you and you'll have to be ready to 5-bet with hands that are much less than premium, as seen in earlier examples.

Personally, I'm more in favor of a balanced loose-aggressive style than a full-fledged hyper-LAG strategy. If you steal only once in a while, as opposed to systematically, it will take more time for your opponents to figure out what you're doing, and stealing may actually be a little easier, because opponents won't come over the top too often. To play an effective hyper-LAG style, you'll also need to be able to change gears at different tournament stages.

Key Point

If you already have a big stack, avoid high-variance situations. Your play must vary depending on the size of your stack; the negative value of losing x chips is greater than the positive value of gaining x chips when you already have a big stack, especially if you believe you have an edge on the rest of the table.

How to Defend Against the Hyper-LAG Style

Difficulties

In the modern game, defending against the LAG and hyper-LAG styles is arguably the most difficult thing to do. These opponents mix up their game so much that they'll almost invariably put you to a tough decision. It's especially difficult to play against them OOP.

Close to the bubble is the toughest time to face hyper-LAGs, because you're forced to fight back with a lighter range at times, or to give up control of the table at this crucial juncture.

Oversized 3-bets all-in, even though they're obviously high-variance, can be a good counter against hyper-LAGs at bubble time, with hands such as medium pairs (where you wouldn't normally like to make the same move against other opponents). For instance, let's say you have 66 with 60 BB in the big blind. A hyper-LAG has 25-30 BB and raises from the cutoff. This may be a good spot to for you to shove, because it'll be hard for him to call with less than 88+. He may not be ready to play for his tournament life if he's holding KJs, KQs, or QJs. However, if you make only a standard 3-bet, he'll very likely re-shove with such holdings. Therefore, especially around bubble time, a lot of your decisions should account for stack sizes and position, and you need to have fold equity on your side so you can pressure the hyper-LAGs with the threat of elimination.

At the final table, the situation is pretty similar to the bubble. Stack sizes matter a lot. To the best of your ability, confront hyper-LAGs when you're in position, because it'll be much less of a headache. However, as fewer and fewer players remain, you'll definitely have to be ready to play a higher-variance game, dictated mostly by the behavior of your hyper-LAG opponent.

Heads-up, especially when your opponent's 3-betting frequency is high and stacks are fairly shallow, limping on the button more frequently may be a good strategy. Whereas your opponent may move all-in when you open with a min-raise, he won't be able to do so if you just limp, which should enable you to see more flops, especially with hands that have good flopping value. Of course, you'll have to mix up your limping range as well, from weak holdings to premium hands. When you limp with a monster and get raised, I think it's best just to call and trap your opponent, as he'll often take one or more stabs at bluffing. Hopefully, by the time you get to play heads-up against your opponent, you'll have assessed his style well enough to set a trap at the right time!

We'll talk more about heads-up play in Chapters 15 and 16.

What To Do

To play against hyper-LAGs, you have to increase your game variance. These are definitely the type of opponents against whom you can make some hero calls, since you know they seldom give up when they engage in a big bluff. They'll 3-barrel bluff quite often.

Hyper-LAGs tend to think that people will make a lot of moves on them. Therefore, it may be easier to set a squeeze trap for them with a premium hand.

Avoid squeeze attempts with marginal hands against hyper-LAGs. Their 4-betting frequency is way too high for squeezes to be profitable in the long run. Therefore, unless you're ready to play for all your chips, it's better not to re-raise pre-flop too often against hyper-LAGs. Calling 4-bets from hyper-LAGs, especially out of position, is optimal only with monsters.

There's no middle ground. Either play really tight or really aggressively to fight back. If you decide to play back at them, you should do so once antes commence, rather than early on when pots are smaller. Before antes, I think the best strategy against hyper-LAGs is to wait for a big hand and try to set a trap. For instance, you may just flat-call a raise from the BB with KK and check-call all the way, unless the board is really too scary, because your opponent will usually fire three times. However, as always, you need to use good judgment and be able to adjust. Indeed, the good hyper-LAG players have an extraordinary ability to sense troublesome situations and dodge bullets. If you make a stand against a hyper-LAG, it's better if you play tighter than your image may suggest, because it'll be easier for you to trap your opponent.

Try to get involved when you're in position. More than against any other opponent's profile, you should try to control pot sizes against hyper-LAG players, which is always easier to do when you're in position. Additionally, you should try to play a little tighter than the hyper-LAG opponent's pre-flop range. However, there's no getting around the fact that you need to prepare yourself to play big pots.

Hyper-LAGs call light as well, so avoid shoving speculative hands such as 76s, as Muenz did at the WSOP.

It might sometimes be possible to 4-bet light if you decide to use counter-aggression and project a tight image, but first make sure your opponent is not crazy enough to 5-bet all-in with air!

If you decide to 3-bet with AK against a hyper-LAG early on, you should be ready to play for all your chips pre-flop, because you're usually ahead of your opponent's range. This is nevertheless a very high-variance spot.

If you have a big stack or your table is about to break soon, tighten up and avoid clashes.

Beware of weak leads and fake blocking bets from hyper-LAGs; your opponent could actually have a big hand. If you raise, it gives him an opportunity to come over the top to represent a strong hand.

Against predictable players, you can sometimes raise for information (with the intention of folding to a re-raise) and take down pots this way. This isn't a move likely to work against hyper-LAGs, though, not to mention that by doing so, you're the one potentially increasing variance in a significant manner. Again, you should focus on pot control and raise when you have a hand with which you're ready to commit.

Suppose there's only one hyper-LAG at the table and you have a comfortable stack. When stacks are deep and you're getting a decent share of table control, you'll sometimes be better off avoiding the overaggressive opponent—even if you have to fold hands that are way ahead of his range. This is especially true if you have to play OOP. Your range should be tighter OOP, unless another bad player is already in the pot, because this will serve as some kind of protection for you. Smarter hyper-LAGs will seldom bluff the biggest calling stations. So if, for example, you're in the big blind and a hyper-LAG opens from mid-position and gets called by a calling station in the small blind, it's a decent spot to get in with a bit of a wider range than you'd usually call with heads-up. The hyper-LAG will bluff less, plus the value you can get from the calling station makes this play feasible. But be wary of all parameters and how good, or smart, the hyper-LAG is. Maniacs don't care about calling stations and are just going to rapid-fire anyway.

Check/raising your big hands, especially on the river, is a good strategy to extract maximum value against hyper-LAGs, who will 3-barrel a lot.

Thin value bets could also be effective against hyper-LAGs, because they tend to call down very frequently, thinking their opponent may be making moves on them.

There is, unfortunately, no single counter-strategy to universally employ against hyper-LAGs, which is why their style is so effective. You simply have to be ready to play high variance and bigger pots, closely observe your opponent's tendencies, and exercise good judgment to pick the right spots.

Ranges and Pot Control

The Hyper-LAG's Range and Yours

When you decide to play against hyper-LAGs, stay away from hands that don't have very strong flopping value. Otherwise, you'll get pushed off pots way too often after the flop. When you face a hyper-LAG, your range should go from pocket pairs to big Broadway cards that can flop top pair. You probably won't be able to semi-bluff with draws as you would versus more "regular" players.

If you're deep and the hyper-LAG opponent tends to 3-bet you too much, you can loosen up your calling range a little bit (e.g., with KJ suited, even OOP sometimes), mostly because you don't want him to think he can bully you all the time.

Examples

Lex Veldhuis and Dario Minieri are arguably the most famous hyper-LAG pros in today's game. Dario is a borderline maniac sometimes. At the WSOP HU championships 2009, Dario 5-bet all-in with 83o, since his opponent had 4-bet a third of his stack already with KK. Regardless, both Dario and Lex are extremely problematic to play against. They float a lot, lead a lot, and raise a lot. In addition, they never seem to be ready to give up on a hand once they get involved.

At the EPT Deauville Hi-Roller 2009, I have 100+ BB in the hijack. Villain 1, Dario Minieri, has 200+ BB on the button. Villain 2, a French pro in the BB, has 100+ BB with 9♣7♣.

I hadn't opened a pot for a while. I raise 2.5 BB from the hijack and Dario 3-bets to 6.5 BB from the button. From the BB, a good French pro 4-bets to 18 BB. Of course, it's an easy fold for me. The action comes back to Dario, who 5-bets really big. The player in the BB folds, but shows 9♣7♣. To return the favor, Dario shows Q♥T♥! As you can see, you're walking through an unpredictable minefield when playing against hyper-LAGS!

River Play

Playing the river against hyper-LAGs presents both danger and opportunity. Whether to check-call or value bet hands such as top pair is opponent-dependent.

For example, on the river against a crazy opponent with a medium-strong holding, it might be better to check and call any bet, hoping to catch a bluff (unless you have enough history and/or clues that tell you your bet will look exactly like a value bet with a strong hand, though not the nuts). If your opponent would raise you there as a bluff a good part of the time and you're prepared to call, it can be very profitable. It's also the highest-variance choice possible.

Examples

You have KJ on a board of K♥-T♥-6♠-5♣-4♥.

If you bet on the river here, your opponent might put you on QJ or hearts. He might not raise with the weaker flushes. This is dependent on action on previous streets and the size of your bet, though. If you've check/called twice and now lead for anything more than 66% of the pot on the river, he probably won't raise with anything lower than a Q-high flush. However, if you check/called on the flop and the turn went check/check, he'll probably raise with all flushes (also depending, on what kind of image he has of you), but will raise most of the time if there's no other way to win the pot. If you bet and he's hyper-laggy, he'll raise with all the hands he would have bet had you checked. He's aware also that it's much easier to bluff you off your hand after you've led out, since his raise will look much stronger than just betting when you check to him. Taking all this into account, the standard river line would be to check and evaluate, but usually call, because his betting range is so wide, and frequently your hand will be good.

Against some hyper-LAGS, I like to bet about a third of the pot as a fake blocking bet, planning to call a raise. They'll frequently just get called by worse kings, but will also pick off a number of bluff-raises. Once again, mix it up very well, because the smarter hyper-LAGs will pick up on what you're doing fairly quickly and value raise tons of hands after that—anything two pair or better, I believe.

If you have a monster out of position, mixing it up on the river either by check-raising or leading weak and hoping to get raised is effective. Leading big is suboptimal, because when you lead big on the river, you frequently won't leave a hyper-LAG with enough fold equity to make an aggressive river bluff-raise. A hyper-LAG isn't the kind of opponent who misses a lot of value bets, so the likely range of hands with which he'll call your big bet is all hands he'd have bet anyway if you checked, and he'd also make a decent number of bluffs as well.

For metagame purposes, understand that you shouldn't try to float OOP with weaker hands and attempt river bluffs, especially if you rarely lead big on the river with your monsters. True, your opponent may not have enough history with you to realize that this line differs from the way you'd normally play monsters, but a move like this isn't crucial and, frankly, there are better spots for your money than playing against hyper-LAGs and maniacs OOP and running a big river bluff! Against these styles, it's almost always preferable to play a tighter range.

Be aware that even maniacs tend to tighten up a bit when they get shorter-stacked, especially the smarter ones who realize that their bullying power goes down a level after losing a bunch of chips. Adjust accordingly.

3

Having a Plan

In drama school, when creating a character, actors are taught to ask themselves, "What's my motivation?" When you play a hand of poker, you should always know the answer to the comparable question, which I would phrase as, "What's my plan and what am I trying to accomplish?"

I used to ask for strategy advice on a lot of hands, and a response I repeatedly received from better players was, "What are you trying to do here?" The common mistake I was making in my post-flop play was that I simply wasn't thinking through my decisions and understanding the motivation for my actions. The essence of this idea is: Every time you take an action in a poker hand, you need to know specifically what you're trying to accomplish by making that move. At the beginning or intermediate stages of your poker career, you need to spend even more time thinking through your actions, because you won't have repeated actions enough for situations to be automatic. Even as you become more advanced, it's still important to slow down and think over why you're doing what you're doing and what your plan is, depending on your opponents' actions.

Here's a straightforward example. You often see players raise the flop, get re-raised, then go into the tank, unsure of what to do. If you're going to raise the flop, you first need to think about what you're trying to accomplish. Is it:

- A total bluff?
- A semi-bluff?
- A value raise that hopes to get re-raised?
- A value raise that will fold to a re-raise?

Then, you need to consider how your opponents will react to your raise, based on their holding. You need to assign them ranges, and attempt to anticipate how each part of their ranges will influence their responses to the raise you're thinking about making. After that, you need to consider what your plan is on future streets, based on your opponents' reactions to your raise, and consider how you're going to proceed on various turn cards.

On the surface it sounds like an awful lot to consider, but the more you play and the more situations you go over, the more automatic it becomes. However, at no point should it become so automatic that you don't put any critical thinking into it, because poker has so many complicated variables that, unless you have a computer implanted in your brain, it's impossible to instantly make the optimal decision every time.

The main reason to have a plan is to prevent getting caught up in an unexpected moment, then making a mistake. How many times have you watched a player under 30 BB make a pre-flop 3-bet, then get shoved on, and suddenly have no idea how to react? Players often wind up folding in this situation. This is almost certainly mathematically incorrect against their opponent's range, but in the moment, the player becomes overly concerned about his tournament life and makes a mistake.

You can counteract these kind of errors by thinking through your actions before you make them; if you realize that in a situation like the example above, you aren't comfortable calling a 4-bet, you should simply flat-call instead and make sure you never get pushed off your hand when you have somewhere between 25%-35% of your stack in the middle.

It's perfectly acceptable to make a play, then have something happen that you didn't anticipate and need to think things over.

Having a plan for every potential variable when you open-raise pre-flop is impossible—there are simply too many variables. Numerous times during an average online session, I have to sit back and slowly think everything over when one of my opponents does something I didn't expect him to do. However, because so much tournament poker is played with shorter stacks (particularly online), throughout my day, I usually know what I'll be doing no matter what happens after I take my action, especially in a heads-up pot. Naturally, the more players in the hand, the more complicated things get, due to the increased number of variables.

Here are a couple of ideas for how to practice this concept. Take a day to play just one table online and in every hand that's not incredibly obvious, sit back and ask yourself, "What am I trying to accomplish here?" Don't take any action until you feel fully confident you've thought through every necessary angle.

You can also play heads-up against someone whose game you respect for a meaningful amount of money. During the writing of this book, co-author Lee Nelson and I played a heads-up SNG most nights, and because I know my opponent is thinking so thoroughly about everything I'm trying to do, I find myself sitting back and thinking through everything I believe to be going on in his head too. Even though there's always just one opponent and he's always the same in every hand, because we're so aware of each other's thought process, I'm forced to think on much deeper levels about what I anticipate him doing, what he anticipates me doing, what I anticipate he anticipates me doing, and so forth. Too bad he's beating me at the time of this writing.

When designing plans, you should always think as far ahead as possible. Also, be flexible, accepting that some parts of each plan might change along the way.

On any given street of play, you should have different plans of actions prepared, depending on which opponent you're facing. Let's say you have a big stack and raise 74o from MP to steal the blinds. If a short stack shoves on you, you'll obviously fold 100% of the time. Therefore, before electing to raise, you should definitely consider whether any short stacks will be acting after you. In another case, if you get 3-bet by a big stack you know likes to re-raise for information, you might have a plan to 4-bet with the intention to fold to a 5-bet.

As the hand develops, you should also have different contingencies that depend on what card comes on the next street. Let's say you have K♥T♠ on a Q♥-J♣-2♥ board, and you call a check/raise on the flop. At this point, you should have assessed your opponent's check-raising range and how he might react if the turn either completes a flush or straight draw or bricks out. Your opponent may check/raise on a draw or only with made hands. Based on that evaluation, you should have different plans prepared for what turn and river cards come out. Of course, you'll often need to re-evaluate at each street, but the more different plans you have in your repertoire, the more quickly you'll be able to adjust.

In order to plan right, you must be able to observe and study your opponents as closely as possible, knowing full well that you'll always miss some information. For instance, at the WPT Bay 101 2010, ElkY folded a big missed combination draw in a huge pot when his opponent shoved on the river within the first 30 minutes of play. The next few hands that ElkY watched him play convinced him that this player was very aggressive. A few hours later, he saw that same opponent 4-bet a third of his stack PF with QQ and fold to a 5-bet shove! Obviously, his initial assessment was probably not accurate, and he had to re-evaluate this opponent. This is simply an example to illustrate how important it is to try and assess your opponents' profiles as best you can in order to design appropriate plans, realizing that you must stay aware and flexible enough to re-evaluate periodically based on new information.

4

Hand Reading

Everyone in poker wants to be good at hand reading and it's an excellent skill to possess. Accurate hand reading in modern tournament hold 'em requires calibrating a number of external and internal variables during the hand in an attempt to form a clear image of your opponents' holdings. The external factors are everything outside the immediate hand involved in making your decision; the internal factors are simply the actions in the hand itself.

External Factors

The external factors are everything outside of and leading up to that specific hand. Here they are, in no particular order.

What Your Opponent Looks Like. Is it a he or she? How old is he? What's his nationality? How is he dressed? Does he have any logos on him? Does he look tired and disinterested or alert and attentive? Does he know complicated chip tricks? Does he fumble his cards?

When in doubt, use generalizations and stereotypes. Remember, however, that you should constantly try to acquire and process new information at the table, so you don't have to rely on such broad generalizations.

Gender. Most women players, especially older ones, tend to be more passive than their male counterparts. It's also safe to assume that the men on the table will perceive women to be passive and weak, and therefore may attempt to bully them. There may be ample situations where you might punish players attempting to bully women on the table. Additionally, women's raises tend to get more respect—especially large raises post-flop and all-in bets pre-flop. Female players should take advantage of this perception.

Age. For the most part, older poker players tend toward being tight, passive, and straightforward. Co-author Lee Nelson, who's in his golden years, enjoys taking advantage of this perception on a regular basis. Some have been playing for decades and are prone to habits of old-school strategy, while others are simply new and recreational players with some dispensable income or savings. Young players frequently come from an online background, particularly those in a higher-buy-in live tournament, since most men under the age of 30 aren't wealthy enough to fork over $3,000 or more just to take a shot at a poker tournament purely for enjoyment.

Nationality. Many online players we know consider a player's location to be one of the most important pieces of information when making a read. At the table, it may be more difficult to discern where opponents are from when you first sit down, unless you overhear a certain language or players voluntarily discuss their background.

It's hard to generalize about Americans, because there are so many of them and they're culturally diverse, but as a whole, tournaments on American soil are often the toughest, because the game is the oldest and most developed there.

The English seem to have a mostly tight, sensible, and logical approach to poker. The Scandinavians seem to have a cool and calm table presence, mixed with a highly loose-aggressive playing style that employs maximum risk-taking for maximum benefit. A simple rule for Scandinavians goes, "Never bluff, never fold, and value bet thin." Southern Europeans tend to play a bit more loosely than their Northern peers and often seem more emotionally invested than their English or Scandinavian counterparts.

Asian players have a certain degree of creative and unpredictable style to their play, as the game is still in its infancy in many of those countries. Some have very strong luck-based beliefs tied into their game, such as the Chinese belief that the number eight is inherently lucky. The new breed of young Korean players is hyper-loose-aggressive, bordering on the maniacal! As a group, they're probably the most aggressive of any in the game today.

Dress. Very few poker players seem to put serious thought into their clothing for a tournament. Some dress in high style, in which case you should assume that they're successful professionals outside of the poker world, playing the tournament on a mostly recreational basis. A notable exception to this generalization is contributor Tony Dunst, who arrives at all live events in sartorial splendor in Zegna or Hugo Boss suits. Many very wealthy individuals actually have a casual and toned-down style of dress, yet often give themselves away with simple yet noticeable details—an extremely expensive watch or piece of jewelry, or expensive shoes. If a player is wearing an online site's gear, he's one of two things: an online qualifier who is contractually obligated (after winning a satellite) to wear the site's clothes, or a poker enthusiast and aspiring professional not yet aware that most serious professionals wouldn't be caught dead in such attire without being compensated. If a player is wearing both an online site's gear and a patch from that site, he's probably a sponsored professional.

Emotional State. It's very difficult for most people to completely disguise their emotional state at the table. If possible, don't let on about your current emotional state while playing or do anything that is overtly reactionary. Some people make it obvious for you by erupting at the table, taking a walk, or swearing under their breath. Some might take a horrendous beat in stride, yet you'll notice that their play opens up and they become more aggressive, less risk-averse, sometimes making a really bad decision that can cost them the tournament (tilt). Anyone who's tired will likely be more risk-averse and tight, whereas alert and focused players are more likely to have better-developed reads on both you and other players at the table and look for exploitive situations.

Chip and card handling. It should be pretty obvious that someone who's competent at a number of chip tricks or handles his cards elegantly has significant experience at live poker. Additionally, you can probably assume that the opponent isn't predominately an on-line player, since most of them don't spend enough time with chips in their hands to develop such dexterous abilities.

Conversation. With whom has your opponent been chatting? Has he been talking to professionals you recognize in a way that would suggest they're friendly? Has he been talking to a bunch of young guys who are probably online players (when in doubt, assume young guys are online players, particularly if wearing a site's logo)? Has he been discussing strategy at the table (never do this!)? Has he said things that would indicate he's a wealthy professional outside of poker and the money at risk likely isn't important? Have the two of you had any friendly banter that would make you believe he'll play you honestly and straightforwardly (beware of pros, however, who will be friendly, then try to rob you blind!)?

Listening to what a player says leading up to and outside a hand you're involved in informs you of the relevance of what he says when you're his target. Some players, authors included, *never* speak during a hand, and this is what we recommend for readers. There's no bet-ter time to listen in than when a player discusses strategy at the ta-ble, giving away pieces of his thought process to anyone who might bother to overhear.

Paul Phillips, a WPT winner a few years ago, is an excellent example of giving away the store. Lee played with him on a number of occasions and never heard him utter anything that wasn't spot on. He routinely discussed strategy at the table, and his advice was amazingly accurate and insightful, chock full of pearls of wisdom. Not only was this counter-productive, because it wised up the less informed players, but it also gave better players the information they needed to adjust their games when involved with him.

Players often banter after the hand about what they had, what they think their opponent had, why they played their hand the way they did, etc. Although it can be tempting to vent or explain yourself, don't fall into this habit, unless you intend to fill your opponents' heads with false information for a specified purpose. Away from the table, honesty might be the best policy, but on it you should lie, lie, lie! If you bluff a tight opponent, tell him what a good fold he made with top pair against your set. Then bluff him again and ask him if you did something to give away the strength of your hand. Make him feel good about his folds, so you can continue to take advantage of him.

Stage of the tournament. This simple detail can have a great deal of effect on what your opponent is capable of at that moment. Many opponents aren't capable of running a major bluff early in the tournament or in a crucial bubble situation. Conversely, some opponents are especially capable of running a major bluff in a bubble situation, because they know the pressure on their opponent is highest at that moment. Others tighten up so dramatically on a money bubble that they won't get their chips in with less than aces, or as one player, one off the money bubble, put it to Tony after he inquired what would have happened had Tony shoved (with 83o) against his KK pre-flop on a WSOP $1500 event bubble, "Of course I would have folded my kings if you shoved and had me covered. I didn't come all the way from Alaska just to finish 271st!" after having flipped up his 83o and telling him, "You're lucky I'm such a nice guy!" A number of opponents will seem to play quite tight pre-flop up until the moment that antes kick in, then go berserk! Some players are much less risk-averse at the very start, or very end, of a day of play, because busting out results in their feeling as if they've wasted their time.

Previous betting patterns and reads. Most opponents use similar, if not identical, betting patterns in comparable situations. Less-developed opponents are nice enough to even make their pre-flop range highly transparent, simply with their bet sizing. Some might have a standard raise of 2.5X or 3X the BB, but raise to 4X the BB with good hands that are difficult (in their mind) to play post-flop—a range such as 77-JJ, AQ, and AK. Some are the type to continuation bet an enormous percentage of flops, but give up almost every time on the turn when they don't have it, check/folding. Many weaker players only min-raise pre-flop when they have an absolute monster. These players also tend to min-raise post-flop only with a monster, or only with a polarized range (either a very good or a very bad hand).

Normally, the way you discover such details is through observation. When playing optimally, you should watch every single street of every hand at the table and be especially aware of hands that get shown down.

Let's be honest here, though. For most people, that's not particularly realistic. If you know you're the type to get easily distracted by your peers, the TV, the cocktail waitress, or an improbable Kalashnikov-brandishing robber (EPT Berlin 2010), simply make a point to get a sense of how active each player is pre-flop, how wide they defend their blinds, how much they 3-bet pre-flop, whether they take mostly passive or aggressive lines post-flop, and what gets shown down.

Internal Factors

The internal factors in a hand are everything immediately relevant during the hand itself. Here they are, again in no particular order.

Stack Sizes

Always be aware of the stack sizes on the table. Try to make a habit of keeping an eye on what the stacks are like at the table, instead of being forced to ask a player during the hand (unless you're trying to get him to talk to assess how relaxed or nervous he appears to be). Why? Asking has two potential issues. For one, your opponent might miscount or simply lie to you. For another, you give your opponent an insight into your thought process and clue him in that you're intelligent enough to be concerned with that particular detail. However, if you're involved in a hand where you simply don't know how much he has and your view of his stack is obstructed, always go ahead and ask instead of attempting to guess.

Also, always take into consideration how aware your opponent is of stack sizes.

Position

You should, of course, be aware of this detail in every hand you enter. In terms of hand reading, using position is particularly useful when narrowing down an opponent's pre-flop range.

Action on Previous Streets

A great deal of the method used during an actual hand for narrowing and sharpening an opponent's range is essentially a process of elimination. How has the action on previous streets led you to eliminate, or reduce, the probability of certain holdings from your opponent's range, and how has the action affected the way your opponent perceives your likely holdings?

If you've ever attempted to play multiple tables online at the same time, you've probably run into the situation where you've arrived at the turn, or river, but can't remember what happened leading up to that, because you had so much action and so many distractions at other tables. Attempting to make sense of your opponent's range at this moment is extremely difficult. Luckily, such a situation will never happen to you when you're playing live.

Metagame and History with Opponent

You need to think about how the specific history between you and this player affects the variables and ranges of the current hand. Additionally, you need to weigh how your overall image and metagame affect his perception of you and his perception of how you perceive him.

If you have a ton of history with an opponent, you may find yourself in what's known as a leveling war, where both opponents attempt to out-guess each other as to which level of thinking they anticipate the other being on. At times, when you're playing against intelligent opponents and find yourself in a leveling war, an always-safe option is to balance your ranges by playing your hand exactly as you would with your entire range in that situation. This will prevent others from reading any particular pattern or skillfully out-guessing you.

For example, let's assume you've been sitting at the same table for a long time and having a raising and re-raising war with an opponent. You raise from LP and he's the only caller from OOP. The flop is K-2-2. Instead of leveling each other, you should bet, as he might check-raise you with air and you then have to re-raise, etc. An option to avoid the war is to check literally 100% of your range there. That way, you're no longer giving him any information.

Another example would be when there's an A and a flush draw on the turn, and you check-raise your opponent. The river completes the flush draw, and you have only a pot-size bet left. In such a spot, if you have a lot of history with your opponent, you should shove with all your range, whether you have a busted flush draw, a set, the flush, or anything else.

In the same way, let's say you raise with a stack of 35 BB and that same opponent, with a stack of 45 BB, 3-bets you, as he has done many times. If you think his only purpose is to play the leveling war with you, you may have to move all-in with the vast majority of your range in that spot.

Of course, in each of the above examples, you need to be successful in your assessment that your opponent has been playing the leveling war; otherwise, you may end up making costly mistakes.

Basically, all the situations in that spot would be quite marginal, but if you think you're a better player than your opponent, you still might be able to out-guess him. Of course, you risk those costly mistakes, but he'll make them more often!

Sometimes, you'll have to play 100% of your range the same way, but it's better to do it in situations like the K-2-2 flop, where it *decreases* variance, as opposed to the 4-bet shove 100% with 35 BB, where it most likely *increases* it.

Against better players, the betting line you take may vary, but the line you select should have a balanced hand range for unpredictability and take variance into consideration. For example, instead of being ready to 4-bet shove 100% of our range with 35 BB when we get 3-bet by some specific players, another way to be unexploitable is to raise in those particular spots only with hands that you'll happily play for effective stacks, obviously a variable range depending on how many high-frequency 3-betting players are still left to act behind and the different stack sizes. ElkY likes to caution players against increasing variance by doing "automatic" plays, even against better players; even though it might be the best strategy at the time, it's usually not a good way to improve. Marginal situations are the toughest spots in poker, but by avoiding them too much, it could prevent your game from reaching another level, and spots such as these are marginal! If you're at a really tough table, on rare occasion high-variance plays like this may be your only option, and picking the right spot with the right frequency may present the best opportunity. Most often, though, you can set your sights on the highly exploitable players that are usually at the table. That reduces variance, so marginal plays should often be avoided. This is especially true in live play.

Making a read during the hand requires weighing each of these details, calibrating their importance, then reconstructing the hand in an attempt to narrow down your opponent's range to something specific. Here's a hand that Tony Dunst played in the $5,000 WSOP NLHE event in 2008: "The hand occurred with about 45 players left. We were already well into the money and play had gone back to normal, since the bubble had burst some time ago. My opponent was a young and plainly dressed guy who had been quite aggressive with open-raises and had raised with 92o, then called a push for an amount that he was committed to call from a very short-stacked tight player in the big blind. I'd also witnessed him speaking in a familiar and friendly manner with expert online players Ike Haxton and Scott Seiver, so I made the assumption that he, too, was an experienced online player. There was no particular history between the two of us leading up to this hand.

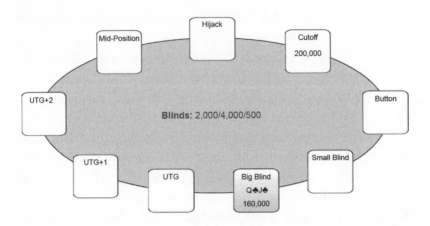

"I hold Q♣J♣ in the BB. Pre-flop, it folds to the cutoff (CO), who raises to 11,000; it's folded around to me and I call. Everything seems pretty standard up to this point. The flop is 4♥-7♠-T♦. I check and the CO checks behind. His check behind seems a bit strange, as I anticipated that he'd c-bet most of his air, all his top pairs, most of his middle or bottom pairs, and any potential draw, such as 65, 86, or 98. It's not unreasonable to think that he'd check behind with strong middle pairs or weak top pairs, for pot control and to induce bluffs from me in order to snap me off on the turn, and probably the river.

"The turn comes Q♥. I lead out 16,000. The CO thinks briefly and announces all-in. I think things over and make the call.

"The turn lead seems pretty standard, though you could check-call as well against some opponents. Given that the board is drawy, I think a bet is better, particularly since I think some of his check-back range is hands with showdown value that could pick off my bluffs.

"When he shoves, though, I have to re-think all the details of the hand and start eliminating pieces of his range. Would he play a set or two pair like this? Probably not, as most of the time he'll either bet the flop with a set or, if he decides to raise the turn, he'll make it an amount that leaves me room to shove over the top, such as raising to something between 40,000 and 50,000. Would he do this with an over-pair? The over-pair seems to be of similar value to the set or two pair, though I think it's even more probable that he bets the flop, and less probable that he simply shoves the turn, since there are very few worse hands he can anticipate getting value out of by taking this line. What about KQ or AQ? Those two hands have almost the exact same value as an over-pair and almost certainly wouldn't be played like this.

"So, what hands could he shove? We know from previous action that he opens an enormous amount of hands pre-flop, so it's possible that he has any number of draw combinations. He can have any of the straight draws, or a hand that's a straight-and flush-draw mix, such as something like J♥9♥, K♥J♥, A♥9♥, etc. He might have a pair-plus-flush-draw combination, such as 7♥6♥, and decide that his showdown value is marginal, and that by shoving I'll fold every ten and most of my queens.

"The more I think about his range, the more it seems likely to contain very few hands that beat me that he'd raise this way for value, and quite a number of hands that have excellent draw equity, but weak showdown value. When I make the call, my opponent taps the table and turns over J♥7♥."

Two More Examples from ElkY

This first example is a hand played in the EPT Monaco Hi-Roller event in 2009.

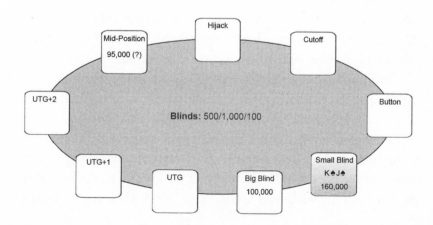

ElkY holds K♠J♠ in the SB. His thought process was this: "I had witnessed the player in MP raise fairly frequently with marginal hands, and he had doubled up on the previous hand with K9 vs. JJ all-in pre-flop.

"Pre-flop, it folds to MP; MP opens to 2,800, then it folds to me in the SB. One line I can use is to 3-bet and call an all-in, but that would be high variance, since I'd probably be facing a coin flip at best. Therefore, I decide to control the variance and flat-call instead. My opponent's stack size is ideal for me to possibly check-raise him all-in on a semi-bluff if I get the right flop, especially if I think he missed the flop. Additionally, it will be no problem for me to commit my stack if I flop top pair or a solid draw.

"Behind me, the BB calls as well. In this kind of situation, I almost entirely rule out the possibility that the BB is holding a strong hand. Indeed, should he have a premium hand, he'd certainly try to isolate the initial raiser with a re-raise. As a result, I can rule out all hands stronger than 99. However, it's certainly possible he could hold a small pair or suited connectors.

"The flop is 3♠-5♠-7♦. With a king-high flush draw and two overcards, my plan is to check-raise the initial raiser, because I think he'll likely continuation bet, which should give me a lot of equity. I check, but unfortunately both my opponents check behind.

"The turn is A♥—arguably the worst card in the deck for my hand. If my opponent is holding an ace, I'm now far behind and my initial plan to check-raise all-in won't get him off the hand now. As a result, I'm ready to give up on the hand should he make a bet. I check, and the BB bets 6,000 into the pot of 11,000. The initial raiser folds and I now have to reassess the situation. Since we're both so deep in chips, it's possible that the BB is holding a lower flush draw than mine. I still believe it's unlikely for him to hold an ace, since he didn't re-raise pre-flop, so I just call out of position.

"The river is 5♥. I check and my opponent bets 18,000. I mentally review all his possible holdings. He could have a small pair such as 44 or 66, which would have given him a gutshot straight draw on the flop, but I think he'd check the river. With a weak ace, I believe he'd also check the river to control the size of the pot. The more I analyze the hand, the more I think my opponent's range is very polarized. Either he's holding a very big hand, such as 75, or he's got a busted draw. I decide to follow my read and call. The BB turns over 9♥8♥ for a busted gutshot straight draw. I rake the pot with K high, gaining chips and a lot of respect from my opponents at the table."

Here's the second example, from a hand ElkY played at the Wynn Classic 2010 Main Event.

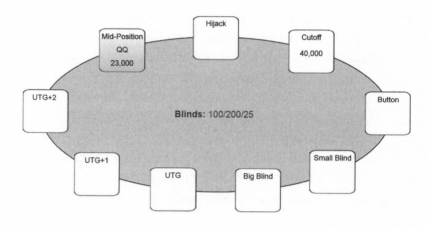

ElkY's read: "I raise 500 with QQ from MP and my opponent calls from the CO. I've seen him play several hands and I think his calling range is very wide.

"The flop is J-8-6 rainbow and I check. In this spot, I check about 30% of the time. Against this specific opponent, the intent of my check is to deceive him by disguising the strength of my hand. I don't like to check-raise in such situations, because I think it increases the variance too much at early stages when stacks are still deep. Rather, my plan is to use a tricky line, such as check-calling both the flop and turn, then betting the river if the board isn't scary. Of course, I'm exposing myself to getting bluffed on the river by a raise sometimes, but I think it's profitable against some opponents, in this case especially if the villain holds a J. The villain checks behind.

"Again, I've seen him play a few hands and he's shown a tendency to bet on straight or flush draws, and even gutshot straight draws. At this point, because he rarely slow-plays his hands, his checking behind tells me I have the best hand.

"The turn is 9♥, which opens the heart flush draw. I don't think this card changes the situation much. Sometimes, the villain can hold 98 or 96, but it's not very likely. If he has 99, I think he would have bet the flop.

"So I still think that I'm ahead, and I decide to take the lead here in order to extract value if he holds a 9, a J, or some kind of a draw. I bet 775 and, to my surprise, he raises me to 2,100. Considering the information I gathered by watching him play earlier hands, I think it's highly unlikely he has QT or T7 in this spot. I think the only likely hands in his range to raise me here are 96, 98, maybe J9, and various draws. I determine that calling here is the best course of action, with a plan to check-call any river card that doesn't complete a straight or a flush draw.

"The river is 4♦. I check and, after tanking for a while, he checks behind. He then shows A♥T♥. As it turned out, my opponent saved himself a river bet, because I would have called."

Another Example from Lee

An interesting hand came up at the October 2010 Poker Stars ANZPT. Lee had about 65,000 chips and the player on his right had recently sat down with 110,000. With blinds and antes of 800/1,600/200, Lee, holding pocket queens, opened UTG to 3,700. It was passed to the new player in the BB, who 3-bet to 10,000. With no history with this player, Lee considered this out-of-position 3-bet after an UTG raise to represent a narrow range: AJs+, AQ+, JJ+. In fact, most players wouldn't 3-bet in that spot with less than AK or JJ+. Lee opted to call in position and re-evaluate on the flop, which came down J-4-4. The 3-bettor checked and Lee checked back, realizing that based on his range determination, he was either way ahead or way behind. The turn was a 7. Lee's opponent now bet 20,000.

Lee tanked, then called. His thinking was that either his opponent had AK or AQ (unlikely) and was taking a stab at the pot, or else he had Lee crushed with JJ, KK, or AA. AJs was also a possibility and his opponent might now be betting for value after Lee's check on the flop. The river brought a third 4. The board now read J-4-4-7-4.

Lee's opponent checked! Lee thought for over a minute before deciding, based on his read, to check it back. If his opponent held AK or AQ, he would fold if Lee bet; if he had JJ, KK, or AA, he'd clearly call. The only hand within his assumed range that Lee could beat was AJ and he wasn't even sure if that hand was in his 3-bet range. QQ was also a remote possibility, but that was also a call. Lee concluded that betting for value was decidedly negative EV. His opponent showed down AA and Lee was still alive in the tournament. Playing the hand any other way would have resulted in elimination.

Part Two

Tournament Play

5

Early-Stage Play
(No Antes, First 3 Levels)

The most significant aspect of early-stage play is the composition of your table. This factor is far more important than hand selection (see *Kill Everyone* for the lowdown on hand selection), especially for the loose-aggressive style of play.

In the early going, it's critical to identify and characterize each of the players at your table. Important variables include the number of hands each player is involved in; whether they limp in or bring it in with a raise; the frequency with which they re-raise an initial raiser (3-bet) both in and out of position; how they respond when they're 3-bet; whether they 4-bet and if so, with what hands; whether they often call a raise pre-flop, then check/fold on the flop, etc. We can't emphasize strongly enough how important it is to pay close attention to the action, especially when you're not involved in the hand. Resist the temptation to chat with other players, to watch the game that's on TV in the poker room to see how your sports bet is doing, or to let personal problems intrude on your observations. *Pay particular attention to hands that are shown down and reconstruct the betting sequence.*

Once you have a handle on every player at your table, you can modify your play to best exploit each opponent. Be aware, however, that a player's style may change as the tournament progresses. For example, a tight player may suddenly get considerably more aggressive and widen his range for raises and 3-bets once the antes kick in. Stay alert and adapt accordingly.

Playing Against Tight Opponents

The normal distribution of player types in a typical high-buy-in deep-stack live tournament is predominantly composed of tight players, one LAG, and one pro. Online, you might encounter more good players, especially in the frequent high-buy-in tournaments that attract a consistent group of tournament regulars. Tight-passive players (weak-tight) are prime targets for loose-aggressive adepts. The timid weak-tight player often limps in pre-flop with a variety of hands, such as small to medium pairs, suited connectors, and non-premium suited Broadway cards, such as ATs, KJs, QTs, etc.

We like to raise to isolate these limpers with a wide range of hands, such as unsuited connectors, K7o+, any suited ace, king, queen, or jack, and suited connectors with up to 3 gaps. If a number of weak-tight players are at your table and several of them have already limped in, don't hesitate to raise when you have position on them. A good guideline is to raise three times the big blind plus one additional big blind for each limper. With blinds of 50 and 100, for example, if three players have limped before the action gets to you, raise to 600. Against weak-tight opponents, you should bet most flops, betting roughly 60% of the pot. If opponents consistently fold when you make these continuation bets, widen the range of hands used to isolate these limpers even further!

You have major earning potential against players of this ilk. Target them and continue to pound on them until either they start to resist and fight back or, more likely, another good player at the table picks up on what you're doing and starts 3-betting you.

If a good player picks up on the "raise-to-isolate-limpers" strategy and starts re-raising in position, start limping more frequently, but make sure you adjust your hand selection. Whereas you may be able to isolate a limper with 95s or 65o for instance, if you start limping more frequently, your range should be tighter, from 1- or 2-gappers to suited connectors and small pairs. Also, be prepared to either call raises more often with speculative hands in position against thinking LAGs or consider 4-betting as a countermeasure. However, avoid playing speculative hands OOP against good LAGs and hyper-LAGs. This is a negative EV play, because it's tough to play hands OOP against these types of players and you won't flop a monster often enough to compensate for the chips you'll bleed while trying. In position, you have more control and more options to make the risk worthwhile.

It's also OK to call a 2-bet from a LAG who raises after several limpers (to isolate) if you have position and are pretty sure that none of the limpers is likely to re-raise. Three-betting a LAG in position with a speculative hand, such as suited connectors and small pairs when he's made what appears to be a raise to isolate limpers, is also a possibility, but this is very player dependent. In today's game, aggressive LAGs and hyper-LAGs won't hesitate to 4-bet you light, and you may have to 5-bet (often all-in) or fold. Obviously, this dramatically increases variance and there are often softer players at the table to exploit. Sometimes, however, you may have to make moves such as this or lose any semblance of control over the table.

Playing "Bust-em" Hands

We first heard the term "bust-em hands" from Daniel Negreanu. A bust-em hand is a speculative hand that usually misses the flop, but when it hits, can produce an unsuspected hand that can bust opponents willing to go to the mat with one-pair hands. When deep-stacked, pros control the size of the pot with one-pair hands, such as AA, KK, or AK (when an ace or king flops), to avoid getting stacked by a bust-em hand. The vast majority of tight players, however, who have been sitting back and waiting for big pairs, are your unsuspecting quarry. Identifying and exploiting this type of player is a critical part of early chip accumulation. Playing unpredictable hands against predictable players is one key to success in the early stages of tournaments. Calling raises from tight players when you're in position can be done with a wide range of hands.

ElkY likes to play small to medium pairs, suited connectors

down to 32, all 1-gap and 2-gap suited connectors down to 42 and 52, respectively, and any two suited Broadway cards, because they're potential bust-em hands. If stacks are deep enough, suited aces and 3-gap suited connectors are also playable (from 3%-6% of your stack, depending on position and your control over the opponent). When you flop two pair or better with a hand such as A♥3♥ on a flop of A-7-3 or A-3-3, you can win a big pot from an opponent who overplays his AK. We prefer A2s-A5s over A6s-A9s because of the straight potential combined with the deceptiveness of hitting flops such as 2-2-x (with A2) and 3-3-x (with A3).

Similarly, playing hands as weak as 32 suited early on can have value. The reason is simple—unpredictability. If a player has a big pair (and remember, we're targeting players who get married to these and will stack off), a flop such as 9-2-2 or J-3-3 looks pretty innocuous in a pot that's been raised pre-flop. This is why a hand such as 32 suited is preferable to hands such as Q7 suited. A flop of Q-Q-x is far more likely to scare off an opponent and prevent him from losing his stack than a flop of 2-2-x. Furthermore, on a flop of Q-Q-x, it's possible that your opponent may be holding a better queen, whereas on a flop of 2-2-x, it's highly unlikely for your tight opponent to be holding a deuce. Flops such as 2-2-x, 3-3-x, A-4-5, and K-2-3 appear to be extremely benign and many players have difficulty not stacking off with AK or a big overpair to the flop.

Additionally, when players see that you're capable of playing 32 suited, they realized that you're capable of playing virtually any two cards, which substantially increases your fear equity (see *Kill Everyone* for more information on fear equity).

When playing out of position, reduce your range to mainly pairs and occasionally suited connectors. However, there are several factors to consider in playing suited connectors OOP. If you're going to be heads-up (HU) against an opponent who tends to raise big pre-flop (5-6 BB) and bet pot-size on the flop, you'll have a hard time going to the river and you probably won't out-flop him often enough to make your play profitable in the long run. If the pre-flop raise is smaller and the flop bets are likely to be 50%-70% of the size of the pot, we frequently call with suited connectors OOP against weaker opponents. Against good players unlikely to play for stacks with one-pair hands, it's usually best to fold. In 3- or 4-way pots, we suggest you call with suited connectors OOP most of the time.

Key Point

Play unpredictable hands against predictable players.

Re-Raising (3-Betting) in Position

Three-betting tight predictable players when you have position has positive expected value. Often they'll fold pre-flop. When they do see a flop, many of these tight players will play "fit or fold" on the flop. You'll be able to take down the pot on the flop about two-thirds of the time when they don't connect and it gets checked to you. If you get check-raised on the flop, you can throw your hand away in most circumstances, knowing you're beat. Of course, sometimes you'll flop a big hand, making an unsuspected set or two pair or picking up a monster draw, and win a big pot.

Playing Against Calling Stations

Another rich source of chips early in the tournament comes from players who call too frequently. These so-called "calling stations" are overly curious, overly suspicious, or overly dumb! Calling stations can be early-stage cash cows and can help you build a big stack quickly. Whenever you identify this type of player, be particularly careful about bluffing them. Bets will only sometimes scare them off when their tournament life is on the line. Early on, this is rarely the case, so avoid bluffing them. Instead, overbet your strong hands when you're both deep-stacked, betting 1-1.5 times the size of the pot on each street. So long as they have chips left, they disregard bet-sizing and pot odds.

When they get short-stacked, however, they're more likely to fold to an overbet. A good rule to follow against a short-stacked calling station when you have the better hand is to size your bets so that you leave him with 25% of his stack.

It's important to assess the profile of short-stacked calling stations. Those who tighten up when their tournament life is on the line are capable of being bluffed by an all-in bet, but may very well call off 75% of their stack. It's important to exploit these players early, because they're rarely around after the first few levels.

In general, rather than figuring out the ratio between the bets and the size of the pot, calling stations are mostly concerned with the amount of chips they have left. For example, if the pot is 2,000 on the river and a calling station has 25,000 chips left, a bet of 3,000 or 4,000 may not scare him so much, because he'll still have more than 20,000 chips after making the call. However, if his opponent bets 25,000 into a 50,000 pot, even though he has much better pot odds to call than in the previous example, he's often reluctant to risk his whole tournament.

Key Point

Avoid bluffing calling stations unless it's for their tournament life, but overbet the pot for value, targeting about 75% of their stack.

Blind Stealing in the Early Stages

Expert loose-aggressive players raise in position with a wide range of hands, not in an attempt to steal the blinds, but to build a pot that they'll most likely win on the flop—especially against opponents who call frequently from the blinds—then check the flop and frequently fold to a bet. The weaker your opponent, the looser your pre-flop range should be, because you'll always have an edge post-flop to outplay him, especially when the structure is deep. Playing two cards that are both lower than an eight can be very profitable against predictable opponents when you connect with the flop, because your opponent will never expect you to hold such a hand after they've raised.

Additionally, your two cards will be "live" pre-flop when your opponent doesn't hold a pocket pair. Over the course of several hours' play, observant opponents will realize that you can be holding virtually any two cards, which makes it exceedingly difficult for them to put you on a particular hand. They'll constantly be guessing, but in most cases *their* holdings will be predictable. Constantly putting predictable opponents to a guess with unpredictable holdings, while using position as a strong ally, is fundamental to the loose-aggressive style of play.

Sometimes players give you additional help by showing a big fold. Look to exploit opponents who show big folds, such as top pair. A good example of this type of exploitation was in the 2009 NBC Heads-Up Tournament. In the semi-finals, Huck Seed was paired with Sam Farha. Farha is tough and aggressive post-flop, so when the blinds were up, Seed frequently moved in over Farha's button raises when he was first to act. Farha showed Huck some big pre-flop folds, such as A8 and KT. Seed responded by immediately *widening* his pre-flop pushing range. Finally, Farha found a hand he was willing to play (AQ) and called Seed's push. Seed was dominated, holding A3, but got lucky and won that hand and went on to win the match and ultimately the title. Showing hands is generally counterproductive, but showing big folds to a LAG is downright suicidal!

Identifying and Exploiting Weaknesses and Tendencies

Identifying a player's weaknesses in order to exploit them is one of the most important aspects in poker; all of the authors' games revolve around this important concept. Let's take a look at some examples of patterns and weaknesses that we usually look for in our opponents and try to exploit.

Some Players Don't Defend Their Blinds

If both the small and big blinds are really weak, you can attack them freely. You'll get away with many early-position and mid-position raises pre-flop, when the action is folded around to the weak blinds. If they fold four out of five times to your raises, even if you get 3-bet occasionally and have to fold, you're making a solid profit in the long run. Be aware, however, that your raises will look more suspicious from late position, and if the cutoff and/or the button are good players and realize that you're stealing, they may start playing back at you. Stealing the blinds isn't important in the very early going, but becomes more significant as the blinds increase, and exploiting weak-players' blinds is highly productive once the antes start.

Conversely, some players almost always defend their blinds. If you're in early position, don't raise with weak hands against these players; you'll get called and may find yourself in difficult spots after the flop.

Calling 3-bets out of position. This is another weakness we frequently see, especially in the early tournament stages. In the long run, this play is definitely –EV, because with position, a good player will often force them to fold on the flop or turn. We look for this pattern and capitalize on it.

Opponents who open-raise too frequently. Against this type of foe, 3-betting in position is a very effective and profitable move, provided you pay close attention to stack sizes, bet sizing, and the proclivities of the players left to act behind you.

Identify revealing tendencies and betting patterns. This is especially true in live tournaments, but can also be observed to a lesser degree in online events. Some players bet small when weak and big when strong, and some do the opposite.

Lee was playing an online heads-up stud high-low match as a Poker Stars Pro versus a top online performer who was evidently not that familiar with this form of poker. Whenever Lee's opponent was the forced bring-in (a forced bet by the player showing the lowest card), he consistently brought it in for the maximum when he was strong and for the minimum when he was weak. Obviously, this was highly exploitable. Lee raised whenever he brought it in for the minimum, prompting a fold, and he folded when his opponent brought it in for the maximum, unless he had a strong hand himself. Someone must have pointed out this obvious flaw; after a break, Lee's opponent started correctly bringing it in for the minimum regardless of the strength or weakness of his hand.

Min-raising to steal. Identifying players who raise to 3-4X the big blind when they have a decent hand (but min-raise from late position, because they "know" they're supposed to try to steal the blinds, but don't want to risk many chips) can lead to profitable opportunities. Min-raises such as this usually indicate a fairly weak hand; otherwise, they'd raise their usual 3X-4X BB. Three-bet these players frequently from both blinds pre-flop and follow up with a bet on the flop, if called. You'll usually take down the pot pre-flop when they fold (the most likely scenario), or in most cases take down a larger pot when they fold to your bet on the flop.

A more complex example that incorporates a number of the ideas discussed so far occurred on day one of the 2009 EPT Championship event in Monte Carlo. Lee observed the following tendencies in a Russian player:

• He consistently raised 2.5X the big blind from late position when he was weak, but 4X the big blind when he was strong.

• Post-flop, he habitually overbet the pot when he was weak, but made more normal two-thirds pot bets when he was strong.

• Being a calling station, he called down other players even when he had a very marginal hand, such as second or third pair.

A hand came up where Lee held K8 offsuit in the big blind. With blinds and antes of 150/300/25, the Russian player bet 750 from the cutoff. Both Lee and the Russian were deep-stacked with more than 50,000 chips at the start of this hand. Lee interpreted the 2.5-times-big-blind bet as weak, but also knew that a 3-bet would most likely be called and he'd have to play the hand out of position. Lee called the 750 and saw a flop of K♠-Q♦-T♥. Lee checked and his opponent bet 3,000 into an 1,875 pot (weak); Lee called.

The turn card was dangerous: 9♣. The Russian could easily have a random jack in his hand and have turned a straight. Lee checked and his opponent bet 6,000, a bet size that revealed nothing in terms of what Lee had previously observed. Lee studied his opponent for more than two minutes; the Russian player started breathing more and more heavily. Although not entirely sure how to interpret the markedly increased breathing pattern, it seemed to Lee as though the player was more nervous than excited. Lee called.

The river produced an inconsequential small card. Although Lee thought he was ahead, he didn't want to stake his tournament life on it if he could avoid it. His opponent was a calling station, but was also capable of making a big bluff. If Lee checked, he was afraid that his opponent would move-in, putting him to a very tough decision. Knowing that his opponent would have to be leery that Lee held a jack based on the line he'd taken and after considering for about 30 seconds, Lee bet 11,000 and his opponent called instantly! Thinking that he totally misread the situation, Lee tabled his K8. His opponent flashed a queen and mucked. Putting together several tendencies and weaknesses was the key to taking down this big pot.

Exploiting Betting Patterns Associated with Weakness

Weak players frequently employ betting patterns that give away the strength or weakness of their hand. For example, an amateur player who bets half the pot on the flop followed by a bet of a third of the pot on the turn often connotes weakness. Checking the turn and making a big river bet after an inconsequential-looking river card on a draw-heavy board is also a pattern we've noticed from weak players. Against better players, you can use betting patterns such as these, but instead of having a weak hand, use the betting pattern as a kind of reverse tell by making this series of bets when you're strong rather than weak.

Identifying and Countering Raises on Dry Flops for Information

On A-, K-, or Q-high flops with two low disconnected cards, if you make a c-bet on the flop and your opponent raises you in position, it's usually for information. He'll slow-play if he has a really big hand. Therefore, if you re-raise in spots such as this, you'll often make him fold top pair or a medium pair and take down a decent-sized pot.

Example

You raise from under the gun (UTG) and are called by the player in the hijack. The flop comes down K-6-2 rainbow. You c-bet and get raised. You can discount the probability of your opponent holding KK, because he likely would have 3-bet you pre-flop. If he raises your flop bet, he's seldom holding 66 or 22, because in most cases he'd probably slow play these very strong hands with such a safe board. His most likely holdings, therefore, are KJ or KT, or sometimes a middle-pair hand that can't stand much pressure. You can often make him release hands such as this with the re-raise on the flop. If he calls, you should lead out on the turn, making it untenable for him to continue with a marginal hand.

This example comes from a hand ElkY played during the WPT LAPC in 2010:

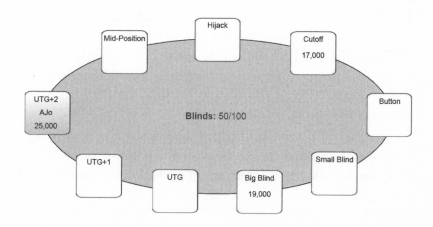

In a previous hand, ElkY witnessed the opponent flat-call a 3-bet pre-flop holding KK. He flopped a set of kings on a dry board and checked out of position on both the flop and turn, then finally check-raised on the river. The subject hand takes place during the second level of the tournament. The blinds are 50/100 and ElkY's got around 25,000 chips. He holds AJo UTG +2, and opens for 250. The player who slow-played top set, with 17,000, calls from the CO, as does the player in the BB (19,000).

The flop comes K-6-2 rainbow and the BB checks. This isn't a bad flop for ElkY, because he thinks he often has the best hand in this spot. Assuming he's ahead in the hand, ElkY doesn't want to check and give any free cards that would improve a hand such as 87, 98, T9, etc., with a turn card opening a straight draw, for instance. Additionally, ElkY thinks the flop is a good spot to scoop the pot. If neither of his opponents is holding a K or a middle pair, they'll probably give up most of the time when ElkY c-bets.

ElkY bets 450; the player who slow-played his set earlier raises him to 1,300, and the BB folds. Based on what ElkY saw earlier, he doesn't think the other player would raise with a really strong hand in this spot. It seems to ElkY that the intent of his raise is probably to get some information with a medium pair (77 to TT) or possibly a K with a low-kicker (maybe KJ at the very most). He might be holding AK, but ElkY thinks he'd have 3-bet pre-flop with such a holding. He may be bluffing here as well. In ElkY's analysis, he rules out a very strong hand and doesn't think it can take a lot of pressure from an aggressive betting scheme. Therefore, his plan is to re-raise him on the flop and bet out big on any turn card, should he call his re-raise on the flop. ElkY re-raises to 3,100. He doesn't think the re-raise needs to be too big here. If the player has raised for information as ElkY suspects, his re-raise simply tells him that ElkY has it. His opponent folds pretty quickly.

Because ElkY has a read that this particular player slow-plays his monsters and that there's almost nothing but monsters he can be raising for value on this texture, ElkY thinks this is an excellent spot to make the 3-bet bluff on the flop. His range almost always consists of bluffs, or one-pair hands that he'll likely fold to a 3-bet. Of course, thinking players will be capable of mixing up their patterns in similar situations, but against this particular opponent, ElkY believed his pattern would be consistent. Average to weak players typically only raise on the flop with a set on a scary board with lots of draws. In this instance, the dry flop of K-6-2 rainbow was anything but scary.

Key Point

In general, it's easier to bluff an opponent who raises your flop c-bet than one who just flat-calls.

Leading on the Flop and Turn

In this section we present a set of example hands, most of which are hands that ElkY played in various events, to help illustrate when to take the betting lead post-flop.

Hand Example 1

Holding KQ and being out of position on a flop of K-7-6 rainbow versus a player capable of raising pre-flop with a fairly wide range of hands, ElkY check-calls a c-bet from the pre-flop raiser of two-thirds the size of the pot. The turn is an 8. ElkY now leads, betting about 70% of the pot, protecting his hand in case his opponent has picked up a straight draw and not allowing his opponent to see any free cards. This type of play confuses many players, and they may call with marginal hands, suspecting a bluff.

Hand Example 2

ElkY in the WSOP Main Event 2009

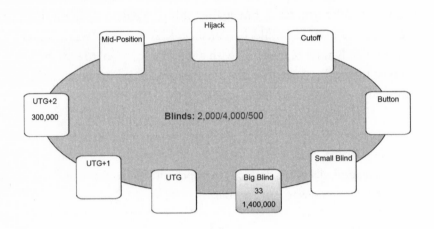

A tight opponent, UTG +2 with a stack of 300,000, raises to 14,000. ElkY, with 1.4 million, calls from the BB with 33. The flop is K-5-3 rainbow. ElkY checks; the opponent bets 25,000, and ElkY calls. The turn is a 4 (no flush draws). ElkY leads with 55,000. His opponent tanks for 20 seconds and goes all-in with KJo. ElkY wins a big pot.

ElkY explains, "My lead of 55,000 with a set is atypical and takes away my opponent's ability to control the size of the pot. He might have thought that the 4 gave me a draw and decided he was willing to play for all his chips with top pair, giving me the wrong price to draw. Unfortunately for him, I had a set."

Hand Example 3

ElkY at Bellagio WPT Championship 2009

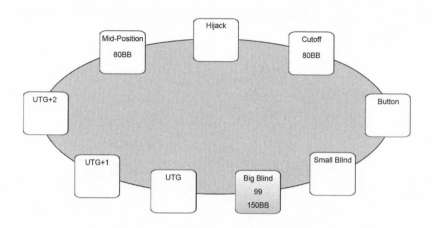

Opponent 1 limps from middle position. Opponent 2 isolates the limper from the cutoff by raising 3.5 BB. ElkY calls from BB with 99. The limper calls. The flop comes T-4-3 rainbow.

ElkY leads out, betting two-thirds of the pot. Both opponents fold quickly.

ElkY didn't want to give his opponents any free cards that could complete a draw. Betting out also blocks potential moves with air from opponents, which would make it difficult for him to know where he stands in the hand.

Hand Example 4

This is a hypothetical example that illustrates how to defend against a surprise lead that appears to be for information.

You raise pre-flop with a speculative hand, such as 65s. One weak opponent calls out of position. The flop is A-x-x (you didn't connect). Now your opponent leads weakly. Often, you should raise right there to represent a strong hand.

Weak opponents usually fold. If you called a raise out of position with 65s and the flop comes down A-x-x and you didn't connect, a strong play is to float a flop bet and lead out on the turn. This is a trend we see good players following more and more frequently. It's a strong deceptive line. Counterbalancing it by sometimes playing top pair, two pair, and sets similarly keeps your opponents off balance and guessing.

Hand Example 5

ElkY at EPT Deauville 2010

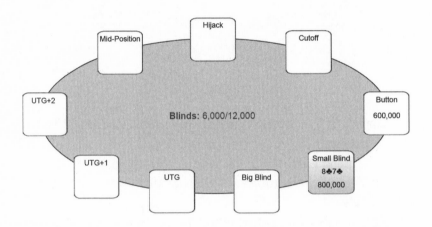

It's Day 3. The blinds are 6,000/12,000. ElkY has 800,000 in the SB. The player on the button, with 600,000, opens for 27,000 and ElkY makes the call with 8♣7♣. He believes his opponent is a weak player he can outplay, even OOP. Also, his image is good, because he hasn't been very active for several rounds. Finally, flat-calling from the small blind represents real strength and the will to see a flop, as opposed to a 3-bet, which may be interpreted as a re-steal. Flat-calling OOP is a play he often makes with 77, 88, or 99. The BB folds. The flop is 5-9-2 rainbow; ElkY leads for half the pot, and the button calls. The turn is a 3, still rainbow. ElkY leads again, assuming that his opponent has probably called a lot of flop bets with A-high or two overcards, then releases if he misses again on the turn, which he does.

Always stay aware of stack sizes. Leading and moving all-in (re-shoving) if re-raised must be done only if you have fold equity. *Leading should not be done as a pure bluff. Lead with either a really strong hand or on a semi-bluff.*

Hand Example 6

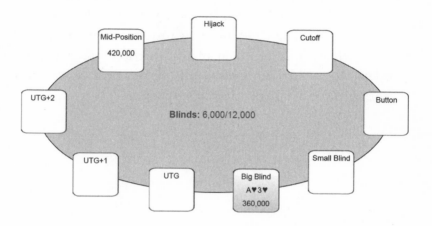

A player in mid-position raises and the button calls. You have A♥3♥ in the BB and your stack is roughly 30 BB. You call. The flop is K♥-9♥-5♣.

Option 1: You can lead for 3.5-4 BB (if your stack is 30-35 BB, you can lead 5 BB) and re-shove if you get raised. Indeed, your opponent may hold a variety of hands (flush draw, gutshot, pair, combination draws, such as a pair and a flush draw, etc.). Some of your opponents may just be raising for information. If you're called by a hand such as AK or KQ, you still have outs to win the hand.

Key Point

With a stack size of 30-35 BB, size your bets so that the all-in bet is about 20 BB. Otherwise you'll lose fold equity.

Your initial bet size for the lead needs to take into account your opponents' tendencies when they raise. Online players nowadays usually raise 2-2.6 times the amount of the initial raise, whereas live players usually raise much bigger and they're not always aware of pot odds.

Option 2: If you know that your opponent tends to c-bet too often, you can also check-raise big enough so that you don't leave him with any fold equity. It will then be difficult for him to call you, but if he does, you still have substantial equity and must call.

Note when leading OOP, the more players involved in the pot, the less likely you'll be raised on a bluff. Therefore, you might not have fold equity with such a move in multi-way pots. Reserve this line for when you're up against a single opponent.

6

Playing the Flop
Hands with Flopping Value

In ElkY's opinion, a hand with good flop value is one that has good potential to connect very strongly with the flop or a lot of opportunities to semi-bluff on later streets, because they will often connect with the board.

For example, in a multi-way pot, hands with flopping value include suited connectors (9♠8♠) or suited one-gappers (6♥4♥), any two suited cards that are both 8 higher, and any pocket pair. On the other hand, unsuited 2 gappers (96o) have poor flopping value, because they rarely connect with the board. Of course, it all depends on the situation and the depth of the stacks.

Another thing to consider is the skill of the players in the hand, and how much you think you can outplay them.

For instance, whereas ElkY often calls a raise IP with T♥9♥, he never does so with A7o. With the latter, there's not a lot of value you can get from your hand post-flop, unless you flop two pair or trips (even trip aces can be dominated and it's not the best hand to play for a lot of chips with a 7 kicker). If stacks are shallow, he sometimes makes a move by 3-betting with a hand such as A7o, if he thinks he has enough fold equity. However, he's much more eager, generally speaking, to see a flop IP with hands such as 9♠8♠, T♠9♠, etc.

Playing Difficult Flops

In poker, more often than not, you'll encounter problematic flops and won't always know what line to use. In this section, we give you some basic guidelines you'll find helpful.

Let's say that you've raised pre-flop, got called by one opponent in position, and hit second or bottom pair on the flop. In such a situation versus a weak player, we suggest betting out 90% of the time. Against stronger opponents, who may play back at you, you probably should mix it up a little more, betting 60% of the time and check-calling 40% of the time.

To go further with this example, let's assume you're still heads-up after the flop; your opponent has called your c-bet, or you've both checked, or you've check-called. If the turn "bricks out" (neither opens any draws nor pairs the board), you still need to adjust your line based on your assessment of your opponent's skills.

When facing a weak opponent, we think you should fire again 80% of the time and check-fold 20%. If he calls again, you go heads-up to the river, and you don't improve your hand, you should then check 95% of the time, since timid players will often check behind with top pair to avoid getting raised, which will save you a bet.

Against a stronger opponent, when the turn bricks out and you still have a marginal pair, you should check-call 40%, check-fold 55%, and check-raise 5% of the time (only if you have a good read that your opponent is making a move on you).

Multi-way pots are also often a source of headaches, especially when you catch a small piece of the flop. When you completely miss the flop, there are two ways to proceed, depending on whether you think your opponents have connected: Take a stab at it or give up right there. Against amateur players, you can sometimes get away with c-betting when a scare card, such as an ace, flops. Against tough opponents, it's more dangerous to take a shot at bluffing on the flop, because you might put yourself in situations where you also have to double- or triple-barrel bluff on later streets, which substantially increases variance. When playing against good laggy opponents who are capable of putting you to a difficult decision, it's usually best to control the size of the pot.

Now, let's say you raise with AQ from middle position and both blinds call. The flop comes 2-8-9. Both villains check to you and you c-bet, since you're still likely to hold the best hand at this juncture. Only a loose-aggressive player in the small blind calls and a Q comes on the turn. The small blind checks again. We think you should check behind in that spot, to avoid getting check-raised if your opponent holds JT, J9, Q9, 98, or a set. Even if your opponent check-raises you on a semi-bluff, it'll be a tough call to make and you're now involved in a high-variance hand. So you should check for pot control. If the river is a brick, your opponent may lead out on a missed draw and give you a fairly easy call. If he checks on the river, you can now value bet.

When it comes to difficult flops, it's also important for you to have a good idea of your opponents' styles. If you're facing several calling stations in a multi-way pot, you should try to "punish" them as much as possible by betting big when you make a strong hand on the flop. If you miss the flop, you should take a small stab at it, then give up if called. Remember, when a calling station gets even a very small piece of the flop, it'll be very difficult for you to get him off his hand, whatever the board texture may be.

One sophisticated move to use a calling station to your advantage takes place when a good player is also involved in the hand. For instance, you're facing a good player and a calling station in a 3-way pot IP. The good player—the initial raiser—bets the flop and is called by the calling station. If you raise IP, the good player will tend to think you must be really strong to re-raise with a calling station in a 3-way pot, and will often give up, reasoning that your raise most likely isn't a bluff. However, you still need to get rid of the calling station. For that reason, ElkY mostly makes this move on a semi-bluff, or if he knows for sure how to make the calling station fold on a later street.

Along the same lines, you should keep in mind that most good players won't try to bluff calling stations. Therefore, when the good player plays well in a 3-way pot with you and a calling station, use that information and get out of the way most of the time. This is part of the metagame, as discussed in Chapter 2.

In multi-way pots against LAGs, your priority should be to control the pot size most of the time.

Due to the unpredictability of laggy opponents, you should always be very careful in multi-way pots against them; their range is so large that there's always the possibility that they actually hit the flop! Therefore, especially in the early stages, pot control should be your main focus in such situations.

In order to protect your ability to control the size of the pot by checking on the river when you're OOP, you should also check the nuts on the river with some frequency against laggy players. They'll take many stabs at stealing the pot on the river and if they know you can check the nuts to trap them occasionally, they'll think twice about firing on the river again, which may allow you to show down marginal holdings.

Once again, the line of play to select is highly player-dependent, based mainly on the patterns you observe in your opponents.

Continuation Bets (C-Bets)

Ever since Dan Harrington first described continuation bets in his excellent tournament-book series *Harrington on Hold'em*, players around the globe have been making this play. What's the best way to employ this move in today's game? Let's take a look at the c-bet against both weak opponents and strong competitors.

C-Betting Versus Weak Players Out of Position

If we've raised pre-flop and are heads-up out of position against a weak opponent, here's our strategy.

- With unconnected flops (example K♥-8♣-3♦), c-bet 80% to 90% of the time on dry flops (unconnected and no flush draws) if an A or K flops.

- If an A or a K flops and our continuation bet is called, we'll bet again on the turn (double-barrel) about 25% of the time, checking and folding to a bet the rest of the time. On flops such as these, most straightforward tight players will fold unless they have top pair or a strong underpair, such as 99-QQ, and many tight players will fold these as well. Some opponents will call on the flop with hands such as these or second pair, but give up when faced with a bet on the turn. When we identify players such as this, we increase our frequency of turn bets with good results.

- On connected flops such as J♥-T♣-8♥, if we totally miss the flop (we have 6♣5♣), we'll bet 80%-90% of the time if our image is strong and we've been winning a lot of hands and c-bet 50%-60% of the time if we've recently lost a few pots.

- If ElkY's opponent calls his c-bet and the turn doesn't fill any straights or flushes, he'll bet about 80% of the pot. The main strength in double-barreling like this is that it forces his opponent to reveal the strength of his hand. If his opponent calls his turn bet, ElkY will usually continue with his bluff and bet the river. A triple-barrel bluff such as this often wins against all pairs and draws, and gives a tight opponent a tough decision if he holds AJ.

- When ElkY has a hand such as AK and has decided to double-barrel with it, if the river card fails to complete the flush or straight, he bets the river about 70% of the time, checks and calls a river bet 20% of the time, and checks and folds to a river bet 10% of the time when out of position. If he's in position, however, he checks behind 75% of the time if his opponent checks on the river. AK has substantial showdown value in a situation such as this, when his opponent may have been on a draw that missed. Most times, he sees no reason to expose himself to a possible check-raise bluff on the river. Of course, this risk is much higher against a good player than a straightforward tight opponent.

- We try to identify players who like to make small raises for information on K- and A-high flops, such as K♦-6♥-2♣, after we've c-bet. Against such players, we'll often 3-bet the flop and bet the turn.

- On paired boards, an effective line is to check the flop and call if your opponent bets, then bet out on most turn cards. If the action on the flop goes check/check, lead out with a bet on the turn.

- On a flop with three connected low cards, if you c-bet against a weak opponent, get called, and the turn is an A or a K, it's usually a good spot to bet again, because weak players often aren't advanced enough to float the flop with A- or K-high. They rarely hold an A or K, and most often they will be scared by the high card combined with your turn bet. Most of the time, this will result in them giving up on the hand.

C-Betting Versus Weak Players in Position

- When we have position, we check the flop more frequently with the intention of betting the turn if our opponent checks again. This "delayed c-bet" picks up the pot most of the time. Weak players frequently view the check on the flop as highly suspicious for an aggressive player and are happy to fold to our turn bet. We use the delayed c-bet about 60% to 70% of the time on uncoordinated or paired boards. To balance this, we sometimes check back with top pair. However, this is a move that we make far more frequently against strong players.

- On boards that could complete draws, it's often effective to check the flop and the turn against weaker players. Weak players will generally bet any kind of a made hand on the river. If your opponent checks the river, bet 95% of the time.

C-Betting Versus Good Players Out of Position

- On unconnected ace- or king-high flops, c-bet 60% to 80% of the time, and be prepared to double-barrel by betting the turn most of the time. Check and fold to a bet 20% to 40% of the time.

Good players will often call your c-bet with a wide range of hands. This tactic, commonly known as floating, is becoming more and more prevalent among better players. Because of this, we need to mix up our play on the turn. A good mix is to double-barrel 50% to 60% of the time, check-raise on the turn about 25% of the time, and check with the intention of folding if your opponent bets 10% to 20% of the time.

• On paired boards, check and call on the flop about 60% to 70% of the time, then mix up your turn play by either leading out or check-raising; check and fold if your opponent bets the flop the other 30% to 40% of the time.

• With connected flops, most of the time, check hands that have value, such as overpairs, in order to control the size of the pot. For example, with AA on a board of J-T-9, we'll often check, because the c-bet would give a strong opponent a chance to bluff us right there.

• When we miss the flop completely, we'll c-bet 60% to 70% of the time and give up the hand if our opponent bets the rest of the time. Don't try to beat the same opponent out of every pot, especially if he's a good player. The most efficient approach is to sometimes let go of smaller pots, but fight for the big ones.

• When you connect with the flop, often check-raise the turn! For instance, if you hold KQ on a flop of J-T-9, check the flop frequently and call when your opponent bets, as you would with an overpair for purposes of pot control, then check-raise the turn. If you have a hand such as QT on this flop, check-raise the turn about 25% of the time, unless you have 25-35 BB, in which case you should check-raise all-in.

C-Betting Versus Good Players In Position

• C-betting a lot of flops against good players, especially laggy ones, is dangerous. They're quite capable of check-raising you, both with a hand and with air. Use a delayed c-bet with great frequency against good players, but balance this play by checking back top pair or better about 50% of the time. Against loose-aggressive players, check back top pair even more frequently. If a laggy player leads into you on the flop and you have top pair, be careful about raising and putting yourself in a position where you might be faced with a tough decision when you have a hand with significant showdown value. However, if he bets the turn and river, be prepared to play for all your chips if you have 40 BB or less.

• Against a LAG, when you have top pair, your opponent checks the flop, and you've checked it back, if he checks the turn, check back a second time about 10% to 20% of the time. If your laggy opponent checks the river, overbet the pot by betting about 1.3-1.5X the size of the pot. Laggy opponents frequently call you down with second pair or worse. In the event that your opponent makes a small bet on the river, consider raising.

For example, you have KQ and the board reads K-6-2-T-5. This play protects your delayed c-bets, as well as future bluffs. Be aware, though, that crazier players may re-raise you, even with a busted draw. Whether to raise or call on the river depends a lot on your read. If you think your opponent is betting for value, raising has a positive expectation, but if you think your opponent is bluffing, calling is the best option.

C-Betting in Multi-Way Pots

Early on in the tournament, in order to accumulate chips, you'll need to consider many parameters when you get involved in multi-way pots. Important factors include the strength of your hand, your position, the opponents you're facing, and having a well-designed plan.

When playing OOP in a multi-way pot, it's difficult to get three streets of value, even with a very strong hand, because players tend to be highly cautious. For this reason, I usually like to control the size of the pot and set traps at the same time. For instance, if I hold top pair in a multi-way pot, I rarely 3-barrel for value; I do that much more often in HU play. I think multi-way pots fall into two categories: the ones where you have the lead and the ones where you don't.

When you have the lead, the c-betting range may vary a lot. However, I think it's still +EV to c-bet quite often on a single A-high or K-high board. Of course, it depends on how many players are in the hand, and what range of hands they're likely to have. If the player in the BB is really loose and defends with virtually any two cards, then you shouldn't be so worried about the high card on the board, which you should be able to bluff at a decent percentage of the time. Indeed, most players tend to play very tight in the early stages, and mostly set mine (which means to play pocket pairs to try and flop a set) or wait for very big hands. *A good thing about leading in a multi-way pot is that you can make a relatively small c-bet.*

Let's say the blinds are 50/100, you raise to 250 from EP, and you get three callers. The pot is now 1,000. The flop comes A-2-2 or K-7-2. Often, unless one of your opponents has hit top pair, a bet of 325 on the flop will win the pot right there. You'd win 1,000 chips for 325, which means your move only has to work one out of three times to have positive EV. In my experience, this move works between 50% to 60% of the time.

In multi-way pots, you should expect your opponents to play in a relatively straightforward style. This means that if an opponent—let's say a good player who has players still left to act behind him—calls your c-bet, he'll have hit top pair most of the time. If the caller closes the action, his range may be a little wider. With all of that in mind, when you're the initial raiser in a multi-way pot, you should try to keep the lead in the hand by c-betting the flop. If your initial raise was to isolate a limper, you should assess how often that opponent may hold an ace or how often he'd 3-bet pre-flop with AK, so you can get a read and adjust your decision on whether or not to c-bet. You should try to take into consideration as much as possible what kind of hands the initial limpers could limp with, because some players are very weak-tight and won't even limp in with most of the small-suited aces. So in that spot, your c-betting frequency on A-high boards should be high.

In multi-way pots, it's important to determine the frequency that a third player will 3-bet with AK after one or more limpers and a raise. For example, take a hand where a weak player limps in middle position. I raise to isolate with T9o from the hijack, and the button, who seems like a decent player, flat calls, as does the first player. Here, in order to fine tune your c-betting range properly on dry, high-card boards, you have to assess how often the button would 3-bet with AQs or AK. Most of the players picking on the isolating raise would 3-bet in position with that kind of holding on the Internet. However, some live players would never 3-bet a hand like AK. Obviously, the more likely he is to 3-bet AK, the more inclined you should be to c-bet A- or K-high flops when he just calls your pre-flop raise.

When you're not the initial raiser, position definitely becomes the key factor. If the initial raiser, let's assume a weak player, bets small or checks the flop, in my experience he's usually ready to release his hand, so I 3-barrel quite often. Let's say the flop is K-T-2 with no flush draw and the initial raiser checks to you in a 3-way pot. You take a stab with 76 and your opponent calls. The turn is a 9 and your opponent checks again. I'd take another stab at it, and maybe even a third one on the river, probably for the size of the pot, because I think it's unlikely the initial raiser would play AK or KT that way. If he has QQ or JJ, he'll often fold his hand when faced with a big river bet. Of course, you'll sometimes run into tricky players who check a set or a strong hand, but even then, I think it's unlikely they'd check-call twice.

As a basic rule, when I have absolutely nothing in a 3-way pot IP, I'll fire on the flop if the action is checked to me. Suppose you're on the button and there is a MP raise called by the cutoff and you. On a flop of Q-9-2, it's checked around to you. If the initial raiser checks, he probably hasn't connected with the board, since if he had, he'd almost certainly try to keep the lead. The player in the cutoff would most likely bet a Q, but he checked to you as well. You should definitely take a stab at the pot. If you're called, you need to re-assess whether you can make your opponent fold a medium pair, which is what he's holding most of the time in this situation.

When I'm OOP and didn't make the initial raise in a multi-way pot, I like to lead much of the time. Of course, you shouldn't make this move if you think one of your opponents is holding a monster, in which case you should be cautious and exercise pot control. For instance if I'm in the SB, and three players call a MP raise, I like to fire on the flop for several reasons. First, it helps me define the hand better, because my bet will generate a lot of information based on my opponents' reactions to it. Additionally, weak players usually play very differently against a lead from the blinds on the flop, folding most of the time, whereas they may c-bet up to 90% of the time if the action is checked to them.

Key Point

It's frequently best to lead out on the flop against weak players who have raised pre-flop and been called multi-way.

Say I called a pre-flop raise from the small blind with Q♥J♥ and the flop comes K-7-2 rainbow in a 3-way pot. A small bet won't cost me much compared with the benefits of quickly assessing my opponents' hands. If I held 77 or 22 in that spot, I'd fire, because I believe that, should one of my opponents hold a K, he'd have difficulty releasing it. Additionally, leading out with big hands balances my leads when I hold nothing but air, keeping me unpredictable. Sharp players will be unable to identify a consistent pattern. By mixing it up, I maintain my unpredictable image and preserve fear equity.

When I flop a set, I'll play the hand in a variety of ways, depending on my read of my opponents' tendencies and my table image at the time. Sometimes, I'll lead on the flop and fire again on both the turn and river; occasionally, I'll try to check-raise the flop and sometimes I'll bet the flop and try to check-raise the turn. *Betting the flop and check-raising the turn is often a good line to use against hyper-aggressive players.* They may even re-raise on the turn if they think they have substantial fold equity. If they check back on the turn, I like to over-bet on the river, because an over-bet sometimes looks like a desperate attempt to steal the pot and confuses many players.

Another benefit of leading from OOP in multi-way pots is that you can control the pot. Regardless of the amount you decide to lead out with (I like to bet a third of the size of the pot), it will be difficult for any of your opponents to raise you. Therefore, you should bet pretty small, keeping the lead and controlling the amount of money that goes into the pot (unless, of course, you get raised). This is a good tool to use for seeing a turn card relatively cheaply. If both opponents call your flop c-bet in a 3-way pot, you should give up on the turn, unless you've picked up a draw that you can semi-bluff.

Let's go back to the situation where you hold Q♥J♥ on a K♥-7♠-2♣ board. You lead for a third of the size of the pot and get called once. The turn is either a heart, a ten, or an ace. You should probably lead again, which will let you see the river less expensively than if you check to your opponent's top pair.

Key Point

A small c-bet in a multi-way pot allows you to keep the lead and control the size of the pot; it also results in an immediate win more than 50% of the time, in my experience.

In a multi-way pot when I'm OOP, in the blinds for instance, I also like leading out. When a timid player raises from the cutoff and gets called in three spots, depending on the profile of the initial raiser, I like to lead OOP. When the initial raiser is one of those players who knows he's supposed to raise from late position to steal the blinds, but isn't advanced enough to know how to float a flop bet, I think a bet out from the blinds in such a multi-way pot shows a lot of strength, and often takes the pot right there.

Example: This is a hand I played at the WPT Commerce in 2009. A player raises from MP, the button calls, and I call from the SB with Q♣J♣. The BB makes the call as well. The flop is 2-4-7, with one club. I think my opponents are weak, and are most likely holding big cards. Obviously, one of them could have a pair or even a set. However, I like to lead in this situation, because I can get away with betting one-third of the pot most of the time and I can quickly tell from my opponents' reactions whether I'm dominated. Everybody folds to my bet, and I rake an effortless pot!

If you want to use this move, you need to have a plan for later streets. In this example, the plan would be to fire again on any club on the turn. If the turn is a Q or J, I would check-call 50% of the time and fire again the other 50% of the time, depending on how frequently I think my opponent may be trapping me with a set. On the river, if my hand improves again (to two pair, trips, or a flush), I think check-raising is often a good move, especially against opponents who value bet thin, because my hand will be very well-disguised. Your ability to make such a move depends first and foremost on your assessment of the opponents you're facing.

Positional Play

Playing in position is always the most comfortable situation in the game. The many advantages make positional play arguably the key concept, not only in Texas hold 'em, but also in most variations of poker. In this section, ElkY describes the advantages of positional play, then gives you some guidelines on how to capitalize on it.

The first advantage of playing a pot IP is that, since you're the last player to act after the flop, you can gather the maximum information about what's going on in the hand. More than from any other position, the player on the button can recognize who is strong and who is weak.

Also, playing IP definitely helps you control the size of the pots. You can sometimes check behind your opponents when you don't think you can extract value from your hand, or if you're unwilling to move-in. Checking behind also allows you to sometimes get free cards, which can be extremely valuable when you are on a big draw, for instance.

The ability to bluff more hands is also an advantage of playing IP. If you recognize weakness from all your opponents and it's checked to you, you can sometimes rake the pot with total air by betting on the appropriate street.

Playing IP, if you do it right, enables you to maximize the value of your hand in several ways. For example, if your opponent checks a scary river card to you, you have the option to value bet thin. Thin value bets are profitable in today's trends, as players tend to make more and more hero calls, especially online. Also, when you have position, you are able to see flops and to get out of troublesome hands at a cheap cost most often.

Finally, if you use your position adequately, you should be able to constantly put your opponents to a guess.

7

Pot Control

Pot control involves attempting to keep the size of the pot at a smaller, more manageable amount in order to reduce variance. It's usually used in hands that have decent showdown equity, such as top pair, but with which you wouldn't want to play a really huge pot or be subjected to big bet pressure from an aggressive laggy foe.

To control the pot size, you can call rather than raise pre-flop, or check rather than bet either on the flop or the turn. Players who fail to exercise pot control in certain situations find themselves in spots where they're unsure of the strength of their hand against their opponent's range and they face a bet that's much larger than they had originally hoped to risk.

An argument can be made that there is too much pot control in the current game. ElkY believes this trend can sometimes be exploited. In order to control pots, most players today tend to check behind on the flop and on the turn. Therefore, *when you have a big hand OOP, you should try to check-raise the flop whenever possible.* If you miss your check raise on the flop, ElkY thinks you should try the same move on the turn, and go for an oversize check raise, to finally lead big on the river. Another way to exploit the trend of pot control may be to lead on every street with a strong hand, especially if you have an aggressive image. By leading every street, you prevent your opponent from controlling the pot size. A third line may also be to check-call on the flop, check the turn, and check-raise the river. *The point here is to not let your opponents control the size of the pot when you have a big hand.*

Controlling the Pot Pre-Flop

Pot controlling pre-flop isn't nearly as common as on the flop or turn, but there are still numerous situations where at first glance your hand looks strong enough for a re-raise, but if you contemplate all the variables in the hand, you may realize that calling is preferable. Pre-flop pot controlling is almost always done while stacks are still quite deep and is often used as a way to reduce variance and difficult decisions against an excellent-thinking and highly aggressive player.

Here's a simple example. The effective stacks are 30,000. Blinds are 100/200 with a 25 ante. You hold A♠A♣ in the BB. You haven't done any pre-flop re-raising yet and overall have a very tight image. Your opponent is cash-game sensation Tom "Durrrr" Dwan, who is on the cutoff.

Pre-flop; it folds around to Dwan, who raises to 500; the button and small blind both fold.

In a situation like this, it may actually be preferable to exercise pot control pre-flop and simply call. Opponents as unpredictable and talented as Dwan will call your re-raise with an enormous range of hands and make a highly specific read on your range because you've been so tight. Additionally, a player like this is willing to take creative and aggressive lines post-flop that will bloat the size of the pot and put you in very difficult situations with a pair, potentially to the detriment of your entire stack. By exercising pot control pre-flop and just calling, you disguise your hand well; you could be calling with a wide range out of the BB. You'll then be able to call your opponent down comfortably on the vast majority of boards and allow him to use his aggression to hang himself at stakes that won't cripple you in the event he sucks out. It will be highly tempting for him to bluff more, because you've underrepresented your hand.

Pot Control on the Flop

Naturally, the concept of controlling the pot size in order to make easier decisions on future streets carries over to checking the flop for pot control as well. However, pot controlling on the flop is particularly effective, because your opponents are expecting that as an aggressive and thinking player, you will be continuation betting a very high percentage of flops. When aggressive players check or check behind on the flop, it's often because they've completely missed and have almost zero equity in the hand, or when they think it's likely their opponent won't fold to a continuation bet, or because they hit a very small piece, or small draw, and want to take a free card instead of risking being raised off their hand. In order to balance your range for the times when you make this play, you should incorporate pot control on the flop as a trap into your arsenal as well.

Here's an example hand played by ElkY in the WSOP $40,000-buy-in event in 2009:

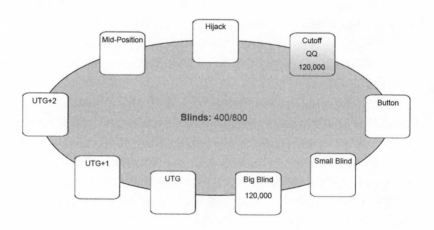

ElkY holds QQ on the cutoff. The opponent is European pro Ludovic Lacay, who is aware of ElkY's aggressive style of play and reputation. Pre-flop, it folds around to ElkY on the CO, who raises to 2,000. The button and SB fold. Lacay calls from the BB.

The flop comes 9♥-8♠-2♥. Lacay checks and ElkY checks behind, trying to make his hand look weaker than it actually is. The turn: 3♣. Lacay bets 3,000. ElkY calls. The river is 7♥. Lacay bets 7,000, ElkY calls, and Lacay instantly mucks his hand.

ElkY managed to extract what was likely maximum value from his hand by *not betting the flop*. This hand can also add value in future plays when ElkY uses the delayed continuation bet, as players will be more cautious about making a bet on the turn when he checks the flop.

Pot Control on the Turn

The turn is the most common street in which players exercise pot control. They often realize that if they bet the turn and are raised, they'll be unsure as to the strength of their hand. Or they think that they probably can't extract three streets of value from their opponent, so they attempt to appear weak by checking on the turn.

Using the line of bet flop, check turn, and bet large on river is an excellent way to get two streets of value against non-thinking or mid-level opponents.

However, against many talented and thinking players, you're usually better off betting the flop, betting the turn, and checking the river, because other aggressive players anticipate your having a fairly wide double-barrel range (which you should also keep balanced by betting on the turn for value more frequently). Here's an example:

The effective stacks are 20,000. The blinds are 200/400 with 50 ante. You hold A♠T♠ in mid-position.

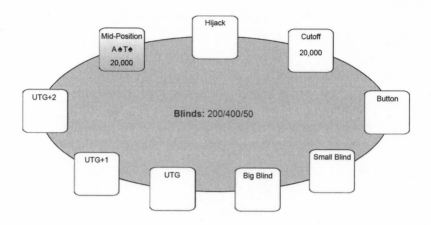

Your opponent is an average player who has been on the table with you for some time. He regards you as aggressive, but not crazy. He's mostly tight pre-flop, but not excessively so. Pre-flop, it's folded to you in mid-position. You raise to 1,000. It folds to the CO, who calls, and everyone else folds. The flop is A♣-J♦-3♥. You bet 1,500; your opponent calls.

The turn is 7♥. This is a good spot to exercise pot control. If you bet the turn and you opponent calls, it will be difficult to extract a third street of value from second pair (which will often fold to your turn bet in the first place) and there aren't many worse aces in his pre-flop calling range. If you're raised on the turn, you'll be forced to fold against this opponent, and you know that if you check, you can call a bet from him comfortably. Also, if you go for three streets of value here by betting on both the turn and river, his entire calling range will probably be better hands, none of which is likely to fold on this board. You check and he checks behind.

The river is 4♣. You should now bet something between 3,000 and 6,000 for value, depending on what bet size you think he'll call with second pair, or weak ace-type hands.

Here's an example from EPT Snowfest 2010:

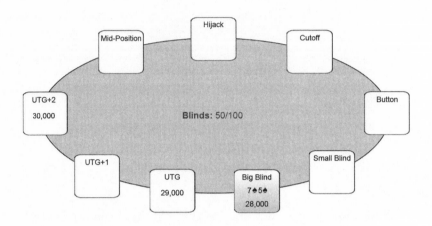

Villain 1 opens UTG for 300 and a Scandinavian player calls from UTG+2. ElkY has no reads, and the effective stack size is 28,000; ElkY calls from the big blind with 5♠7♠. The flop is 3-4-6 rainbow; all players check.

The turn is T♥; now two hearts show on the board. This is a really good card for him, because any player will most likely bet with hearts and/or a ten. Based on the flop checks, it's likely everyone missed. ElkY checks. Villain 1 checks. The Scandi bets 650; ElkY makes it 2,000; Villian 1 calls quite quickly. The river is an off-suit 6 and ElkY bets 4,400; Villian 1 tank-calls and mucks when he sees ElkY's hand. The key in the current game is to counter pot-control tendencies when you have strong hands and when you want to bluff. This puts your opponents in a really tough spot by frustrating their ability to pot control.

If the flop is bet, you can also usually get two streets of value on decent boards by check-calling on the flop, check-calling the turn, and check-raising on the river. This is a good line.

Here are three ways to defend KJs. The flop is K♥-J♥-2♥. You check; your opponent checks behind. The turn is 8♦. If you lead in that spot, you'll get only two streets of value from a king and your opponent will most likely fold other hands. You'll maybe get one street from the jack, but probably not two. On the other hand, if you check, he'll most likely bet a king and weak draws like T9, as well as lots of air. By getting a check-raise here, especially if the river blanks out, you might get a lot from a king, and he might become crazy and 4-bet with air, since your line is definitely non-standard. Still, don't count on the last option too much, unless your opponent is a hyper-LAG or borderline maniac.

Another tricky and deceptive pot-control-related play that ElkY likes to make is flat-calling with pairs such as QQ and JJ pre-flop when in position and in heads-up pots. Many opponents in a live tournament fold many of the hands you beat if you re-raise, but never fold the hands that beat you; by calling, you allow them the opportunity to flop a pair or draw and you can take down a nice pot, over which you'll have control in position. However, the play loses much of its appeal and value if the pot becomes multi-way. Then, re-raise pre-flop, because hands such as QQ and JJ don't play nearly as well in multi-way pots, especially out of position and while stacks are still moderately deep. Make sure to balance these re-raises by occasionally having non-premium hands in your squeezing range.

Another hand ElkY likes to mix into his pre-flop 3-bet range when the situation is right is AQ, with which he'll re-raise 10% to 20% of the time. The situations he looks for are when the initial raiser is particularly weak and a pre-flop 3-bet is likely to take down the pot right then, or if an aggressive player in the blinds is subject to try a squeeze play if ElkY just smooth-calls. By 3-betting in position, ElkY preempts this move. The problem with flat-calling with AQ in this situation is that if it gets 3-bet and folded back to you, you'll be faced with an awkward decision. Although AQ is probably ahead of the laggy squeezer's range, if you 4-bet, he'll fold all hands that you beat, but may come over the top and move-in with his strong hands. Flat-calling his squeeze is also not a very attractive option, since you'll miss the flop two-thirds of the time and will probably be in an uncomfortable position post-flop against an aggressive foe. By taking the initiative and 3-betting in position, it takes the play away from your strong opponent. Additionally, early in the tournament,

ElkY likes to 3-bet with AK in this same situation 20% to 40% of the time, and more frequently when out of position.

ElkY explains, "This depends on the opening raiser's stack. If he has 20-30 BB, I would 3-bet 90% of the time, because I am very comfortable getting the money in PF against his range. Indeed, a stack size of 20-30 BB is shallow enough for him to not have reverse implied odds in that spot. As a result, he will probably re-shove with AQ or a pair. In the mid-to-late stages he increases his 3-bet frequency to 70% to 80% in position, and nearly always when out of position."

8

Monitoring Your Image

Your table image affects every move you make, along with your opponents' perception of your style and strategy. The key aspect of this concept is the difference between perception and reality. Your table image isn't linked to your style or technique. Rather, it's tied to the way your opponents view and analyze your play. The hands you show down, the frequency of your raises and 3-bets, and the number of times you check-fold post-flop are the parameters that make up your table image in the mind of your opponents.

For example, if you see three premium hands in one orbit, which you raise or 3-bet without getting any action or showdown, you'll be perceived as a very aggressive player. This might be the case, although any tight player would have played these 3 hands the same way. As a result, your opponents will tend to loosen up their 3-betting range against your raises and you shouldn't expect them to make big folds pre-flop against you. Therefore, when reacting to a 3-bet by an opponent who perceives you in this way, you probably shouldn't 4-bet as light as you might have if you hadn't played a single hand during the last hour, since players will anticipate that you're capable of betting light in that spot with great frequency.

Your opponents' perception of your image may vary considerably, especially in live poker. Live-tournament players come from many different backgrounds and often don't approach the game like most Internet players. Some live players are simply oblivious to the concept of table image. If you can identify players who pay no attention to table image, regardless of whether your image is good or bad, you shouldn't play against them like you would against more observant players.

For example, say you move all-in over the top of a raise with 22 against a player who has 20 BB left. Whereas a pro may understand the thought process behind your move, an amateur might think you're crazy!

There are other situations in which you should be aware of the circumstances with respect to your table image. Let's say you're in a cash game where a player has been sitting out and is just coming back from dinner. If you've been playing tight and showing monsters for the last hour, your table image won't matter to him in the slightest, so you won't be able to make the same kind of moves against him as you could against the rest of the players who have witnessed you turn over hand after hand. The same situation arises in tournaments when a new player is moved to your table.

When it comes to monitoring your image, you must definitely account for your opponents' perceptions based on a number of variables and try to anticipate how they'll react to your plays and your moves against them.

How To Use Your Image

In order to use your image to your advantage, you and your specific opponents must have some history. If you're a regular online player and you've played against an opponent in many sessions over time, you'll be able to use the image of your game he's built up over much time and experience. When you don't have a history with a player, it substantially reduces the range of moves and plays you can make against him, as he may underestimate you or not credit you with the capability of pulling specific moves.

Deception

We believe that it's *key* to play opposite to the current perception of your image. This may change over time based on your actions and the player composition at your table. If you're perceived as a very tight player who is unlikely to make a move, you'll get a lot of credit if you pick the right spot and a big pot for a play, such as a squeeze bet, a pre-flop 4-bet, or a river bluff, regardless of your holding. On the other hand, if you've been re-raising constantly, then you should be aware that at some point, you'll need a real hand to get paid off.

For example, when players such as Dario Minieri and Lex "Raszi" Veldhuis hold a huge hand like KK, they tend to get paid off by weaker holdings, such as 99, 88, AJ, etc., because their opponents no longer believe them after witnessing their constant aggression. However, the downside is that when they're card-dead, they lose a lot of chips with their moves, because the other players start firing back at them with a higher frequency than a normal tight-aggressive player would encounter.

Players with a lot of TV exposure often have an established image as soon as they sit down. This can sometimes be problematic, as unknown players can have a preconceived notion based on what they've observed on television and act accordingly. Only substantial time at the table might change their perception, but often their preconceived image is difficult to shake. ElkY and Lee often have this problem. What makes it particularly difficult is that it's impossible to ascertain which players at the table already have formulated a view on our images. Engaging them in conversation can sometimes be revealing.

Capitalizing

You can capitalize on your image by making plays that are contrary to it. If you're a maniac, you'll get paid off when you actually do hold a big hand. On the other hand, if you're really tight, you shouldn't be surprised if everyone folds when you raise with AA.

Tight players can capitalize by bluffing with air once in a while (and if you don't have the heart to make a play like this, we suggest you take up chess!). Also, you can gain an additional edge by balancing your play and making sure the opponents you pick are aware of your image at the time.

Building your image in a tournament with the intention of manipulating it at a later point is actually a big gamble. The problem is, you never really know when your table will break (although sometimes you can ask the Tournament Director if there is a predetermined table-break order) or if you'll be moved to re-balance tables. Additionally, an opponent against whom you've been doing some image building may get knocked out by someone else or moved to another table, preventing you from taking advantage of your previous set-up work.

As we explain below, avoid losing chips in order to build your image. Negative EV bluffs aren't a smart idea if your sole intent is to use the move to get paid off in future hands. You can never be sure you'll get into such a spot in the future, and you can't guarantee that you'll have enough chips left to make whatever play it is you're planning.

Here's an excerpt from an article ElkY wrote on the subject for *Bluff* magazine in 2010 discussing how to build your table image:

> "First of all, you have to be careful, because one mistake a lot of players make is to do something crazy or something almost plain stupid just to 'build their image.' Your image is only worth as much as the time you can expect to play with your opponents. If your table is about to break or the day is nearly over, you don't want to call short-stack all-ins with small pocket pairs or similar gambling hands just to send your opponents the message that they can't come back over the top of you with air. For example, let's say that there are four more hands to play before the last hand of the day. If you try to steal and someone comes over the top for a decent amount, where the situation is marginally negative EV, or

neutral EV at best, there is no point in calling; just let the hand go and come back with a fresh image the next day.

"In tournaments especially (as explained in Chapter 3), hands should almost always be played with a plan that accounts for all the information you've gathered up to that point; *it's usually much more important to make the right move at the right time rather than trying to build up some image at the cost of EV.* Chips are too important for that. (Cash games are another matter, obviously.) If it's a really deep-stacked tournament and you know your table isn't likely to break, you can take a little more freedom with your image, but it still depends on many different factors.

"Also, as always in anything poker-related, pay close attention to your opponents, especially the ones who are observant of situations and ready to exploit them. On the other hand, you'll also face some players who will be oblivious to the fact that you stole their blind ten times in a row and are just waiting for a premium hand to re-raise you. In that case, even if you hold pocket nines and it's the best hand you've raised their blinds with, it doesn't matter; you can fold safely to their re-raise, because you'll get their blind the next twenty times.

"I don't advise showing bluffs frequently. I only do it when my opponents show me a really bad lay down and I think it might tilt them a bit to show a bluff. That said, when bluffing, make sure it's worth showing, because for the hypothetical chance of throwing a player off his game, you give free information to the rest of the table and that's never a good thing, especially if it's a river bluff. Whereas showing AQ to a player you three-bet pre-flop when he showed you he folded AQ also doesn't give much information to anyone really, showing an elaborate bluff on the river gives away a lot more information on how you played that kind of hand on earlier streets.

"To conclude, always be aware of how your opponents

perceive you and try to react accordingly, but try rarely to sacrifice equity to build some kind of image; in tournament poker, it's never worth it."

How to Change Gears Depending On the Respect You're Getting

If your image is good and people respect your raises and 3-bets, we obviously suggest you keep doing it as long it's profitable. However, be aware that the notion of respect is something that may change quickly and you'll most likely need to readjust several times throughout the tournament.

Monitoring Opponents' Images

Here's another key concept: *Your opponents aren't always aware of their own images.* The better players are aware and do adapt to it, but weaker players simply aren't aware of this concept or don't know how to use it. Once again, it comes down to your ability to identify your opponents' patterns and tendencies.

For example, let's assume the player on your right has been fairly tight for an hour because of some aggressive players on his right, and is now left with a medium-to-short stack. The blinds and antes are getting quite high and everyone folds to him on the cutoff for the first time in several orbits. Your assumption should be that a good player will be raising almost 100% of his hands in this spot and it's therefore a good spot for you to 3-bet him light. On the other hand, if you think he's a weaker player, you might not want to make that move, because his opening range may be the same regardless of his position or his image. In other words, you shouldn't try to overthink or make sophisticated moves against a player who probably doesn't play at a high enough level to understand what you're doing.

Big Calls and Big Folds

The Importance of Big Calls

The most important aspect of making big calls is the effect on the metagame, table image, and, obviously, gaining chips. However, making a big call depends on specific spots; in our opinion, you should never try to make big calls only to build your table image. If the hand is slightly -EV, it's *occasionally* OK to consider a big call. Nevertheless, you need to keep in mind that making big calls will definitely increase the variance of your game, which is not something you should pursue in an effort to build your table image.

From the metagame perspective, making big calls with marginal or weak hands sends your opponents a clear message, and they'll probably avoid floating you with air and trying to outplay you on later streets. Therefore, they'll usually tighten their range against you, which is always a good thing! *Making big calls will strengthen your table image and increase your fear equity.* However, keep in mind that only the players at the table when you made the call will remember it. If a new player comes to the table a few hands after your big call, he may try to bluff you, just like your previous opponent.

Here are some examples that illustrate image-related hands from ElkY.

Example 1

Pokerstars Caribbean Adventure Hi-Roller 2009

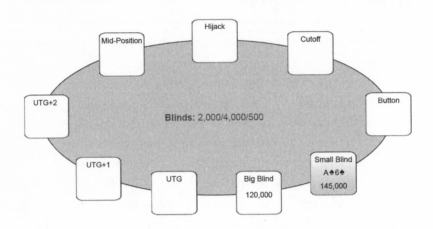

The blinds are 2,000/4,000 with a 500 ante. I have around 145,000; Johan Van Til has around 120,000. I hold A♣6♣ in the SB.

Johan is a very aggressive Internet player against whom I played many hands when I won the WPT Fiesta Al Lago the previous October. He's directly on my left. Since arriving at the table, I've limped many times with weak holdings in SB versus BB situations.

Pre-flop, everyone folds to me in the SB and I decide to limp from the SB. I like to mix up my game in this spot for several reasons. First of all, when out of position, I like to control the pot size. Second, should an ace hit the flop, my hand would be very well-disguised, because I know that Johan, with his aggressive style, would expect me to raise with an ace pre-flop.

I call 2,000. Johan raises it to 12,000 total. I call. The flop comes Q♣-T♦-2♦.

I check and Johan checks behind. At this point, I don't think he'd check a strong made hand on such a dangerous board. He could be checking a ten, but I'm almost certain he'd bet a queen in this spot, knowing that I could try to make a move on this drawy board. Therefore, my read is that he's either on a draw, trying to control the pot, or holding a medium-strength hand with good showdown value. I believe he could be holding KJ, J9, or two small diamond cards. In all three cases, I'd be ahead in the hand.

The turn is a 3♠. Leading out in this spot wouldn't make much sense. In this kind of spot, a turn bet doesn't represent many hands. Additionally, leading out would make me vulnerable to a raise. Johan is a very aggressive player and wouldn't hesitate to put me on the spot should he sense any weakness on my end. Also, he could simply flat-call, which would greatly complicate my decision on the river. Lastly, he could just fold to my bet and I wouldn't extract any value from my hand. If I follow my read from the flop, check calling seems to be the optimal play.

I check and Johan bets 18,000, which would tend to represent a very strong hand. However, it doesn't seem consistent with the previous action. Johan might have made a set on the turn or raised me pre-flop with a holding such as 32, but I don't think either of those is very likely. I call the 18,000, my plan being to check-call the river, because I believe his intention is to continue bluffing. If he has a ten, or a medium pair such as 99 or 88, then the board is already too dangerous for him to value bet big on the river. If he holds a Q♣ then he's played it very well. The river's a 5♥.

I check as planned and he quickly bets 42,000. Now I have to re-evaluate the hand. Johan could have A4, making a gutshot straight on the river. However, his pre-flop raising range is quite wide, and more often he will have two big cards. My hand is weak, merely ace high, but the board now contains multiple busted draws, and against each one of those my ace is likely good. The only card that would justify a value bet in this spot is a Q♣ but I'd discarded that possibility in my analysis of the flop play. Furthermore, it's crucial for me to take control of the table at this stage of the tournament. I know how aggressive Johan is and I don't want to let him bully me. Only 16 players are left and I know that making a big call would greatly benefit my table image.

I call, turn over my cards, and Johan instantly throws his cards in the muck! By following my read throughout the hand, I made a great call, which had three major benefits. I now have a lot of chips, my confidence is boosted, and my opponents are scared to play against me. I have just put myself in a very favorable position to go deep in the tournament.

The Importance of Big Folds

The most important reason for making big folds is to preserve your chip stack. Depending on the stage and chip stacks during a tournament, you can sometimes do more and sometimes do less with your chips.

Let's say you're deep into a tournament and you have 50 BB, with the average at 40 BB. If you get into a situation where you'd play a coin flip for a 50 BB pot, the outcome would leave you with either 75 BB or 25 BB. The decision whether to take the coin flip in this spot is crucial. With 50 BB, you have a lot of fold equity on the majority of your opponents. You can bust a lot of the average and short stacks. You also have enough depth to call some raises in position and try to outplay your opponents on the flop or later streets, with the option of controlling the pot size, if necessary. However, should you lose the flip and be left with 25 BB, you have only one more raise-fold and a round of blinds before you reach the critical stack size of 20 BB, where your game now revolves around a push-fold strategy. When you thoroughly think through the situation, you can see how taking that flip with 50 BB greatly increases your tournament variance, and increased variance is something that better players are best served by avoiding.

Example 2

EPT Deauville 2010

(Note—This hand is analyzed mathematically in the Appendix.)

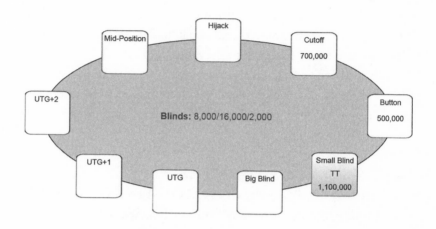

Freddy Deeb has 700,000 in the cutoff and a Romanian player has 500,000 on the button. I'm holding TT in the small blind with 1,100,000.

I played with the Romanian on Day 2 and he hadn't gotten out of line, in my opinion; I considered him to play fairly conservatively and straightforward. Freddy Deeb is an intelligent and successful live pro.

Pre-flop play folds to Freddy on the CO, who raises to 40,000. The Romanian on the button 3-bets him to 110,000.

I think my TT in the SB is very borderline. Obviously, the Romanian player knows Freddy is loose and raises a wide range. However, I don't think he'd 3-bet light or with complete air in such a spot. He could have 99, AQ or AK, probably AJ or AT suited, maybe KQ suited. In addition, Freddy could also have a big hand. Therefore, I believe this situation to sometimes be slightly +EV, but often to be neutral EV. If I 4-bet in this spot, my opponents will probably fold anything less than JJ+ and AK, but should they have any of those hands, I'll have to call their all-in bet.

In a spot like this, I think protecting my stack is the priority.

Indeed, moving from 1.1 million to 1.6 million in chips when the average is 900,000 won't make such a big difference if I win an all-in pot. On the other hand, should my stack drop to 600,000, I'd have much less depth with which to work. In addition, making such a fold can be a good move in tournaments where you think you have a big edge on your opponents and you'll be able to outplay them in better spots. I opted for stack preservation and folded.

We asked Tysen to analyze the math to determine whether ElkY's fold was positive or negative EV compared to an alternative line of play of 4-betting to 250,000. To analyze this, we made the following assumptions:

- Opener will open top 25% of hands.
- 3-bettor will 3-bet with 99+, AQ+, ATs+, KQs (plus 5% as outright bluff, but for purposes of this analysis we eliminated this).
- Opener will shove AK, will shove QQ 75% of time, and JJ 50% of time, and will otherwise fold.
- If opener folds, 3-bettor will shove JJ+, AK, AQs 75% of time, and TT 75% of time, and will fold otherwise.
- If the opener shoves, 3-bettor will still call with KK+.

Without taking into account Independent Chip Model (ICM) considerations, such as the payouts or average chip stacks, I did this analysis using raw-chip EV. Given these assumptions, raising to 250k is slightly -EV compared to folding (-15k vs. -8k)—the details of this calculation are found in the Appendix. However, once you add in bubble factors from the tournament payouts, it will only make the EV worse; it could never be more favorable. Therefore, *folding is absolutely better.* The main contributing factor is that you don't have much fold equity. You take the pot without a contest only 36% of the time, and when you're called, you're likely behind. I'd suspect that with bubble factors, folding JJ is probably correct in this spot as well, but it depends on the stack-size distributions.

Example 3
EPT Warsaw 2009

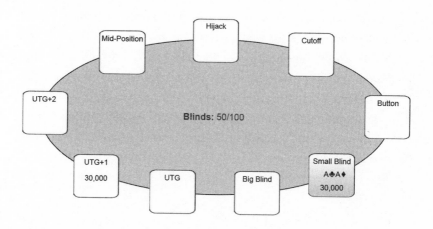

It's very early in the tournament and I don't have much information on my opponents.

Pre-flop, a player in early position raises to 300; it folds around to me in the SB. To mix up my play and disguise the strength of my hand, especially when everyone is still so deep, I decide to call pre-flop rather than re-raising. If I 3-bet out of position so early on, I'm definitely giving away the strength of my hand, as I'll almost never re-steal under these conditions. If my opponent is good, he'll know how good my hand is and will either fold or play all the upcoming streets carefully and optimally. Additionally, I'm giving the player in the BB the opportunity of making a squeeze that will end up costing him severely. At worst, I'll be facing two opponents; not too bad when holding aces. The BB winds up making the call as well. The flop is a J♣-5♣-T♠.

I lead 525 for about half-pot. I like to lead in such a spot, because I'll get instant value from any J and my hand is very much underrepresented. If one of my opponents holds a J, I should be able to get all three streets of value most of the time. The BB calls and the initial raiser folds.

The turn: A♠. I lead for 1,100. The BB thinks for a little while and makes the call. The river: 8♦. I bet 3,300. My opponents tanks for a while, grabs chips, and appears to be thinking about just calling, then finally goes for more chips and raises to 9,600. I think it's nearly impossible for him to raise me for value this early in the tournament with anything other than KQ or Q9. I tank for quite a while, then fold my aces face up. He elects not to show me his hand. Later in the tournament, the same player forced an opponent to fold TT when holding TT himself. He showed his opponent his cards, telling him he made a bad fold. I think this is important to notice, because I believe he would have shown me his cards had he been bluffing or had a worse hand when I folded the aces to him.

Example 4

APPT Macau 2007

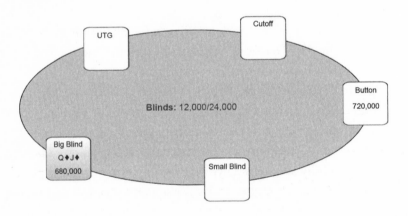

An opponent named Tan raises to 77,000 from the button with A♦Q♥. I re-raise to 197,000 with Q♦J♦, and Tan calls. The pot is 434,000.

The flop is Q♣-8♥-5♥. I check and Tan bets 210,000. I fold.

In this case, I can't really say that I had a tell on my opponent, but I think I made my decision based on metagame and the overall game flow. I'd played with Tan a few days before, and I knew he respected my game and feared me. Therefore, I assumed that his range to call my PF 3-bet was certainly tight. When he bet after I checked the flop, I knew he wouldn't be likely to fire with a medium pair such as JJ, TT, or 99 on such a board; I believe he'd rather have checked behind with such holdings. Additionally, I sensed a lot of confidence in his bet. All in all, from the read I had on him, I think his range to bet there was most likely polarized to a huge hand. As a result, my analysis was that Tan, in that spot, would probably not try to bluff me, and would even less likely have called a PF 3-bet with the intention to bluff me on later streets. Therefore, I opted for a fold.

Fighting for Control of the Table

When To Take Control of the Table

Fighting to control the table is obviously a very important part of the game, but you have to make sure you do it at the right time. For example, it's not cost effective to fight for pots at the early stages of the tournament before the antes kick in and when the blinds are small relative to stack sizes. Rather, during the first levels of a tournament, you should be working on building a strong image by exploiting opponents' weaknesses and by picking the right spots.

With Antes

It's definitely the most appropriate time to start fighting to control the table when antes kick in, as each uncontested raise becomes much more profitable than it was previously.

When Not To Take Control

There's not much point in trying to control a table that is about to break, especially if you have very aggressive opponents who may put your chips at risk. If too much variance is required to fight for table control, you should avoid trying to do so. In fact, at times in the tournament, your chip stack and equity supercede the importance of controlling the table. In such situations, we advocate staying away from high-variance situations. Especially these days, as the trend is to play small ball and gradually increase your stack throughout the tournament, I think good players shouldn't necessarily alter their strategy in order to play massive pots or go for big bluffs.

How to Take Control on the Bubble

Picking your spots is obviously crucial. Try to balance the frequency of your 3-betting abuses of the bubble; if you think a player opens way too light, you may want to 3-bet him once every two orbits, depending on what's been taking place at the table.

Picking your opponents is also very important. It's up to you to identify which players are really abusing the bubble, which ones respect you, and which ones are fearless and ready to play for all their chips, even with a big stack at a crucial stage in the tournament.

Using your image also matters. Whether you're the stealer or you decide to fight back at an overzealous raiser, make sure your opponent respects you and that your moves are credible. Factor in the history at the table, or between you and your opponent if you've played together in the past. If you do a good job at picking weaker opponents to control the table, you'll be perceived as strong by the better players. Therefore, they may decide not to tangle with you.

At the same time, while building your image, you must send the message that you won't fold a lot and are crazy enough to play big pots, when in fact you're actually more conservative than you appear to be. This goes back to the concept of perception versus reality. In fact, you may even want to make a marginally -EV call when you have a big stack in order to effectively send this kind of message. Also, you may choose to 4-bet light and play one or two high-variance pots, if you know you'll be spending a lot of time at your current table and you want to make sure that all of your opponents realize they're best off avoiding you and attacking others at the table.

For example, if you raise to 2.3 BB with 44 from mid-position and a laggy player with 35 BB 3-bets to 6 BB, you could 4-bet all in. If your plan goes well, you'll earn respect and fear equity and most of your opponents will leave you alone. Taking calculated risks such as this is key in taking control of the table and capitalizing on the bubble.

How to Maintain Control If the Momentum Changes

If the momentum changes too much, you sometimes have to give up control and wait for better spots as the tournament progresses. Once again, this depends on several parameters, such as when the table breaks, the format of the structure, etc.

For instance, if your image isn't good (you lost a big flip or a big pot, or you just got caught making a big bluff) at a 9-handed table that is not about to break, you should take some time and temporarily withdraw from the fight. If the structure is fast, though, you may have to just keep up with aggressive play no matter what.

Dangers of Trying Too Hard

The main dangers are trying to control the table with an insufficient stack size or with the wrong timing. If you have 30 BB, for instance, you shouldn't be fighting for control, because you don't have enough options to do so; your opponents with big stacks won't be afraid to tangle with you.

9

Bluffing

In the immortal words of Chris "Jesus" Ferguson, "The first thing you need in order to bluff is a really bad hand." This isn't entirely true, since naked bluffs aren't nearly as common as semi-bluffs, which can have greater expected value than top pair, but you still must improve to win.

Picking Your Opponent

This is probably the single most important variable in bluffing.

Obviously, timid weak-tight players are ideal targets, but thinking players can also be targets of complex multi-street bluffs.

When bluffing, it's crucial that your bets tell a convincing story. Take a classic hand played between Tom "Durrr" Dwan and Phil Ivey on the "High Stakes Poker" TV show. Although Phil Ivey wouldn't generally be considered the ideal player to bluff, Durrr used the information he had to tell a convincing story.

In this hand, Phil Laak raised from early position pre-flop to $3,900 with A9o; Eli Elezra called with A♣7♣ from the cutoff, as did Ivey on the button with A♦6♦, followed by Daniel Negreanu in the small blind. Durrr, holding 9♠8♠, then raised to about $29,000, resulting in folds from Laak and Elezra, a call from Ivey, and a fold from Negreanu. Durrr started the hand with about $750,000 and

Ivey had more than $1 million. This is real money, not tournament chips.

The flop came down K♦-Q♣-T♦. First to act, Durrr bet about $45,000 and Ivey called; the turn was the 3♣. Durrr now bet about $123,000 and after some deliberation, Ivey called. The 6♠ came on the river and after due consideration, Durrr bet approximately $263,000, leaving himself with around $280,000. Ivey went into the tank, thought for an incredibly long time (Elezra fell asleep!), and finally folded.

Looking back over the hand, we can go through the probable thought processes. Durrr's initial re-raise after an early-position raise and three calls represents a premium hand. The flop of K-Q-T with two diamonds could easily have given him a set. He could also have hands such as AK or AA. Durrr's flop bet of $45,000 is consistent with any of these holdings. Ivey, holding the nut-flush draw and an overcard, might have considered raising on the flop, but probably rejected this option, concerned that if he raised on the flop, Durrr could re-raise, forcing him to fold. In this event, Ivey would have lost the substantial equity that his flush draw provided. Having considered all this, Ivey elected to just call on the flop.

On the turn, Durrr's bet continued to be consistent with a big hand; Ivey still had enough implied odds to call, probably thinking that Durrr, if he had the hand he was representing, would have substantial difficulty folding if the diamond came on the river. The 6♠ on the river gave Phil a pretty useless pair. Durrr now continued to paint a picture of a very strong hand by betting over a quarter-million on a triple-barrel bluff.

Ivey, realizing that he probably had no fold equity when Durrr had already committed about 75% of his chips to the pot and knowing that he could beat only a bluff, reluctantly folded and Durrr scooped a huge pot!

A significant piece of information that made this excellent bluff possible is that Ivey had just smooth-called on the flop after an early-position raise and two calls. It's highly unlikely, given this betting sequence, for Ivey to have pocket kings, queens, or aces, but Durrr knew that Ivey couldn't eliminate these hands from *his* range. By playing the hand strongly on all three streets, Durrr got Ivey to fold.

Admittedly, due to Durrr's high bluffing frequency (it was a perfect spot for a pre-flop squeeze play, for instance, which in fact it was), Ivey was suspicious, but all he could beat was a bluff, and Durrr's actions were all perfectly consistent with a big hand, since he led on every street.

Bluffing Opportunities

In other chapters, we cover a number of areas that involve bluffing. C-bets are essentially a bluff on the flop. Double and triple-barreling involves continuing your bluff on the turn and river, respectively. Three-betting and 4-betting light are bluffs that relate to the battle for the blinds and antes during the mid-game. Putting players to a decision for all their chips on the bubble is another example of a high-pressure bluff. The final-table bubble, where players often freeze due to the opportunity to make an appearance on TV, is another setting where bluffs are often highly successful.

Here are some bluffing lines that are likely to be effective, provided you have a solid image. LAGs and hyper-LAGs are often called down more frequently than a solid player, and must pick their spots to bluff more carefully.

Check-raise bluffs on the flop. Check-raising on the flop can often be successful against players who c-bet with high frequency. It's best to do this with a modicum of value, such as bottom pair, a gutshot, or even a backdoor flush draw (one of your suit) on the flop. The preferred board textures to do so are really dependent on your opponent. Against weaker players, any paired non-drawy board is quite good, like Q-5-5, because they won't realize how polarized your range usually is in that situation (basically 5, queens full, or air) and they'd still fold all their ace-high and smaller-pair hands. However, thinking players are aware of this and will either re-raise the flop again, call down with mid-pair, or float to take the pot away from you later. In the current metagame, it's almost better to check/raise on more coordinated boards when you have absolutely zero equity in the hand, because it's much tougher for your opponent to make a move in those spots.

Floating the flop and raising the turn. This is a very strong line. Raising on the turn as a bluff isn't commonly seen and a betting line like this reeks of strength.

Say you have position on an opponent and call his mid-position raise with 7♥6♥ and the flop comes A♥-9♣-2♠. Your opponent bets two-thirds of the pot and you call; the turn is the 5♥ and your opponent bets again. Raising now, representing a set, is a strong play, even though you're actually semi-bluffing with the flush draw that you just picked up on the turn. Whether or not the heart comes on the river, a pot-sized bet is likely to be a winner. Betting the river, both when you hit and when you miss, balances your range. The line you take with both your strong hands and your bluffs is indistinguishable.

Check/min-raising the turn, and moving all-in on the river. This is another strong bluffing line. Out of position after having called a pre-flop raise, this line involves check-calling on the flop, then check/min-raising on the turn, then making a big bet—often all-in—on the river.

River bluffs. Generally speaking, river bluffs are underutilized. They're particularly effective against foes who like to value bet thin on the river, and when your read is that your opponent is making a blocking bet.

Check-raising as a bluff on the river against opponents who value bet thin is a very strong play, since most players aren't capable of making big river bluffs when facing a bet from their opponent. Therefore, your bluff will likely be treated with great respect and your opponent will probably fold all but the strongest hands.

When in position, raising weak leads from straightforward players can be profitable. Often, these are blocking bets, where an opponent is attempting to control the size of the pot. By making a small bet on the river, he's hoping to keep you from making a larger bet (like you would have, had he checked). This type of action can provide a good bluffing opportunity, especially if a card comes on the river that might complete a flush or a straight.

Some tricky players make weak river leads with very strong hands, hoping to be raised. This is, in fact, a good line for you to take against strong laggy players, who are likely to read it as weakness and raise, falling into your trap.

Another good river-bluffing opportunity is when you're on a straight draw and a third flush card hits on the river. Since your action up to that point will be consistent with a draw, your opponent may well be convinced that you hit your flush. This bluff can also be made when you're on a flush draw, but an obvious straight card comes on the river.

Hand Example from ElkY
WCOOP 2009 Event 43

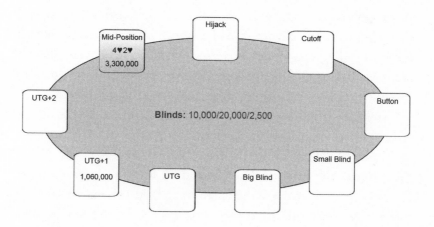

There are 80 players left. I'm a huge chip leader at my table and I've been controlling and bullying my opponents for quite a while now, hitting flops, but also mixing it up with successful bluffs. Very few opponents seem to be ready to make a stand against me, so I keep the trend going!

Villain 1 raises to 50,000 from UTG+1. He's a weak-to-average player. His stack size of around 50 BB is perfect for me to put him in an uncomfortable position with a 3-bet. Indeed, in such a spot, I could very well hold JJ+ or AK+ and be ready to call his all-in. All my opponents left to act behind have stacks too small to have implied odds to call, so I think my 3-bet may force him to fold a strong range, up to TT or AQ. I min-3-bet to 99,000. With the right pot odds, the villain calls. The pot is 250,000.

The flop is T♠-J♠-8♠, obviously very unfavorable to my hand.

The villain checks. Often, I should be able to win the pot right there with a c-bet, but I also like to mix up my play. I believe that checking heads-up IP represents strength. Checking here is a line I often use myself with hands that have good showdown value, but with which I'm not ready to call an all-in on the flop. For instance, I may check behind in this spot with AJ, QQ, KK (no spades), sometimes 7♠7♥ or A♠/K♠.

The turn is the 5♠ and the villain checks again. This is now a good opportunity to take the initiative on the fourth spade, since I no longer have any chance to win at showdown and it's likely that the villain will give up if he has missed. I bet half the pot and the villain calls. I think he's too weak to play A♠ or K♠ this way, although it would be a great line in this case. The pot is roughly 500,000.

The river is the 6♠ and the villain bets 220,000. His lead here scares me less than another check would. At this point, I'm almost certain that he doesn't hold the ace or king of spades, in which case the optimal line in my opinion would be to go for a check raise. According to my analysis, the villain may hold two pair, a set, or a straight with no spades, and try to turn his hand into a bluff on this dangerous board. It's also possible that he is trying to do a semi-value blocking bet with Q♠ or 9♠. I think I'm now in a great spot to put him under a lot of pressure. If I move all-in here, he'll have to make a decision for his tournament life, whereas he'll still be left with a reasonable stack if he folds. Furthermore, even if he makes a hero call, assuming my analysis is correct, I'll still be left with more than 100 BB.

I move all-in and my opponent folds. I show the bluff, and the party goes on!

Picking Off Bluffs

Picking off bluffs is a very important skill for poker. When you think your opponent might be bluffing, you'll need to consider several parameters.

The first thing to consider is your opponent's typical patterns, and whether his line on a given hand is consistent with the plays you've observed previously.

Also, it's important to realize which street you think your opponent may be bluffing. In my opinion, it's generally easier to pick off bluffs on the flop or the turn, as you'll most often face semi-bluffs.

One of the most important aspects is to have assessed your opponent's range and tendencies in a given spot. For example, let's assume your opponent is really tight and doesn't mix up his game too much. He raised from EP. If any 6 makes a straight on the turn and your opponent bets, it's fairly unlikely he's actually holding a 6 in that spot. Indeed, the only probable hand he could hold is 66, and he would most likely have limped with such a holding pre-flop.

To determine whether your opponent is bluffing, you need to be able to reconstruct the hand based on previously observed ranges and betting patterns.

Another aspect linked to picking off bluffs is when you make moves to *induce* bluffs from your opponents. The most obvious situation for this is when you have the nuts OOP and one or more draws missed on the river. If you bet there, your opponent will fold most of his bluffs, unless he's a total maniac and tries to bluff-raise you with complete air (still pretty rare, in my opinion). He'll probably only call you with hands that have decent value. On the other hand, if you check, your opponent will often value-bet with most of the hands he would have called with; he'll also often bluff with his missed draws. Sometimes, your opponent may even get stubborn with his value bet and call your check-raise. As a result, I think that you get more value overall by trying to check-raise the nuts on the river OOP.

When you have a strong hand in the same spot and are unsure whether you have the winning hand, check-calling on the river is a move that can help you control the pot size. Indeed, you'll avoid the headache of facing a tough decision if you get raised there. For example, let's assume you have Q♥Q♦, and the flop is J♦-T♦-8♠. You bet OOP and get called by your opponent both on the flop and the turn, which is the 5♠. The river is the 6♣. When you check there, your opponent will often bet all of his missed draws such as two diamonds, KQ, and may also bet a strong J, depending on the situation. Of course, he'll also value-bet all his two pairs and straights, which beat your hand, but you will at least have dodged the headache of betting the river and getting raised, rendering you no longer able to control the pot size. Overall, I therefore tend to think that this move is +EV.

Polarized Ranges

Another critical concept with regard to picking off bluffs is to identify when your opponent's range is very polarized. A polarized range means your opponent may bet either an extremely strong hand (nuts or second nuts, for instance), bet as a bluff, or check behind with any other hand. Of course, your ability to recognize polarized ranges is based on experience and is very player dependent.

For example, let's say you've observed a specific opponent who tends to check back two pair on a fairly safe board. If the same opponent keeps firing at you on a board that shows a four-card straight, that opponent will often have a range polarized to either the straight or nothing.

I think it's usually easier to recognize polarized ranges against weaker players. For example, you're facing a weak opponent who raises A♠Q♦ from LP and you call from the BB. The flop is A♣-Q♥-2♥ and you check-call your opponent's c-bet. The turn is the 7♦, and you check-call his bet again. The river is the T♥; you check, and your opponent checks behind with top two pair. If you know your opponent tends to check in such a situation, you can also assume that, except when holding a hand such as A♥x♥ (top-pair and nut-flush draw), there's probably no hand that he'll 3-barrel with for value on the board above. Therefore, in situations similar to this one, your weak opponent's range is very polarized, to either the nut flush or air. Against better players, it's usually more difficult to discern such polarized ranges, as they'll be able to value bet thin in a lot of situations on similar boards. For instance, good players may very well value bet thin here with sets, any two pair, AK, or AJ, which will make the call more difficult for you to make.

Sometimes your opponents use lines that just don't seem to make sense, leading you to think that they're bluffing. However, it's important to realize one fact: Players around the table all have different skills, playing experience, and strategic concepts. As a result, a line that doesn't make sense to some amateur may be perfectly understandable to pro players, and vice versa. Therefore, it's important to keep this concept in mind before making a decision, because the key often lies in your ability to put yourself in your opponent's mind.

ElkY remembers a hand that took place during the Wynn Classic 2009 between Jimmy Fricke and Scott Seiver. He doesn't exactly recall all the action, but on a board something like KT and 3 rags, Scott Seiver moved all-in on the river. Fricke tanked for a long time before making the call. Seiver instantly mucked his 22, thinking he was way dominated. However, Fricke had only AQ, which held up only because Seiver had already thrown his hand away!

This anecdote simply illustrates the fact that, especially when it comes to polarized ranges, the best move or the best read is always the one that accounts for the way your opponent thinks.

Bet sizes can also give you valuable information when trying to pick off bluffs. Good players usually plan ahead with their bet-sizing.

For example, if they bluff by check-raising the turn with the intention of betting the river, they'll make sure they have at least 75% of the pot size left to bet. On the other side, weaker players, although it always varies, tend to bet small with big hands and overbet when bluffing. In my opinion, this pattern is probably the worst possible EV, as you don't win enough with big hands, but may lose a lot when called bluffing. In general, I believe there's a bet-sizing threshold to your fold equity on river bets as bluffs. *If you bluff-bet 75% to 100% of the pot on the river, that is the point where you have the maximum fold equity relative to the risk of losing your chips if you get called.*

Another thing to consider is the fact that, when deciding whether to call your bet, your opponent will typically ask himself what he would have done in your shoes. Therefore, if you're able to use reverse psychology in such situations, you should be able to extract value from some of your moves. The idea, as always, is to try and mislead your opponents as much as possible.

Some players have a strong tendency to bluff too much when they have a big stack. If you can identify that, it may allow you to make some big calls in opportune situations.

When it comes to physical tells, ElkY doesn't consider himself an expert at picking off bluffs in such a way. However, he usually tries to pay attention to reaction time in his opponent's moves. For instance, players who usually take a long time to make decisions are often bluffing if they suddenly act fast.

For physical tells, as well as any other tells that help you pick off bluffs, it's crucial that you've established a baseline by carefully observing your opponent's behavior. Whenever your opponent's action or behavior deviates from that baseline, you may start suspecting a bluff. Conversely, when you have a strong hand, you might make your opponents think you're bluffing by occasionally using tricky and unexpected lines compared to what you have been showing previously.

10

Min-Raises

Min-raises are the smallest possible raise—equal to the blinds or the last bet. I have only one thing to say about min-raises: I hate them. It's not that I think they aren't a viable playing option. It's just that they're annoying to play against. I've made all kinds of posts on the poker forum twoplustwo.com, where I've described being min-raised and I wasn't sure how to react, because they're often such a different dynamic than being raised in a more standard way. Luckily, most people's patterns with their min-raises tend to be fairly consistent, and while you can never be 100% certain, you can make some confident generalizations about them.

Min-raises need to be discussed on a street-by-street basis. How you interpret them and what their overall indication means are quite different, depending on which street you get min-raised on. We'll discuss both how to use them and how to combat them.

Pre-Flop

When Your Opponent Opens With a Min-Raise

What a min-raise means from an opponent often depends on what stage of the tournament you're in and what position he's in. Early in a tournament, people min-raise from numerous positions with all kinds of random stuff. You can often (but not always) discount big pairs, since most people are more interested in protecting them during the early stages than getting tons of players into the pot. Sometimes they'll show up with hands like suited connectors or small pairs, trying to make sure they see a flop cheaply. But people's min-raising range early in a tournament can end up including all sorts of things, including big face cards, strong pairs, or just random junk.

Meanwhile, min-raises during the late stages of tournaments very often represent a big pair, especially if the player has been making standard raises, then suddenly elects to min-raise. This is especially true with min-raises coming from early position, but much less consistent with min-raises from the cutoff or button. In fact, I give such little credit to button min-raises that I 3-bet them at a very high frequency, anticipating getting many folds. I'm especially paranoid about min-raises from UTG deep in a tournament; those very often wind up being a big pair.

How You Should Use Min-Raises Pre-Flop

This depends a lot on your table. Early in the tournament, I rarely min-raise, but at the middle or late stages, I see plenty of situations where they could become useful. If you have a table that tolerates them and lets you steal the blinds with them, I'd encourage min-raising as a steal quite often. Additionally, many high-stakes tournaments online have gotten to the point where nearly everyone opens for a min-raise, because most all players are generally playing 3-bet-or-fold poker.

Whether you should pull stunts like min-raising your big pairs in order to get action depends on the intelligence of the players on your table. If you're on a $100-re-buy table online and have been employing all normal raises, then suddenly min-raise, your opponents are sure to know something's up. Knowing this, it's possible, once in a while, to use a min-raise from early position as a steal-raise. If you're on a table full of weak players who will simply see a smaller raise and start calling more, I'd encourage you to go ahead and make this seemingly obvious play: min-raise your big hands.

When Opponents Min-Re-Raise You Pre-Flop

Against non-thinking players, you can count on this being a huge hand they're trying to keep you in with. Some do this with a range that's so small it contains only KK+; others do it with hands such as AQ+/JJ+, not realizing that they're overrepresenting their hand in some cases.

Against thinking players, things get messier. Some thinking players like to make min- or tiny re-raises on your left, just to make your life difficult, because they know that you know it's not profitable to call re-raises—even small ones—out of position with all but a few hands. As a result, they wind up pummelling your open raises and force you to adjust, either by trying to call and getting creative post-flop or by starting to make small 4-bets with a wide range pre-flop. I normally combat players like this by widening my 4-bet range and frequency, but I also add some hands, such as KQs, to my flat-calling range that will often be a push/fold decision if they re-raise a standard amount. Keep in mind that some thinking players use min-re-raises with only big hands too, not aware that you're perceptive enough to be clued in to what they're attempting. This is especially true if your opponent has no idea, or indication, that you're a thinking player too.

How You Should Use Min Re-Raises Pre-Flop

Again, it's highly opponent-dependent. Against non-thinking players who call too wide against small re-raises, but fold against larger ones, I'm fine using a tiny re-raise pre-flop with a big hand in order to trap them. I might also have a wider min-re-raise range against opponents who open-raise frequently, and often flat-call re-raises, but don't 4-bet very much. This is because I can often make a tiny re-raise pre-flop and isolate them out of position in a heads-up pot, then take down a large percentage of the pots with a continuation bet on the flop. However, I wouldn't do this against a player who is apt to adjust and start 4-betting me often.

I don't usually min-re-raise thinking players pre-flop. This is because I want to keep my normal re-raise range balanced by including my big hands, and I don't necessarily want to play a lot of re-raised pots with good players post-flop, since their out-of-position calling range won't have serious leaks in it and they'll do many difficult things against me post-flop.

In the case of more amateur players, if they've been fairly short (10-15 BB) and moving in a lot without doubling up, you should suspect that they hold a monster if, all of a sudden, they open with a min-raise, from any position.

When stacks are 60+ BB, a 4-bet min-raise PF is a very powerful move with almost all your range, in my opinion. It forces your opponent to make a decision. Because play is still pretty deep, it's fairly rare that an opponent will 5-bet all-in with anything less than a premium hand, in which case you'll have the information you need to fold.

Let's say Player A raises from UTG+1 and Player B 3-bets from MP. If you min-reraise as a 4-bet from the button, you put both players in a very tough spot. Even though you're giving them odds to call, you may also hold a monster in that spot. Therefore, if either one comes over the top with a shove, you can fairly easily release any hand other than AA or KK.

Flop Min-Raises

When Your Opponent Min-Raises You On the Flop

Flop min-raises are the hardest to play against and dissect. So many players min-raise the flop, for so many reasons, that you normally need a decent amount of experience with a player to get a sense of what his specific min-raise means. If I have absolutely zero read on a player and he min-raises me on the flop, my assumption is that he has a big hand, but it's nowhere near as consistent as on other streets.

Most flop min-raises seem to be one of four things; the challenge is to figure out which. It could be:

1) A big hand looking to keep you in and extract value.

2) A drawing hand (likely in position, unless the player's an amateur) where the opponent is looking to create a little fold equity, plus give himself the chance to check back the turn, making the price to see cards cheaper.

3) A hand such as top pair raising to see where it's at, likely because the opponent isn't very good and thinks that raising for information is a clever idea—not realizing that he may in fact have turned a hand like top pair into a bluff against most of your range.

4) A cheap shot at bluffing on a flop that has an excellent texture. For example, you raise in mid-position, your opponent calls in late position, and everyone else folds. The flop is A-5-2 and you continuation bet (as you're going to do a very high percentage of the time on an ace-high flop) and he min-raises you, affording him a very cheap way to take the pot away from you in a spot that's hard for you to continue without top pair or better.

One of the counters ElkY likes to make, especially against the craziest hyper-LAGs and/or thinking players, is to flat-call (float) the min-raise OOP, as they'll most often make the move when IP themselves. Therefore, if you decide to float OOP, even with complete air, you become the one representing a very strong hand: at least a big ace, if not better. Most of the time, you can then check the turn, since your opponent will likely check behind to avoid a check-raise, then take the pot with a bet on the river. When you make such a move, it's usually preferable to have some kind of a backdoor draw, which leaves you with some outs in case your read was wrong. Unless your opponents are very strong and recognize what you're doing, ElkY believes this is a good counter move in such situations.

For instance, let's say you open 2.5 BB pre-flop (no antes) and get two callers IP. Everyone has around 50-60 BB. The flop is A-7-2 rainbow and you c-bet for 3.5 BB. One player folds and the player on the button raises you to 7 BB. If you re-raise to represent strength, you'll likely have to make it 18-20 BB, thus greatly increasing the variance. Therefore, by flat-calling here, not only are you representing great strength, but you're also saving some chips. On the river, assuming you both check the turn, you should be able to take the pot down with a bet as small as 8 BB.

If you notice that a villain tends to min-raise the flop only with big hands, naturally you fold when he raises. If you think he does it with both big and drawing hands, you're mostly stuck calling with hands that have decent showdown value. If you think he often does it with top pair to find out where he's at, then you should add a lot of hands to your flop 3-bet bluff/semi-bluff range, because you'll get him to fold a surprisingly good hand. If he does it with all four (or simply options 1, 2, and 4), then he's balanced it pretty well and playing against him will be annoying.

How To Use Min-Raises On the Flop

You can use min-raises in all the same ways villains use them against you—except for option 3, because taking a hand with very strong showdown value and essentially turning it into a bluff against a continuation bet is almost always a terrible idea.

Min-raises for value with huge hands are a good option against tight-weak players who get scared to put a large amount of chips in the pot without being very sure of their hand. These types often won't fold something like top pair to a min-raise, but they might fold it if you raise big on the flop, then follow it up with an appropriately sized bet on the turn. Opting for a flop min-raise instead ties them to the hand, since players like this normally don't think too much about ranges. If your villain is a massive calling station, you're likely better off going with a normal-sized raise.

Min-raising a draw in position can be a very good play against opponents who tend to double-barrel top pair or bluffs on the turn with large bets, but will be slowed down on the flop by your min-raise and likely not 3-bet the flop when faced with your raise. Against a single opponent, you'll also have some fold equity on the flop with certain boards, so the min-raise performs multiple functions.

Min-raising as a total bluff on an uncoordinated board with one high card can be a good play, as long as your opponent is either straightforward enough to fold when he doesn't catch a piece of the flop or you've balanced this by doing it with big hands and draws against thinking players.

I don't really use min-raises online much, because most players are aware that if I have a good hand, I'll go with a normal raise. But some players are straightforward enough that you can make this play and reduce how much you commit on your bluff attempts. The best possible flops for this kind of play are A-x-x, K-x-x, and Q-x-x, since your opponent will c-bet a high percentage of the time and be forced to fold most of the time against your raise when he has no showdown value, unless he feels like getting creative and 3-betting back with air (and most of them don't).

Turn Min-Raises

The turn is usually the last street you'll see people min-raise on a bluff. Overall, most turn min-raises are used for value with big hands, but occasionally, players will throw you curve balls and do it with a semi-bluff or complete air. It's not too likely as a semi-bluff on the turn; often the pot is so large at that point that they're better off moving all-in. But during the early or middle stages of a tournament when stacks are still deep, some people will use them.

This is especially true of very good players who are aware that you've seen them min-raise the turn for value; by doing it with bluffs/semi-bluffs, they balance their range against another thinking player. Aggressive players are also capable of making a big river bet after min-raising the turn, both for value with hands such as sets, or as a bluff on a missed draw. If you don't have this move in your arsenal, you should add it; it's a very strong line and, with a balanced range of monsters and bluffs, can give opponents plenty of headaches!

Most straightforward players rarely min-raise the turn without a monster. They're aware that people rarely fold to a raise of that size with so much committed and they want to keep their opponent in, so that they can extract a bit more value on the river. Be aware that if you have a draw and someone min-raises the turn against you, odds are you have excellent implied odds, since you can weight their range toward big hands, though this is less true when your draw is fairly obvious (such as the board becoming four to a straight, or a flush being the only reasonable hand you're drawing to).

It's the rare situation where I'd personally use a min-raise on a turn, but again, if you're in a spot with a very big hand against a player who you think would fold for more, it can be a good option. This is especially true if you have a full house on a board with a flush draw; if you make the raise too big, any decent opponent will realize he doesn't have correct odds to call and will fold, but if you min-raise, he'll almost always stay in and get smashed on the river if he makes his hand. Also, if a good player sees you min-raise the turn for value, you can consider min-raising the turn as a bluff against him in a later hand, if you think he'll believe you're only doing that with good hands.

ElkY and Lee min-raise the turn more frequently than I do. Against good thinking players, min-raising the turn as a bluff can sometimes work very well, if you choose your spots appropriately. If you think your opponent double-barrels as a bluff quite often, min-raising the turn will completely freeze his action.

Example
ElkY, EPT Copenhagen 2010

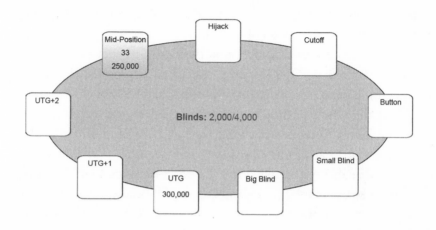

The opponent against whom ElkY played this hand is a good player. Here are ElkY's description and thought process:

From a hand I played against him the previous day, I assessed that he respects my game and that he likes to control pot sizes when stacks are deep. The blinds are 2,000/4,000. The villain is UTG with 300,000; I'm in middle position with 250,000.

The villain raises to 10,500 and I call with 33. My call may be a little borderline, but my opponent has been opening quite a lot of pots. I'm also hoping that one of the weak players in the blinds will get involved. I also have a good image, as I've been playing fairly tight for several orbits; this gives me a little more room to maneuver. The SB, a pretty weak player, calls as well.

The flop is 4-7-9 rainbow. The SB checks and the villain bets 21,000. Even though it may be a little larger than usual, it seems like a pretty standard continuation bet. At this point, folding would be acceptable. However, on a board that might have entirely missed both of us, he'll likely c-bet his entire range. So I call, preparing to re-evaluate on the turn. The SB folds.

The turn is a 5♦, which opens the diamond flush draw and gives me a gutshot. The villain bets 32,000. My reasoning is that he'd probably check with a decent hand if he was trying to exercise pot control, as is his tendency. His bet is really small and seems weak to me. He may well be bluffing in this spot. He might also have a hand that is difficult to play on the turn, such as 98 or 88. Therefore, his bet may also be some kind of a block.

Given my analysis, I now think this is a good spot to min-raise him, so I make it 77,000 (a little more than a min-raise, but close enough). Unless he's playing a very strong hand in a tricky manner, I don't think he'll be able to come over the top, and my min-raise will definitely freeze his potential plan to 3-barrel bluff. Unless he holds a big pair and makes the call, I think my move is +EV, because it should enable me to take down the pot often enough in this situation to be profitable. In addition, even if he calls, I probably still have six outs on the river. And if a diamond comes on the river, it will be an excellent card for a river bluff, since my opponent knows I'm capable of semi-bluff min-raising the turn with a flush draw. The villain folds.

I don't recommend making this move against amateur players at earlier stages of the tournament. Rather, you should use it sometimes against thinking players you have some history with. Not only will you be able to freeze their plan to 3-barrel, but you could also sometimes make them fold the best hand.

River Min-Raises

No one bluff min-raises the river. Ever. I think I've seen it less than three times in my career, and it's always a huge hand. If you don't have a monster, just fold.

That said, such a bluff can be very effective against a pro, because this play represents extreme strength and he just may not be able to believe you're capable of bluffing in this manner.

Another spot to consider min-raising on the river is against opponents likely to fold for more.

A final situation where you might use a river min-raise is when you have a hand like a hidden weak two pair on a fairly dry board. Your opponent is pretty straightforward and calls readily. If the two of you are still fairly deep, you can min-raise his river bet with the intention of folding to a further re-raise (knowing he basically always has better than a weak two pair), but you can often gain value if he gets married to one pair and can't say no to the price. Just because you'll fold to a re-raise doesn't mean you're bluffing. It means you're aware that you gain more chips from moves like this than you lose when you fold to a re-raise. He'll have one-pair hands and call far more frequently than he will re-raise and you'll fold, resulting in positive EV.

11

Mid-Stage Play
(Antes to Bubble)

We consider the mid-stage of a tournament to be everything between the antes kicking in and the bubble becoming a relevant factor.

In major live tournaments, the middle stages often last one or two days, depending on the speed and quality of the structure. Currently, most live structures start you with 10,000 to 20,000 chips and the antes often kick in at the second 100-200 level, generally with a 25 ante. You get one level of deeper-stack play at the first level with antes, but when the blinds increase to 150/300, the average stack is often reduced to about 75 BB and it normally continues to fall as the blinds escalate. Most live-tournament mid-stage play seems to hover around the 50-BB-average mark, though the size of stacks you'll encounter will generally be everything from very short (10 BB or less) to the chip leaders who may be holding 200 BB or more. As a result, you need the tools to play fairly deep-stacked poker with antes involved, which means having a variety of plays in your arsenal and the ability to think about deep-stacked poker on an advanced level.

The most obvious and immediate change you'll likely notice when the antes kick in is that professional players start opening more frequently and for smaller amounts. In live tournaments, many players settle into raising about 2.5 times the BB as their standard opening raise; online, at the time of this writing, it's dropped well under that to the 2.3-BB region, and in many cases even smaller.

Another immediate change is that the majority of thinking players also considerably widen their 3-betting range and start incorporating light 3-bets and 4-bets. You shouldn't anticipate too much of this from the weaker players on your table, but those capable of these plays will start initiating them at these stages.

You should follow suit with the professionals and cut your raise size, as well as look for good opportunities to 3-bet the table's more aggressive players, or the players who give too much credence to your 3-bets. We think that during the mid-stages, while stacks are still quite deep, you should generally plan to make 3-bets that are a full three times the size of the original raise, especially when you're out of position. In position, you can 3-bet a smaller amount against some tight and sensible players who are aware they shouldn't call re-raises light OOP in the 50-BB vicinity. But many players are willing to take a flop if the pot odds they're getting are favorable and they believe that stacks are deep enough to justify it.

In essence, *the moment antes kick in, you should open up your range for just about everything you're capable of doing pre-flop.* While the antes are still small, we don't recommend that you start 4-betting heavily, since stacks are generally still too deep for this and it's likely that there isn't enough built-up history with most opponents that getting it in with a wide range can be profitable.

But every now and then you'll find yourself up against a particularly aggressive 3-bettor who needs occasional reminding that you can't be pushed around all day. Also, consider 4-betting people who like to 3-bet for information or without much plan, in order to make them fold a better hand (especially when stacks are deep). If they 3-bet you with AQ, or 77 to TT when effective stacks are 60+ BB, it's super tough when you 4-bet them. Pick your spots carefully, though. Some hyper-LAGs have banned the word "folding" from their active vocabulary. Indeed, some of these fearless players will 5-bet you light if they think they have fold equity!

In order to get a more thorough sense of what we're discussing here, let's break down our mid-stakes play according to our stack size.

100 BB and Above

In a hand with antes, all kinds of possibilities are open when effective stacks are 100 BB or above. Your opening range can be as wide as you think is profitable, depending on your position and the player line-up behind you. You have room to attempt pretty much any conceivable play post-flop, and in some cases, not even wind up risking your tournament life. You can even triple-barrel without risking a gigantic portion of your stack; if you open for 2.5 times and are called by another stack that's 100 BB deep, there's now about 7 BB in the pot. Assuming you follow it up with a bet of about 3-5 BB on the flop, you now have a pot of roughly 15 BB on the turn, which will likely see a bet of around 9-12 BB, resulting in a pot of approximately 35 BB on the river. Assuming you fire a river bet of 20-30 BB (let's call it 25 BB in this specific example), you've now risked approximately 40 BB over the course of the hand, meaning that even if your play fails, you're left with 60 BB and tons of breathing room.

You can also 4-bet with the intention of folding when stacks are this deep without committing yourself. If you raise to 2.5 BB and are 3-bet to approximately 7.5 BB, you can certainly make it something between 18 and 23 BB and have plenty of fold equity with your raise, yet room to fold if your opponent shoves. This isn't something you should attempt too often, but it's certainly a play worth having in your arsenal if you wind up on an aggressive table.

A situation where you 4-bet two players who have raised and re-raised prior to the action reaching you represents a strong move, especially from the blinds. Here's a good example: A weak player limps from early position and a good player on his immediate left raises. Then, in late position, another good player realizes that the initial raiser was probably raising to isolate and outplay the limper and he 3-bets. If you 4-bet from the small blind, you'll frequently force everyone to fold, unless one of them is holding a monster.

When you 3-bet at these effective stack sizes, you need to be aware that you'll get called and have to play post-flop considerably more than at the later stages of the tournament when stack sizes are considerably smaller relative to the blinds. Generally, you can anticipate most opponents playing a bit more cautiously and straightforward in re-raised pots, but this isn't necessarily the case when playing against experts or maniacs.

75 to 100 BB

Play at these stacks is comparable to those at 100+ BB, but a few alterations in strategy need to be made. You still have room to open and 3-bet with enormous flexibility, though 4-betting has now become a more awkward enterprise. Certainly, at the upper limits of this stack size, you have room to make the 4-bet and fold to a 5-bet, but once you get below about 80 BB, it becomes increasingly questionable. You need to become particularly aware of your opponent's 3-bet size, what it indicates about his range, and whether you'll have room for such an elaborate play based on his sizing.

Say you open 2.5X and your opponent goes to 9X (and many will re-raise on the larger side while still so deep); if you hold a stack of 80 BB, it's questionable whether you really have the room to 4-bet and fold. If you elect to make it, say, 25 BB and your opponent shoves, you're now getting an excellent price to call. Granted, your opponent is rarely 5-betting light, especially in live events, so you can feel pretty good folding a great proportion of your range.

Online, where 4-betting light is more common than in live play, some players are capable of adding hands to their 5-bet value range if they observe a player 4-betting and folding to a 5-bet with any regularity. Tracking software can help identify players like this.

50 to 75 BB

This is the level where stacks will remain for much of the early-to mid-stage play. Assuming you start the tournament with 20,000 (as the majority of major tournaments do these days) and maintain exactly that stack, when you reach the 150/300 level, you'll have roughly 67 BB; at 200/400, you'll have 50. These stacks require a somewhat different approach to strategy than larger ones. Your open-raising flexibility is essentially still the same, since losing 2 BB to 3 BB on this stack is basically irrelevant. However, other plays we've discussed in this chapter need adjustment.

The 50- to 75-BB stack size is the optimal range to 3-bet your opponents with a fairly wide range of hands, especially when you have position on them. There are a couple of reasons for this. First, you're not risking a major portion of your stack and it will have little effect on your opening range and flexibility in future hands. Second, the stack sizes are such that your opponent is often making a greater mistake in calling your 3-bet when he's out of position than he would with deeper stacks.

Although 3-betting with a wide range is favorable at these stack sizes, you should 4-bet with a narrow range, as the only realistic and available 4-bet is all-in and doing so risks an enormous number of chips (not to mention your tournament life) for relatively little potential gain. Four-betting light is suboptimal and should be avoided. Most of the time, if your opponent 5-bets, you no longer have the room to 4-bet and fold, and moving all-in in hopes of inducing a fold is doing so with the worst possible odds.

Say you open a 65-BB stack to 2.5X the big blind and are 3-bet to 7.5X the BB. You can't realistically 4-bet to 20 BB with the intention of folding, as you have nearly a third of your stack in the pot. Moving all-in is an equally unappealing option, as you're risking an additional 62.5 BB to win the roughly 12 BB in the pot. Increasing your stack by this margin is not overly helpful, yet risking a stack of this size, then getting called and finding out that you're dominated, can result in a tragic end to your tournament life. Therefore, if you do 4-bet with this stack size, do so with a hand strong enough to play for all your chips, either pre-flop or on the flop.

You still have reasonable flexibility to make moves post-flop, but you'll now be risking most, if not all, of your chips. If you start a hand with 65 BB and bet the flop, turn, and river on a bluff that involves opening to 2.5X the BB, continuation betting approximately 4X the BB, and betting about 10X the BB on the turn, you now have a pot with roughly 35 BB and your remaining stack is 49 BB, making for a somewhat awkward river decision.

Now, there's nothing wrong with electing to continue if you believe your opponent is weak. But do the calculations: By betting, say, 24 BB, you'll be left with only a 25-BB stack when called. If you attempt this same play starting with 55 BB, then you reach the river with 39 BB in your stack, then the only sensible bet size is all-in.

It's still important to have these plays in your arsenal against other good players, so you're not lacking in balance, but their frequency should be cut down from the times when you have 100 BB or more.

40 to 50 BB

As the blinds escalate through the mid-levels, the average stack often settles in this range for quite some time. This is still a stack that allows for decent flexibility, particularly in your pre-flop options. Whereas with the previous size, we recommended against doing much light 4-betting, with this stack size, you have a near-optimal stack to 4-bet with a wide range (particularly with closer to 40 BB), when you suspect an opponent is often 3-betting you with less than premium hands.

Say you open-raise to 2.5X the BB and your opponent makes it 7.5X. If you now go all-in, you have substantial fold equity, because your opponent is not yet pot-committed. You're risking substantially less than at the previous stack size, while making the same gain and maintaining almost identical fold equity against his range. You should reserve this move to use against laggy players who 3-bet with some regularity, but are unlikely to call your 4-bet with less than JJ+ or AK. If a tight player 3-bets you from one of the blinds, however, he rarely has a light holding and your fold equity is diminished.

A strong play that ElkY likes to use is to 4-bet against a raise and re-raise. This is especially effective when you do it from the blinds. If the situation is right, you can make this move from anywhere, but usually it's versus a mid-position open and late position 3-bet. The likelihood of your opponents having monster hands increases when it's both an early opener and 3-bettor. Also, if you make that move on the button, there's always a small chance that the blinds will wake up with a monster. And sometimes they're short-stacked enough that they'll get it in with a wider range of hands due to good odds. To make this move profitably, you need a good read on your opponents and should pick the right spot. A mid- to late-position raise followed by a button re-raise by an aggressive thinking player can be a good spot for an all-in push from one of the blinds. This play is especially threatening when made from the small blind, since a big 4-bet from this position represents extreme strength.

With this stack size, you can still open-raise as wide as you deem profitable. Three-betting is also still a viable option, although the frequency of 4-bets you encounter will increase, because good opponents also understand the stack-size dynamics and the risk-reward ratio. Also, some hands that might fold or call a 3-bet at effective stacks (the lesser of your and your opponent's stacks) of 65 BB might move in when in the low 40 BB.

For example, your opponent opens in UTG+2 to 2.5X the BB and you 3-bet him to 7X from the button with effective stacks of 42 BB. If you have an aggressive image or history with him, he'll likely go all-in with hands such as 99, TT, and AQo, whereas if you were 65 BB deep, he might just fold or call instead. Watch your table and make mental notes about which players will widen their 4-betting range due to the difference in stack sizes, and which are oblivious to these fluctuations.

At this stack size, any multi-street aggression will wind up being a shove by the river. If you open a 45-BB stack for 2.5X the big blind and get called, then continuation bet 4X the BB having missed the flop, and double-barrel bluff by betting 10X the BB on the turn, you've now committed 16.5 BB, leaving yourself 28.5 BB in a pot with roughly 35 BB in it. The only river bet that makes sense in this situation is all-in (unless you have an absolute monster and you feel your opponent simultaneously believes all-in bets to be inordinately strong, but might call a slightly lesser bet of, say, 20 BB).

This stack size also opens up another opportunity for creative play: 3-betting pre-flop out of position, then checking the flop and moving all-in if your opponent bets. Say you begin the hand with 45 BB again and have T♥8♥ in the small blind. An active opponent opens from late position and, because you have a tight image and a hand that can connect fairly well if you get called, you 3-bet him. Assuming we use the same bet sizes as in the prior examples and he's raised 2.5X and you've made it 7.5X, if he calls, there will be roughly 18 BB in the pot and you'll have 38.5 BB left in your stack. If you get a flop that gives you a flush draw, an open-ended straight draw, a pair plus a gutshot, or a gutshot plus overcards, you can consider checking, then pushing all-in if he bets, because when you check he'll likely bet between 9 and 13 BB, perfectly sizing your all-in check-raise to create maximum fold equity while risking the minimum amount of chips. And if you're called, you'll often have significant equity. Make sure not to use this play on opponents who habitually flat-call with big pairs against re-raises. A good player who smooth-calls a 3-bet with effective stack sizes of 45 BB will probably smooth-call in a situation like this with big pairs, otherwise 4-betting all-in or folding. Fortunately, many live players call much too loose in these situations pre-flop and you'll have very good fold equity with this play.

An alternative option when 3-betting light pre-flop and you flop a hand with decent equity is to bet the flop with the intention of moving all-in on the majority of turns. Whether you check-raise all-in on the flop or lead with the intention of moving in on the turn depends on a few factors. First, how wide a range do you believe your opponent has when he calls your pre-flop 3-bet? Second, how frequently do you expect your opponent to bet the flop as a bluff if you check to him on the flop? Third, how wide do you feel your opponent will peel to a flop continuation bet, yet fold to a turn shove? Fourth, is the texture of the board such that if you bet the flop, your opponent will often have semi-bluffs that he'll be able to shove on you (and if you have good equity, that means you'll be forced to call, but lose all the potential for added fold equity)? Fifth, which line do you believe your opponent anticipates you taking for value with your big hands: leading or check-raising the flop?

It's very difficult to have an accurate answer to all these questions without an enormous amount of history with your opponent or considerable insight to his thought process. The best you can do is try to take everything you know from your history, and what you've seen him do and say at the table, then start estimating.

The 40- to 50-BB stack is also the lowest stack size in which you'll be making some of your looser flat-calls pre-flop. For example, too much below 40 BB and you no longer have the implied odds to flat with many small pairs and suited connectors against sensible opponents in a heads-up pot. There will be some exceptions—your opponent is a truly awful poker player prone to stacking off light, or you have a history that leads you to believe he'll pay you off more than usual. But for the most part, consider this stack size to be about as shallow as you can flat those types of hands against a standard open of about 2.5X. In fact, when holding 40 BB and facing a full 3X raise (which many opponents still do), you probably shouldn't be flatting your small pairs in an attempt to set mine in a heads-up pot against most opponents. Your implied odds simply aren't large enough.

30 to 40 BB

At this stack size, your options are still pretty varied, but you'll almost always be playing for your entire stack. Thus, you need to be more selective about the situations you attempt to manipulate and the spots you pick.

You can still 4-bet light with a stack of 35-40 BB, but as a whole, attempting to get a fold by 4-betting light when you have less than 35 BB is a bad idea, since your opponent will be getting an excellent price to call and, if he's smart, likely knows that he can't really 3-bet you with that stack without intending to call your 4 bet all-in. This isn't 100% accurate; there are still many situations where you're open-raising very small and your opponent will use frequent small 3-bets to bully you, in which case moving in with a stack of this size with a fairly wide range of hands can be appropriate.

Depending on the size of your opponent's opening raise, you still sometimes have room to 3-bet light pre-flop, but the frequency is certainly decreased from earlier stack sizes. Your opponents will now be pushing all-in with a considerably wider range for value against you, as well as occasionally attempting light 4-bets when you have the upper-half of this stack size and they have fold equity. If a villain opens a full 3X the BB or close to it, you should generally not attempt to 3-bet him with the intention of folding if you're 35 BB or below, since you'll be getting an excellent price to call his all-in bet. Again, there are a few exceptions to this rule, but they're best executed when you know your opponent will fold to a 3-bet of a smaller size (such as re-raising by only 2.5X the amount of his raise, as opposed to a full 3X his raise or greater), and you have a very tight image that will result in your opponent folding a large amount of his opening range to you.

Additionally, many experienced and intelligent opponents know that they should rarely flat-call a re-raise when effective stacks are 30 to 40 BB deep, so if your opponent does this to you and you know he's good at poker, major alarm bells should go off in your head. With many very good tournament players, the only time they flat-call a 3-bet with stacks this deep is when they have kings or aces and they believe their opponent isn't intelligent enough to realize how small his range is in this scenario. This is an excellent play to use yourself when a bad player 3-bets you and you know he'll probably fold to a 4-bet too frequently pre-flop, yet will probably commit himself post-flop, either with a lesser pair or on a bluff, when you simply call his re-raise. This is one of those spots where, even though it may be obvious to most of the players that your range is super narrow (KK, AA), as long as the 3-bettor you're actually facing in the hand doesn't know it, there's absolutely no reason ever to mix up your range by making suboptimal decisions.

You still have complete flexibility with your open-raising range at this stack size, although if you're at the blind stage where the average stack has fallen into this area, you should be more careful, since many players will often 3-bet around these stack sizes. Some won't realize that below 35 BB, they're often getting excellent pot odds for calling a 4-bet all-in from you, so they may actually 3-bet, then fold, when you move-in with a wider range than is correct.

Still, just because they commit this blunder doesn't make them any less annoying to play against. The way to counteract it is to widen up your 4-bet value-pushing range. At this stack size, your open-raising range and frequency should reflect the composition of the players at your table. If they're highly aggressive and 3-bet more than normal, or call and get creative post-flop often, tighten up your open-raising range. If they're playing too tight and allowing you to take too many blinds uncontested when the antes have gotten to a significant stage, naturally, increase your open-raise frequency.

Another aspect to become aware of is that firing three barrels as a bluff becomes less appealing as the game goes on; by the time you reach the river, your opponent will be getting an excellent price if you push all-in. Say you start the hand with 35 BB, open to 2.5X the BB, and are called. There's now about 7 BB in the pot and again you bet 4 BB, followed up by a turn bet of 10 BB. At this stage you've now committed 16.5 BB, leaving you with 18.5 BB in a 35-BB or so pot. Although your river all-in bet technically still has fold equity, your opponent will be getting more than 3-to-1 odds to call you, meaning he can justify calling quite often, since he needs to be good only 25% of the time.

The second aspect to consider is that when you fire a turn bet of that size and percentage of your stack and your opponent flat-calls, it's highly suspicious. Unless he's completely brain-dead, your opponent should realize on the turn that, with the majority of his draws, he no longer has the implied odds to make a call correct and, therefore, can probably call your triple-barrel bluff. Sometimes, he'll be holding one or two pairs on boards that get increasingly scary and he'll be forced to release on the river, but there's a big chance your opponent is trapping you when you bet such a large percentage of your stack on the turn. The probability of a trap is substantially larger than a draw in this scenario.

At this stack size, you should greatly reduce your flat-calling range to open-raises pre-flop. In heads-up pots, small- to medium-suited connectors and small pairs should almost always be folded. Against early-position raises with a stack of this size, we recommend a pretty tight flat-calling range that includes hands such as AQ, 99-JJ, and, against some loose or bad opponents, hands like AJs, KQs, JTs, QJs, and T9s (against many opponents, flat-calling even these hands would be a mistake).

Against middle-position raises, we recommend a flat-call with hands such as AJ, ATs, KQ, KJs, QJs, JTs, and T9s, and against some opponents, the weaker end of this range should be folded. Against most mid-position raises, hands such as 99-JJ and AQ should be 3-bet with the intention of calling a 4-bet all-in, but sometimes you'll encounter opponents with a tight 4-betting range against you, in which case you should flat-call with these hands, as you'd be forced to fold them if your opponent jams on you.

Against late-position raises, if you're in position, you can consider flat-calling with hands such as AJ (sometimes a hand with which you 3-bet and call an all-in), ATs, KQ, KJs, QJs, JTs, and T9s. Most of the time, pairs should be re-raise-or-fold decisions. However, you can still trap with JJ+, especially against players who open light. They can't 4-bet all-in anymore, because they know you'll call and they'll just fold to your 3-bet. If you smooth-call, they might lose more on the flop. Also if some 15- to 20-BB players are yet to act, they could 3-bet all-in with a wide range, but if you 3-bet, they'll probably fold everything except TT+ and AQs+. When you're in the small blind at these stacks, you should have a very tight flat-calling range. Against early-position raises, you should either 3-bet or fold, rather than flat call. When facing a mid- or late-position raise, flat-call with hands such as AJ, AJs, ATs, KQs and QJs. You can sometimes flat a bit more wide if your opponents are raising extremely small, but generally this stack size is very difficult to play out of the small blind.

25 to 30 BB

This is a particularly awkward stack size to play and there's a reason that co-author ElkY makes such a point of maintaining his stack size in situations that would drop him to this level. Your options and flexibility are greatly reduced in almost every aspect of aggression and you'll often find yourself playing a fairly straightforward style when at this stack size (correctly so). *Light 3-betting is almost entirely out of the question, particularly if you intend to 3-bet and fold to further aggression.* At this point, you've committed far too large a percentage of your stack to lay the hand down. Additionally, if you're contemplating 3-bet shoving all-in as a bluff, you're risking the maximum amount of chips in order to gain a relatively small pot.

For example, if you start the hand with 25 BB and your opponent open raises to 2.5X the BB, you'll be risking your 25 BB for the roughly 5 BB in the pot. Going from 25 to 30 BB changes very little in your overall flexibility and strategy, but going from 25 to 0 is obviously fatal (although yes, you'll sometimes suck out and go from 25 to a bit over 50). Against many opponents in late position, shoving 25 BB over the top will be correct with any pair, any suited ace roughly A8s or above, ATo+, KQo+, and KJs+. This, of course, depends on how wide you believe your opponent will raise or call you, and is something that fellow author Tysen Streib discusses at length and with charts that explain the correct ranges in Chapter 13.

You can still open-raise this stack size pretty wide, and your conditions for doing so shouldn't be all that different from the 30- to 40-BB level. But the closer you slip toward 25 BB, the wider your opponent's range will be when moving in over the top of you. However, your flexibility in flat-calling raises is greatly reduced, because you'll rarely have the implied odds necessary to make the call profitable.

One move you can make at this stack size, though, is flat-calling with big pairs such as QQ+. Many of your opponents won't be aware that you actually have a pretty tight flat-calling range with this stack size, because they themselves don't have a very tight flat-calling range. Additionally, the stacks will be such that getting your hand all-in post-flop will be pretty easy and correct on the vast majority of flop textures, since your opponent will rarely fold a hand such as top pair when you have only about 20 BB left.

18 to 25 BB

This is the stack size in which it's best to move over the top of opponents' open-raises. ElkY calls a 20 BB stack the "sweet spot" for all-in 3-bets. Charts with optimal move-in ranges were provided by Tysen Streib in *Kill Everyone*.

Outside of shoving over people's raises, this can be a highly awkward stack to play. You now have to become much more selective about the spots in which you open-raise, because your stack size is such that many aggressive opponents will move in over the top of you. Tough opponents will pressure you with 3-bets and you'll have your tournament life on the line. It's far better when you're the aggressor and have fold equity on your side than when you must make a tough call such as this. In many situations we recommend that you significantly cut down your open-raise size, often to the area of about 2.2X the BB. Becoming increasingly popular online is to open-raise all-in with a 20-BB stack. This avoids the awkward position of facing a 3-bet from an opponent for all your chips. On the plus side, if you're in this stack-size area, it normally only takes winning the blinds and antes a couple of times to get you back into a more comfortable playing zone.

Lee was playing a tournament recently and had John Juanda on his right after the bubble broke. Lee and the big blind had about 20 BB and Juanda had about 40 BB. The first time it was passed around to Juanda on the button, he open-raised to about 3X the BB and Lee pushed all-in from the small blind. That was enough for Juanda! The next three orbits when Juanda was on the button and it was folded around to him, he moved all-in.

With the higher side of this stack size, it can be good to pull off a squeeze play, but once you get to around 21 BB or below, your opponents will be getting such an excellent price on calling your all-in squeeze attempt that it becomes far less effective. You can also still consider flat-calling with very big hands with this stack size, especially if your opponents are oblivious to the fact that this call indicates a monster. You should have virtually no other hands in your flat-calling range, except in occasional situations where there's a raise and one or more callers to you in the BB and you're getting excellent odds with a hand that can flop well and play easily post-flop, but isn't quite good enough to shove pre-flop (such as medium-sized suited connectors). Small pairs can also be called when it's four ways and you know your shove will get called pre-flop.

13 to 17 BB

This stack size lends itself predominately to pre-flop all-ins; the ranges for doing so as an open-raise were provided in *Kill Every-one*. It should be noted that against some players, this is simply not enough chips to move over the top when they open-raise. Against others, it's more than enough.

One major factor in how much fold equity you have when moving in over the top of someone with this stack is their stack size. A player who has opened a stack of 25 BB will be much more hesitant to call when losing will cripple him than a player with 50 BB; he'll still be somewhere in the mid-30-BB range if he loses and may still feel comfortable. ElkY, however, thinks that stack preservation in the 40- to 50-BB range has such great value in terms of flexibility that he tends to avoid calling if he thinks the situation is borderline, based on probable ranges.

This stack size isn't necessarily a push or fold though pre-flop in all situations. You'll encounter spots where the opponents behind you are incredibly tight and will only move over the top or call you with a premium hand, so then it becomes correct to raise/fold a stack of this size. Also, while you're normally better off moving in over the top, you'll occasionally encounter a player or a table line-up where flat-calling with a big hand on this stack size can be better than moving all-in. This would happen against a very bad opponent who is clueless about stack sizes and is very tight in his calling range of all-ins, no matter what kind of pot odds he's getting. This can also be good even if the open-raiser isn't fooled by your flat-call, or if you have many highly aggressive short-stack players behind you who are clueless about what your flat-call means (though spots like these are increasingly rare).

12 BB and Under

Pretty much all decisions are push or fold pre-flop with this stack. You no longer have room to move over the top of an open-raiser, so you're essentially waiting for a spot to be the first one to move in yourself. The optimal ranges to do this were provided by Tysen Streib in *Kill Everyone*.

If you get especially crippled and are around 5 BB or below, be aware that you no longer really have fold equity on a shove, and should instead wait until you have a hand that has high showdown value or good suck-out potential—so fold your absolute garbage.

Example of Adjustments Based on Stack Sizes

Let's take a look at some examples of how your play should differ based on the effective stack sizes.

You hold A♥K♥ in mid-position. You raise to 2.5X the BB pre-flop and it folds to an opponent in position who calls. The blinds fold and there's now roughly 8 BB in the pot. The flop is T♥-6♥-2♠.

If you have less than 30 BB, it's best to check-raise all-in. Your opponent will frequently take a stab at this pot and sometimes make the mistake of folding mid-pairs when he convinces himself you have a ten or an overpair. At this stack size, you simply don't have the room to bet, then 3-bet all-in.

If you have 30-50 BB, you should lead with the intention of 3-betting all-in if you're raised. The size of your lead should depend on the effective stack sizes on the flop. If you get to the flop with 30 BB left, then lead 3-4 BB so your opponent has room to make the mistake of raise-folding some hands, since his raise size will generally be to 9-12 BB and your all-in shove will be 30 BB in total. If you have 50 BB, lead on the larger side, roughly 5-6 BB; if your opponent raises to the 15- to 18-BB range, you have room to get a fold when you move in for 50 BB in total. However, if your opponent habitually bets when checked to, you should go for a check-raise with the intention of making a bet that commits you (and him) on the turn. Additionally, if you have a read that your opponent believes min-raises to be very strong hands, you can lead with the intention of min-re-raising on the flop followed by moving all-in on the turn.

If you have 50-75 BB, you should lead on the flop with the intention of re-evaluating your decision based largely on your opponent. If you get to the flop with 70 BB, bet out 5 BB, and are raised, your course of action should depend on the frequency of your opponent's flop aggression. If he's very laggy, you should re-raise with the intention of getting it all-in, because your opponent may be bluff-raising the flop fairly often and even when called, your hand will have excellent equity against his range. If your opponent is very tight and straightforward, you should call on the flop with the intention of re-evaluating on the turn, because he'll have a tight flop-raising range that has basically no bluffs, very few hands that would fold to an all-in, and numerous hands that will have you getting it all-in with 50% equity at the very best and nine outs at the worst (and if he has a set or an improbable two pair, he'll have redraws).

12

Equilibrium Solutions for 3- and 4-Betting

The Truth About Equilibrium Strategies

Over the years, we've heard a lot of people give their opinions about equilibrium strategies. Many times they're confused or even wrong about what an equilibrium strategy entails. Let me address the more common concerns people have about them and try to put some issues to rest.

The Equilibrium Strategy Is the Perfect Strategy and Can't Lose

Mostly false. The definition of an equilibrium solution is that if you and your opponent are both playing equilibrium strategies, you can't gain anything by doing something different. It's usually used as a defensive strategy, one that is difficult to exploit. It's a good strategy to use when you don't know who your opponent is or if you know your opponent is a better player than you are. However, it won't always be the perfect strategy in all situations. If your opponent isn't playing perfectly (and who does?), you can make more money by moving away from the equilibrium and trying to take advantage of him, i.e. if he tends to fold too often, then you'll make much more money by bluffing more frequently.

An equilibrium solution can't lose in the long run if only two players are in the game. Unfortunately, that breaks down in a three-plus-player game. Equilibrium solutions still exist, but they don't guarantee a player won't lose. The only comfort we have is that any opponent can't hurt us without hurting himself as well. In these cases, our best course of action isn't necessarily to go with equilibrium. However, I find that studying equilibrium solutions is still useful and can give you some insights about the game that might not be obvious.

Even If the Equilibrium Strategy Can't Lose, It Can't Win Either

False—at least in poker. Most people draw a comparison to the game of rock-paper-scissors. The equilibrium strategy in that game is to choose all three options randomly—each one-third of the time. The problem is that if you choose this strategy, you can't lose or win in the long run, even if your opponent plays poorly. When you play equilibrium, your expectation is to break even, no matter if your opponent is also playing equilibrium or if he picks a substandard strategy, like always picking rock.

This isn't true in poker, where your opponent's mistakes frequently make you money. Take the example of a short-stacked heads-up situation. Blinds are 500/1,000, you have 9,000 chips, and your opponent has you covered. You decide to make the equilibrium play and push with the top 60% of hands. That play is the equilibrium, because if you choose to push different hands, you won't make as much money as you will if you stick with 60%:

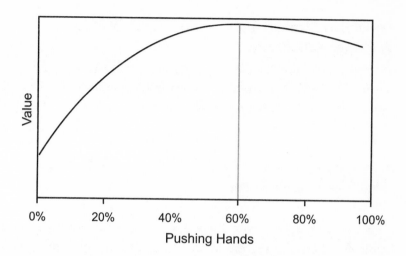

When you make that push, your opponent's best response is to call you about 41% of the time, including with some fairly weak hands like K4o. The following graph shows his value when you're pushing 60%:

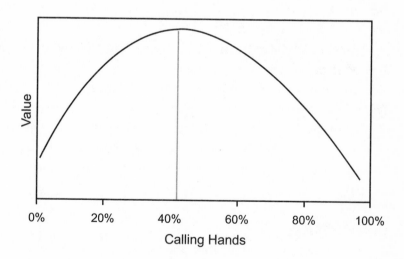

Although the best choice is to maximize his value and call 41%, most players won't call that often. So if he chooses to fold those moderate hands, that extra fold equity will make you money. Any value he loses goes right to you.

Equilibrium Strategy Only Works If Your Opponent Is Playing Equilibrium

False. People who say this don't understand how equilibriums work. We showed above how following the equilibrium strategy is profitable even if our opponent isn't playing optimally.

True Equilibrium Can Only Be Achieved in Toy Games That Aren't Really Poker

Is poker too complicated a game to figure out the equilibrium? This is becoming less true every day. Poker is a very complicated game and there are way too many situations for players to come up with a complete solution. However, a variety of techniques can be used to come up with answers that should be close to the true equilibrium. These techniques are beyond the scope of this book, but we can often compute what is called an "ε-equilibrium." A true equilibrium can't be exploited. We define an ε-equilibrium as a solution that can't be exploited by more than ε, and we ensure that ε is a small number with which we can live.

There are rough approximations for the full game of heads-up deep-stack poker. The best computers in the world right now can use this equilibrium and play at a moderate level, but they're still bested by good human players. Still, computing power and innovative techniques are always being improved. All of my equilibrium solutions presented in this book are for medium- or short-stack situations, which, we feel, are accurate enough to be useful in actual play.

The EQ Strategy

As mentioned earlier in this chapter, figuring out equilibrium solutions to anything more complicated than most push/fold situations is damn hard, if not impossible. But I've never let something like the impossible stop me, so I decided to tackle it head-on. Contained in this chapter is the ultimate guide to 3- and 4-betting from a computer's point of view. I present and describe the equilibrium solutions and contrast how they might differ from other advice we give. To me, the best way to use math-based analysis is to start with the equilibrium solutions as a baseline, then see how we should change that strategy based on our opponent's playing style. So I will also present some exploitive solutions against certain opponents.

Post-flop play is particularly tricky for doing these sorts of solutions; there's no way to deal with it that's both good and easy. Any time you move away from just push/fold and allow your equilibrium solution to consider flat-calling, you have to deal with post-flop play. So how do you determine the EV of flat-calling? In previous studies, I took the simple approach and just used the flat showdown equities of the hands after the call. This is the same as assuming no post-flop betting or that the eventual loser of the hand realizes he's beat and folds after the victor bets. But I've never been too happy with that method; it ignores the value of position, the fact that some hands play better than others, and the chance that the pot could grow post-flop. I wanted some way that I could estimate the EV of calling pre-flop without having to make a full-fledged equilibrium program, one that would end up being sufficient for a Ph.D. thesis.

An exact equilibrium solution is totally out of reach, even for the best programmers today. But I was interested only in an approximate equilibrium. I wanted to study its basic properties and how the solution changed as I changed the variables—stack sizes, raise sizes, positions, etc. After numerous false starts, I decided to use actual played hands for approximating post-flop EVs.

I couldn't just use observed hands from online hand histories, because a bias is introduced when you get to see only the hole cards that go to showdown. Likewise, I couldn't use my own hand histories, or any of the authors', since that also introduces a bias. I finally decided to use hand histories from a computer no-limit competition[1] in which the best computer programs in the world compete. That gave me access to more than a million hands played by strong programs where I could see all the hole cards.

---

[1] The 2009 Association for the Advancement of Artificial Intelligence computer poker competition.

I used those hands to create a model that estimates EV based on many factors (position, stack sizes, pre-flop aggression, and actual cards), so now my equilibrium solutions could recognize that 87s plays better in position than out and when stacks are deeper rather than short. So while you and your opponent probably don't play post-flop like these programs do, it's an unbiased estimator of your EV and should be a very good substitute for the purposes of finding these pseudo-equilibriums.

Before we dive into the actual solutions, let's talk about position and post-flop play in general. We all know that being in position is an advantage. It should also be obvious that the deeper the stacks, the more of an advantage it is to be in position; deeper stacks mean more betting rounds and opportunities to use that advantage. As more of your stack goes in pre-flop, that advantage decreases up to the point where you go all-in (no advantage at all).

So let's say you're in the big blind facing a raise from a mid-position player. You'll be out of position throughout the hand. All other things being equal, would you prefer that more of your stack gets in pre-flop? Well, yes and no. It's true that your positional disadvantage decreases the more you get in pre-flop (good), but you're also building a bigger pot where you're behind strategically (bad). You'd expect that if you combine those factors, once you get to the flop your EV would look something like this:

Hypothetical Positional Disadvantage with 10,000 Chip Stacks

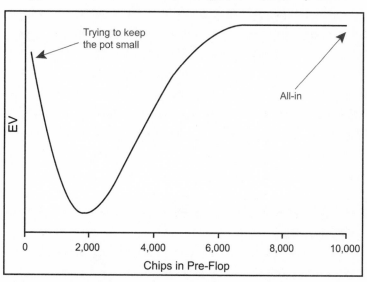

From this graph, you can see two possible strategies for reducing your disadvantage: Either keep the pot small or get it all-in. In this particular example, committing about one-sixth to one-fifth of your stack gives you the worst situation. You've bloated the pot, but stacks are deep enough that there will be post-flop play. On the flop you'll have 2-2.5X the current pot in your stack, an ugly place to be when you're out of position. You'll also see that your positional disadvantage completely disappears once you get about two-thirds of your stack in. In this case, the money's going in the middle anyway, so it doesn't matter if it's now or later.

Obviously, the real EV depends on your hole cards, and the shape of this curve will be different for different hands. With AA, you're always better off getting as much in as possible. With trash hands, the curve never comes back up when you commit more chips; you're simply building a bigger pot that you have a small chance of winning. However, most hands have EV curves similar to the one presented above.

The EV once you see the flop isn't the only factor when making pre-flop decisions. Fold equity obviously plays a big part. Let's say effective stacks are 10,000, blinds are 100/200, and you've got a good hand in the BB facing a raise to 500. A pot-sized 3-bet would be to 1,600, getting close to the worst point on our graph. A larger 3-bet has similar or worse post-flop EV unless you make a *huge* re-raise. However, you might find that a larger-than-pot 3-bet is preferable, simply because you have more fold equity. This is true even if it's on a worse EV point on our curve, since the positional disadvantage kicks in *only if you're called*; the extra fold equity could make up for this loss. This won't always apply; it depends on the particular circumstances, as we'll see in the next section.

Key Point

When out of position, consider either keeping the pot small or try to get all-in. This should be only one factor in your decision; fold equity and the value of your hand are the others.

Equilibrium 3- and 4-Betting

We start by looking at the equilibriums of one particular situation in detail, then show how those solutions change as we change different variables like stack sizes or antes. Then, after examining several equilibrium solutions, we look at exploitive solutions and how to appropriately counter real-world opponents.

One giant disclaimer before we start looking at the equilibrium solutions: *We aren't recommending that you memorize these solutions or try to play them at the table.* While they might be optimal in the specific situation for which they're designed, you'll never face these exact situations. The stacks and antes will be different, your opponent won't make optimal responses, etc. So what good are they? By studying how equilibrium solutions change with different assumptions, we can get an understanding as to what the solution considers important. If we change the effective stacks from 50 BB to 30 BB, how does the solution change? Why? How does it change if the opening raise is 3 BB versus 2.5 BB?

Key Point

The goal of studying equilibrium solutions is to gain an understanding of *why* we should pick a certain strategy, not to follow it blindly.

Our initial example is how the big blind should play against an unknown mid-position raiser. Effective stacks are 10,000, the blinds are 100/200/25, and our opponent just raised 2.5 BB to 500. We also assume that we're far from the money, so prize-distribution effects are negligible and we look just at chip values.

The first question we have to answer is what is the mid-position-player's opening range? If we look at a large sample of online hand histories for early in a tournament, it seems the average person opens with a raise in mid-position about 10% of the time. So should we just put our opponent on a top 10% hand? It should be obvious that this is incorrect, as it assumes that he raises the top hands 100% of the time and never raises with a worse hand. Lots of people occasionally limp with a strong hand and sometimes raise with hands below the top 10%. We need a distribution so that strong hands are frequently opened, moderate hands are occasionally opened, and trash hands are rarely opened. How do we get that distribution?

Some software packages out there (I won't name names) try to predict this by looking just at showdown hands and calculating the percentage of hands raised from that. This is completely wrong; it imposes a very strong bias toward hands that reach showdown. Instead, we have to create a model that intelligently combines our guess at raise frequencies with the chance that the hand type will go to showdown. We can do this for both cases when a player raises and when he doesn't, so we can guess the hand types that don't even go to showdown. We then have to merge and tweak the model, so our predictions match the observed results. It's still a guess, but it's much better than using either (1) the top 10% or (2) biased results from showdowns.

After doing all that, you get the following distribution of raise frequencies for the average player:

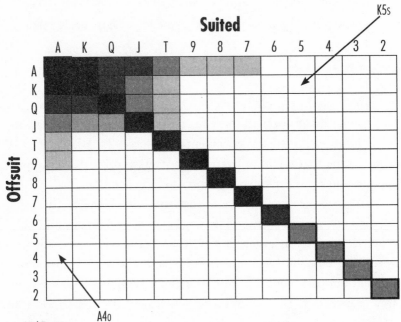

Mid Position
Raise Frequency

90%
80%
70%
60%
50%
40%
30%
20%
10%
0%

This chart is a nice compact representation of all 169 starting hands in hold'em. A color version of this and many other charts can be found on pages 369. Here's how you read it. Find your two hole cards along the top and left sides of the chart. Where they intersect is the entry for your hand. Pairs are along the diagonal, offsuit cards are below the diagonal, and suited cards are above the diagonal. All possible combinations are here.

The most commonly raised hands are raised about 90% of the time and 55 types of hands are raised 5% or more. You might not be able to tell from the shading, but AA is a bit lighter than hands such as JJ or AK, since it's slow-played a bit more frequently. I'm not expecting you to read the exact values off of this graph; it's just here to give you a sense of the opener's assumed distribution.

Now that we've determined the opening-raiser's range, let's see the equilibrium actions of the BB:

Defending Your Big Blind Against a Mid-Position Raiser
(10,000 Stacks, Blinds 100/200/25, Raise to 500)

Suited

	A	K	Q	J	T	9	8	7	6	5	4	3	2
A	P70J	P	P90J	p	p	F60p	F	F	F	F70J	F	F	F
K	J70P	P	C	p70C	C	C	C	C	C	C	C	C	C
Q	p	C	P60J	C	p60C	C	C	C	C	C	C	C	F
J	C	C	C	p	C90p	C	C	C	C	C	C	C	F
T	F	C	C	C	P	C	C	C	C	C	C	C	F
9	F	C	C	C	C	C	C	C	C	C	C	C	F
8	F	C	F	C	C	C	C	C	C	C	C	F	F
7	F	C	F	F	F	C	C	C	C	C	C	C	F
6	F	F	F	F	F	F	F	C	C	C	C	C	F
5	F	F	F	F	F	F	F	F	F	C	C	C	C
4	F	F	F	F	F	F	F	F	F	F	C	C	C
3	F	F	F	F	F	F	F	F	F	F	F	C	C
2	F	F	F	F	F	F	F	F	F	F	F	F	C

Offsuit (row label, vertical)

F	Fold
C	Call
P	Make pot-sized 3-bet and be willing to get it all in
p	Pot 3-bet but fold to 4-bet
J	Jam

X#Y	means do the first action #%

For example:

p70b	= p 70% and b 30%

This chart is a little more complicated to read, since the computer's equilibrium solution often involves mixing strategies, so you don't always do the same thing with the same hand. The letters in the chart are defined in the legend below it and are the basic actions the solution was allowed to consider. In addition to jamming (going all-in), making a pot-sized 3-bet, calling, or folding, the solution was also allowed to make a small re-raise (0.5X the pot) or a big 3-bet (1.5X the pot). The solution elected never to make these smaller or larger re-raises. We'll see them come into play when we consider 4-betting.

An entry like "p60C" for QTs means that the solution randomizes between two actions. The number in the middle is the percentage chance that you should do the first action. So with QTs, you should make a pot-sized 3-bet 60% and call 40%. With QQ, you should make a pot-sized bet 60% and go all-in 40%. (These percentages have been rounded to the nearest 10% for readability, so you won't see any of the actions that occur less than 5% of the time). All of this randomization is to help balance out the strategies, so you won't be too predictable. Mixing allows you to disguise your hands more effectively to increase your overall profitability.

Also notice the difference between the capital "P" compared to the lower-case "p" in the chart. The lower-case letters should make a 3-bet as indicated, but will usually fold if the opponent 4-bets. The capital letters are strong enough to be *willing* to go all-in. This doesn't necessarily mean jamming over a 4-bet, just that you're not intending to fold the hand pre-flop. For example, you have AQs and make a pot-sized raise to 1,825. If your opponent makes a min-raise back, you could flat or push as you please.

Let me note a few things that may seem weird about these 3-betting recommendations, then address each one in turn:

• You defend your blind quite liberally, calling with most suited hands and quite a few unsuited hands.
• It occasionally goes all-in for 10,000, even though the opener's raise was to 500.

- Many hands aren't mixed at all, like KK.
- Weaker hands are sometimes raised preferentially over stronger ones (KJs mostly raises, but KQs always calls, etc.).
- Pocket tens are willing to get all-in, but not pocket jacks.

You defend your blind quite liberally. The reason? Even though we'll be out of position for the rest of the hand, we're getting almost 3.5-to-1 pot odds. That's hard to pass up and something to keep in mind when considering your open-raise size. Against competent players in these situations, a raise to 2.5 BB is smaller than optimum, since it allows the BB to call so frequently. However, this raise size could still be correct in most cases, because your opponents won't defend as often as they should. More successful steals means more profit for you; keeping the raise size smaller means that you won't lose as much when the blinds play back at you.

However, just because other people don't defend their blinds as much as they should doesn't mean you should follow suit. Don't be afraid to call and see a flop. You might get lucky or have a chance to take down a pot when he misses. Some pros, notably Gus Hansen, are notorious for defending their blinds. This has its plusses and minuses, just like every poker decision. On the upside, if people notice that you frequently defend, they'll stop stealing your blinds so often. Gus admits that he gets more than his fair share of walks due to this.

The advantage of *not* defending so often is you might get a little more respect when you do defend. However, folding too often could put a target on your head, so it's all about balance. One additional advantage of playing tighter is that it reduces variance, which could be beneficial. These equilibrium solutions don't care about variance, only EV. To make life easier, many of those trash hands are only marginally +EV, so they can be folded to reduce your variance.

The equilibrium solution won't recommend a liberal defense all the time; this changes when we introduce bubble effects. Also, notice that the solution doesn't recommend calling with weak aces. It does call with K2s and K7o, but not with A9s or ATo. Since the opener's range is fairly strong, weak aces face too many reverse implied-odds situations and can get into big trouble[2].

It occasionally goes all-in for 10,000, even though the opener's raise was to 500. This seems like huge overkill, especially with a hand like aces! Most people's intuition is that a smaller raise would be more profitable. One of the important concepts of equilibrium solutions is that different hands can help each other out. You're actually trying to balance out a complete strategy for all hands, not just one particular hand at a time. Consider, for example, A5s. Pushing these strong hands allows you to push A5s profitably. Strong hands ensure that the opener is fairly tight in calling the push, allowing you to steal with A5s—and A5s turns out to be a great stealing hand when you expect your opponent to be tight. If you only pushed with A5s and other medium hands, the opener could call much more frequently and you'd be in trouble. So it turns out that pushing A5s along with all the strong hands is more profitable than pushing none of them. Remember, equilibrium strategy assumes your opponent is playing optimally. Since few (if any) opponents play a perfect equilibrium strategy, this strategy is quite different from the exploitive strategies that we review later.

Many hands aren't mixed at all, like KK. You may be thinking, isn't this exploitable, since I'm often only doing one thing with each hand? Shouldn't I be mixing it up more often? As I mentioned previously, what's important is that we mix *complete strategies*, not just individual hands. So we need to make sure that each type of action is mixed and not exploitable. So the right question is not, "Is my KK strategy exploitable?" Rather, it's, "Are my pot-sized raises exploitable?" You can see that our pot-sized raises cover a variety of hands that should do well against the opener's fairly tight range.

If there were a certain raise size where only one kind of hand did that action, that *would* be exploitable. Let's say we want to start mixing with KK. We also want to put in some small value raises. So

---

[2] You probably know that an implied-odds situation is one where you have a draw, giving you the opportunity to win a big pot without having to pay anyone off if you miss. A *reverse* implied-odds situation is the opposite, where we have a vulnerable made hand and won't know if we're good on the river. It often means either paying off bets on future streets or possibly folding the best hand.

we change KK to raise a pot-sized amount 80% of the time and a smaller raise 20%. This is exploitable, even though we're doing more mixing than before. No other hand makes a small raise, so whenever the small raise happens, your opponent would know you have KK. In order to counter this, you now have to start making small raises with all sorts of hands, which may decrease their EV. The computer considers this option as it's calculating the equilibrium, but in this case it determined that it was higher EV to stick with pot raises all around instead of adding in a mixture of other sizes. Once we start looking at other solutions, we'll start using those alternate sizes.

Weaker hands are sometimes raised preferentially over stronger ones. There are a number of reasons for this. Part of it is the balancing of our strategy with appropriate mixing. A few raises are bluffs like KJs and QTs that we intend to fold to a 4-bet. However, most of the reason is post-flop playability. The computer thinks that KQs and QJs are much easier to play post-flop than their 1-gap counterparts, and of course they are. But it's a balancing act again. In this case, the solution expects to get more EV out of playing a smaller pot post-flop with a superior hand. Hands like KQs would be put in a tough spot if they 3-bet and faced a 4-bet, since they have to fold. The solution gets more value out of it by denying its opponent the opportunity to 4-bet.

Pocket tens are willing to get all-in, but not pocket jacks. This does seem quite odd. It turns out that pocket tens have more equity than pocket jacks when they face hands like AA and AQ, thanks to their superior straight-making ability. So tens end up being okay against a 4-bet and jacks don't. Strange stuff.

Now that we know the equilibrium 3-betting strategy, let's look at how the opener should 4-bet. We'll have a different strategy against each of the different raise sizes the big blind could make.

4-Betting Over Various 3-Bets
(10,000 Stacks, Blinds 100/200/25)

10,000 Stacks

Hand	His 3-Bet Size			
	Small	Pot	Big	Jam
AA	J60 S20 P20	J	J	C
KK	C	C70 J20 S10	C50J	C
QQ	C	C	C80J	C
JJ	C	C	C	C80F
TT	C	C	C	C90F
99	C	C	C70F	F
88	C	C	F80 C10 J10	F
77	C90J	C50F	F70J	F
66	C	C50 J40 F10	F60J	F
AKs	C	C	C	C
AQs	C	C	C70J	F
AJs	C	F50J	F	F
A8s	F60 J30 p10	F	F	F
A7s	J60 F20 p20	F	F	F
A6s	F70 J20 p10	F	F	F
A5s	J90p	J	F60J	F
A4s	J80 p10 F10	F70J	F80J	F
A3s	J70 p20 F10	F	F90J	F
A2s	J50 F30 p20	F	F	F
AKo	C	C	C	F60C
AQo	C	F90J	F	F
KQs	C	C	F80J	F
KJs	C	C50 J40 s10	F	F
KTs	C70 F20 s10	F80J	F	F

4-Betting Over Various 3-Bets (cont.)

10,000 Stacks

Hand	His 3-Bet Size			
	Small	Pot	Big	Jam
KQo	C	F70C	F	F
KJo	C60 F20 s20	F	F	F
QJs	C	F50C	F	F
76s	F80C	F	F	F
Other calling hands	22+, ATs, JTs, 65s, 54s	none	none	none

F	Fold
C	Call
S	Make small (0.5X pot) 4-bet and be willing to get it all in
s	Small 4-bet but fold to 5-bet
P	Make pot-sized 4-bet and be willing to get it all in
p	Pot 4-bet but fold to 5-bet
J	Jam

The hands are now listed along the left-hand side, and I've listed all the hands that are at least occasionally 4-bet. The four different raise sizes we could be facing are now lists that go down according to the hands on the left. At the bottom of each list, I've also included all the miscellaneous hands that will flat-call the 3-bet. Obviously, these should only call if alternative actions aren't given for them in the table above them.

This chart is a lot more complicated. Not only are we looking at four different raise sizes we have to deal with, but in several special cases, the solution actually mixes between three different actions. For example, against a half-pot 3-bet, the equilibrium solution with A2s is to jam 50% of the time, fold 30%, and make a pot-sized 4-bet 20%.

Even though the equilibrium 3-bet solution never makes a half-pot 3-bet, we still need to calculate a 4-bet response to it. We have to be prepared to handle off-equilibrium actions. Now, unlike the 3-betting chart, we aren't holding a random hand when we make a

4-bet decision; we're much more likely to have a strong holding. I'm not showing hands that are rarely open-raised, although they're still in the model (they all fold anyway). At this stage, a 4-bet is usually a jam, but in a few small cases the solution tries to milk a few more chips in EV by making a non-jam raise.

Again, a few strategies here probably seem strange at first glance, so I'll address them in turn:

• The solution doesn't 4-bet often and flat-calls with hands that most people would 4-bet, such as AK, KK, or QQ, especially when the 3-bet was small.

• The solution folds the suited connectors T9s-87s, but calls with 76s-54s.

The solution doesn't 4-bet often, especially against a small 3-bet. That's because the 3-bettor put the opener in a tough spot with his raise size. That small raise is a little more than 10% of the stacks, meaning that most 4-bets should be pot-committing. So most 4-bets are equivalent to pushing, a bit of an overbet. Granted, the 3-bettor considered pushing when it was even more of an over-bet, but he had a positional disadvantage to overcome. Here we can call in position with some play left in our stack.

Since this small 3-bet puts the opener in an awkward 4-betting situation, why didn't the equilibrium choose this raise size when we looked at 3-bets? Because awkward 4-bets are only a small part of the situation. The small 3-bet has other disadvantages that outweigh this consideration: It gives the opener 3-to-1 pot odds to call in position. Re-raising a pot-sized amount gives opener worse odds to call, even though it makes his 4-betting less troublesome.

The solution folds the suited connectors T9s-87s, but calls with 76s-54s. This has to do with playability against the 3-bettor's range, since he usually expects us to have a strong hand when open-ing. These lower suited connectors do better and are more likely to win a big surprise pot against the 3-bettor. Hurray for the little guy!

These 4-bet strategies obviously get tighter as the 3-bet gets higher. Again, see how TT actually calls more often than JJ against an all-in move. This is the same logic we saw in the 3-betting solution.

In all the cases, a mix of hands are always bluffs in any raise, just to keep from being predictable. In these 4-betting situations, the bluffing hands are usually weak suited aces, especially A5s.

Key Points
- Effective poker strategies often involve mixing it up in order to be unpredictable, but there are really two ways to mix up your play:
    1) With any given hand, you can sometimes take action X and sometimes action Y.
    2) You can make the same play with many different kinds of hands, weak and strong, so that opponents can't put you on a range.

These equilibrium strategies do both, but it's hard for humans to do #1, even when they set their minds to it. It's easier to do #2, and we feel that's usually good enough.

- When making 3- and 4-betting decisions, consider all of these factors when deciding on the best action:
    - What are my direct pot odds, implied odds, and am I in or out of position?
    - What's my opponent's range for making his raise?
    - If I re-raise, how much fold equity do I have? Does my raise size put him in a difficult spot?
    - What's his range for playing back at me? Do I have a plan if he comes back over the top?
    - What's my image and what do I think he'll assume about my ranges?
    - How can I be more unpredictable without losing too much EV?

Changing Stack Sizes, Raise Sizes, and the Ante

Now let's take a look at how our first equilibrium example changes as we change a few factors. Here we compare several situations at the same time, so I present this in a slightly different format for easier comparisons.

Equilibrium 3-Bets With a Variety of Stacks, Raises, and Antes

10,000 Stacks

Hand	100/200/25 Open to 500	100/200/25 Open to 600	100/200 Open to 600
AA	P70J	P80J	P60 J30 B10
KK	P	P	P
QQ	P60J	P60J	P70 B20 J10
JJ	p	p	p
TT	P	p90C	p80C
AKs	P	P	P
AQs	P90J	P	P70J
AJs	p	p90C	C80p
ATs	p	p	p80F
A9s	F60p	F	F
A5s	F70J	F90J	F
A4s	F	F	F
A3s	F	F	F
AKo	J70P	J70P	p50 J40 b10
AQo	p	p	p90b
AJo	C	F	F
KJs	p70C	C90p	C70p
K2s	C	F	F

Equilibrium 3-Bets With a Variety of Stacks, Raises, and Antes (cont.)

10,000 Stacks

Hand	100/200/25 Open to 500	100/200/25 Open to 600	100/200 Open to 600
KJo	C	C80p	C
QTs	p60C	p	C70 p20 b10
QJo	C	C	C
JTs	C90p	C50p	C70p
JTo	C	C	C
Other calling hands	22+, K2s+, K7o+, Q3s+, Q9o+, J3s+, J8o+, T3s+, T8o+, 93s+, 97o+, 84s+, 87o, 73s+, 76o, 63s+, 52s+, 42s+, 32s	22+, K3s+, K9o+, Q5s+, QTo+, J6s+, JTo, T6s+, 95s+, 85s+, 74s+, 64s+, 53s+, 43s	22+, K3s+, K9o+, Q5s+, QTo+, J6s+, JTo, T6s+, 95s+, 85s+, 74s+, 64s+, 53s+, 43s

6,000 Stacks

Hand	100/200/25 Open to 500	100/200/25 Open to 600	100/200 Open to 600
AA	J50 P30 S20	J80S	P50 S30 J20
KK	J60 P30 S10	J90S	P50S
QQ	J	J	J90P
JJ	J	J	P90S
TT	S50P	J60S	s
AKs	P70S	J	S60 P40
AQs	J60 P30 S10	J70S	P80S
AJs	J	J	J
ATs	J	J	J90s
A9s	s50 p30 J20	J	F
A5s	J	J	F90J

Equilibrium 3-Bets With a Variety of Stacks, Raises, and Antes (cont.)

6,000 Stacks

Hand	100/200/25 Open to 500	100/200/25 Open to 600	100/200 Open to 600
A4s	J90F	J	F
A3s	F	F80J	F
AKo	J	J	J80P
AQo	J70 s20 p10	J	p60s
AJo	C	C80s	C
KJs	C	C	C
K2s	C80p	F	F
KJo	C	C	C90p
QTs	C	C	C
QJo	C	C	C70p
JTs	C	C	C70p
JTo	C80p	F	F
Other calling hands	22+, K2s+, K9o+, Q4s+, Q9o+, J5s+, JTo, T6s+, T9o, 95s+, 85s+, 74s+, 64s+, 53s+, 43s	22+, K5s+, KTo+, Q8s+, QJo, J8s+, T7s+, 96s+, 86s+, 75s+, 65s, 54s	22+, K5s+, KTo+, Q8s+, J8s+, T7s+, 96s+, 86s+, 75s+, 65s, 54s

In the tables above, I'm comparing six different situations where we're in the BB facing an opening raise from the same MP player. Some situations use 10,000 effective stacks as before; others use 6,000. The blinds could be 100/200/25 or just 100/200 to see the effect of adding an ante. In addition, the opening raise could be to 500 or 600.

The left-most list in the first table is the same situation we discussed in the previous section; the other five columns are new.

In order to see the overall picture better, I've also made this table, which summarizes the action probabilities of the six situations above.

Equilibrium 3-Bet Action Probabilities
With a Variety of Stacks, Raises, and Antes

	10,000 Chip Stacks			6,000 Chip Stacks		
	100/200/25 Open to 500	100/200/25 Open to 600	100/200 Open to 600	100/200/25 Open to 500	100/200/25 Open to 600	100/200 Open to 600
Fold	56%	72%	72%	68%	77%	78%
Call	38%	22%	23%	26%	16%	16%
Small Raise	0%	0%	0%	1%	1%	2%
Pot Raise	5%	5%	4%	1%	0%	2%
Big Raise	0%	0%	0%	0%	0%	0%
Jam	1%	1%	1%	4%	6%	2%

So, what are the obvious things that jump out at you from these tables? Some things that jumped out at me:

• The solution 3-bets about 6% of the time in all cases.

• For 6,000 stacks with an ante, most raises are pushes.

• When looking at the "other-calling-hands" ranges, the presence of an ante makes no difference.

The solution 3-bets about 6% of the time in all cases. There's some variation, such as raising more often when there is an ante, but it doesn't make much of a difference. When he increases his raise size from 500 to 600, we tighten up our calling range, which is important, but our 3-bet range is almost unchanged. With 10,000 stacks, we 3-bet a bit less and with 6,000, we 3-bet a bit more, but for the most part, it doesn't matter if he opens with 500 or 600. This makes sense, as his strong opening range hasn't changed, only his raise size.

For 6,000 stacks with an ante, most raises are pushes. There are occasional smaller value 3-bets (and bluffs), but most of the time, a raise is a push. His raise is 8%-10% of our stack and we're out of position. We'd hate to make a smaller raise, put in a good chunk of our stack, and still be out of position post-flop. It's better to push all-in and eliminate our positional disadvantage, even though a push is sometimes more than a 4x-pot bet.

When looking at the "other calling hands" ranges, the presence of an ante makes no difference. This really surprised me. When we compare ante versus no ante:

• We are more willing to fight for a pot with an ante (makes sense).

• Our minimum calling standards are almost unchanged (what?!?).

It didn't really make sense to me at first, but a little investigation into the details of the solution hints at an answer.

Our intuition fails us, because we think, "When there's an ante and I lose the pot, I lose the same amount, but when I win, it's a bigger pot. Why wouldn't I play more hands?" The answer is that our opponent will fight a lot more to win a pot that has an ante.

Now this only applies when we're thinking about very weak hands—right on the border between calling and folding. Stronger hands see a bigger +EV boost from the ante, which is why they're more willing to 3-bet, but weak hands see almost no EV gain. When we call an opening raise (early in a tournament) with a hand like J6s or 74s, we're hoping either to strike gold or sometimes take the pot away from our opponent if he missed the flop. But face it, most of the time we're going just to check and fold. We both know that on average, he'll have the better hand on the flop. We can't change that. Trying to bluff the pot away from him too often with weak hands is just spewing chips. All those times we check and fold, it doesn't matter if there's an ante or not; we lose the same amount.

What about when we don't check and fold? Sometimes we'll win a bigger pot if there's an ante. Sometimes we'll lose a bigger pot. The ante creates a bigger starting pot on the flop, so his continuation bets will be bigger. That means worse implied odds on our draws and it's more expensive to chase them and miss. Sometimes we'll float, try to check-raise, or do something else to steal the pot and it won't work. Oops, we just lost more, because those bets and raises are bigger with an ante. But the clincher is this: With more dead money in the pot, he's *less likely to give it up* post-flop.

Put it all together and you see that with weak hands, there's very little EV change with an ante, because the dead money we gain when we win the pot is countered by the fact that we're going to win less often. The flip side is that our stronger hands get a bigger bonus from the ante, because our opponent is less likely to give it up and is more likely to pay us off.

Now let's turn the tables and see how the opener responds to a 3-bet. Because we have to consider all the different 3-bet sizes, I only compare our original example (10,000 stacks, 100/200/25 blinds, opening raise to 500) with the same situation, but 6,000-chip stacks.

Responding to a 3-Bet
(100/200/25 Blinds, Opening Raise to 500)
10,000 Stacks

Hand	His 3-Bet Size			
	Small	Pot	Big	Jam
AA	J60 S20 P20	J	J	C
KK	C	C70 J20 S10	C50J	C
QQ	C	C	C80J	C
JJ	C	C	C	C80F
TT	C	C	C	C90F
99	C	C	C70F	F
88	C	C	F80 C10 J10	F
77	C90J	C50F	F70J	F
66	C	C50 J40 F10	F60J	F
AKs	C	C	C	C
AQs	C	C	C70J	F
AJs	C	F50J	F	F
A8s	F60 J30 p10	F	F	F
A7s	J60 F20 p20	F	F	F
A6s	F70 J20 p10	F	F	F
A5s	J90p	J	F60J	F
A4s	J80 p10 F10	F70J	F80J	F
A3s	J70 p20 F10	F	F90J	F
A2s	J50 F30 p20	F	F	F
AKo	C	C	C	F60C
AQo	C	F90J	F	F
KQs	C	C	F80J	F
KJs	C	C50 J40 s10	F	F

Responding to a 3-Bet (cont.)
(100/200/25 Blinds, Opening Raise to 500)

10,000 Stacks

Hand	His 3-Bet Size			
	Small	Pot	Big	Jam
KTs	C70 F20 s10	F80J	F	F
KQo	C	F70C	F	F
KJo	C60 F20 s20	F	F	F
QJs	C	F50C	F	F
76s	F80C	F	F	F
Other calling hands	22+, ATs, JTs, 65s, 54s	none	none	none

6,000 Stacks

Hand	His 3-Bet Size			
	Small	Pot	Big	Jam
AA	J90S	J	J	C
KK	C	J90C	J90C	C
QQ	C	C50J	J	C
JJ	J90S	J	J	C
TT	C	C60J	J70C	C
99	C	C60F	F60 C30 J10	C70F
88	C	C40 F40 J20	F60 C30 J10	F60C
77	C	F70J	F70 C20 J10	F
66	C	F50J	F70 C20 J10	F
AKs	C	C	J80C	C
AQs	C	C	C	C
AJs	C70J	C	F90C	F

Responding to a 3-Bet (cont.)
(100/200/25 Blinds, Opening Raise to 500)

6,000 Stacks

Hand	His 3-Bet Size			
	Small	Pot	Big	Jam
A8s	F	F	F	F
A7s	F	F	F	F
A6s	F	F	F	F
A5s	F90J	F	F	F
A4s	F	F	F	F
A3s	F	F	F	F
A2s	F	F	F	F
AKo	C60 J30 S10	J60C	J90C	C
AQo	C60J	C40 F30 J30	F70J	F90C
KQs	C	F90C	F	F
KJs	C50J	F80C	F	F
KTs	F	F	F	F
KQo	C	F	F	F
KJo	F70 J20 s10	F	F	F
QJs	C	F	F	F
76s	F	F	F	F
Other calling hands	44+	none	none	none

F	Fold
C	Call
S	Make small (0.5X pot) 4-bet and be willing to get it all in
s	Small 4-bet but fold to 5-bet
P	Make pot-sized 4-bet and be willing to get it all in
p	Pot 4-bet but fold to 5-bet
J	Jam

The first table are the 4-bets we saw in the previous section where we responded to 3-bets of various sizes. The second table is new, where we reduce the effective stacks to 6,000.

One thing to notice is that with 6,000 stacks, 4-bet bluffing is a lot less common. The reason? Lack of fold equity. Even when he puts in a half-pot 3-bet, that's a bet of 1,150 or almost 20% of his stack. When he makes a larger 3-bet, he's even more committed. Surprisingly, the equilibrium solution occasionally flat-calls a big 3-bet, even though it's 40% of our stack. It does this occasionally with good aces, plus some medium pocket pairs and KK. The solution expects that everything goes in the middle post-flop most of the time, but figures it gets the best of it when someone gives up, given that the opener has position.

Changing Position and Tournament Pressures

So far, we've only examined raises from a mid-position raiser and situations with no pressures from the tournament structure. Tournament pressures exist when the money bubble is in sight, giving a value to simply staying alive. The "no-pressure" situation applies only in the first few levels of a major tournament, and even then is only an approximation. More realistic situations are examined below and include "medium-" and "high"-pressure situations[3]. You'll have to decide how high the pressure is on you for any given tournament situation. Pressure obviously increases the closer you get to a prize bubble, be it the money or final-table bubble. Big-stack versus big-stack confrontations are usually high-pressure situations, as is a medium stack going up against a big stack.

---

[3] For those readers familiar with *Kill Everyone*, these two situations equate to bubble factors of 1.5 and 2.0, respectively.

The chart below compares our original mid-position opener with a very aggressive button who opens 50% of the time (again a mix favoring stronger hands). This is more aggressive than most people open on the button, but some players open this much or wider routinely.

Equilibrium 3-Bets Depending on Opener's Position and Tournament Pressures
(10,000 Stacks, Blinds 100/200/25)

Facing a Mid-Position Raise

Hand	No Pressure	Medium Pressure	High Pressure
AA	P70J	P	P90B
KK	P	P	P
QQ	P60J	P	P
JJ	p	P	P
TT	P	p50C	C60p
99	C	C	C
88	C	C	C
77	C	C	C
66	C	C	C
55	C	C	C
44	C	C	C
33	C	C	p70F
22	C	C80p	F
AKs	P	P	p
AQs	P90J	p	p
AJs	p	p	p90b
ATs	p	p80F	p60F
A9s	F60p	F	F
A8s	F	F	F

Equilibrium 3-Bets Depending on Opener's Position and Tournament Pressures (cont.)
(10,000 Stacks, Blinds 100/200/25)
Facing a Mid-Position Raise

Hand	No Pressure	Medium Pressure	High Pressure
A7s	F	F	F
A6s	F	F	F
A5s	F70J	F	F
A4s	F	F	F
A3s	F	F	F
A2s	F	F	F
AKo	J70P	P	p90B
AQo	p	p	p
AJo	C	F	F
ATo	F	F	F
A9o	F	F	F
A8o	F	F	F
A7o	F	F	F
A6o	F	F	F
A5o	F	F	F
A4o	F	F	F
A3o	F	F	F
A2o	F	F	F
KQs	C	C	C
KJs	p70C	C	p90b
K8s	C	C	c90p
K7s	C	C	F70 p20 b10
K6s	C	C	F60p
K5s	C	C	F80p

Equilibrium 3-Bets Depending on Opener's Position and Tournament Pressures (cont.)
(10,000 Stacks, Blinds 100/200/25)

Facing a Mid-Position Raise

Hand	No Pressure	Medium Pressure	High Pressure
KQo	C	C	C
KJo	C	p80C	F90p
K2o	F	F	F
QJs	C	C	C
QTs	p60C	p	p
QJo	C	F90p	F
JTs	C90p	p	p
J9s	C	C	F80p
JTo	C	F	F
J6o	F	F	F
J5o	F	F	F
T9s	C	C	p80F
T2s	F	F	F
T9o	C	F	F
T6o	F	F	F
T5o	F	F	F
92s	F	F	F
98o	C	F	F
82s	F	F	F
87o	C	F	F
73s	C	F	F
72s	F	F	F
76o	C	F	F
75o	F	F	F

Equilibrium 3-Bets Depending on Opener's Position and Tournament Pressures (cont.)

(10,000 Stacks, Blinds 100/200/25)

Facing a Mid-Position Raise

Hand	No Pressure	Medium Pressure	High Pressure
63s	C	F	F
62s	F	F	F
52s	C	F	F
Other calling hands	K2s+, K7o+, Q3s+, Q9o+, J8o+, T3s+, T8o+, 93s+, 97o+, 84s+, 87o, 73s+, 76o, 63s+, 52s+, 42s+, 32s	K5s+, KTo+, Q7s+, J7s+, T7s+, 96s+, 86s+, 75s+, 65s, 54s	K8s+, KQo, Q9s+

Facing an Aggressive Button Raise

Hand	No Pressure	Medium Pressure	High Pressure
AA	P	P	P
KK	P	P	P
QQ	P80B	P90B	P70B
JJ	P70B	B90P	P
TT	B80P	B	P50 S40 B10
99	J	B90P	s50 p40 b10
88	J	P70B	p70s
77	J	P70B	p80 s10 b10
66	J60 P30 B10	C50 P40 B10	p80s
55	B60 P20 C20	C	C70p
44	C	C	C
33	C80J	C	C
22	J90C	C	C70s
AKs	P	P	S90P

Equilibrium 3-Bets Depending on Opener's Position and Tournament Pressures (cont.)
(10,000 Stacks, Blinds 100/200/25)
Facing an Aggressive Button Raise

Hand	No Pressure	Medium Pressure	High Pressure
AQs	B90P	P	P70S
AJs	P	P	P
ATs	P	P	p70S
A9s	P	P	s50 p40 B10
A8s	P	p	p80s
A7s	P80B	B70p	p60 s30 B10
A6s	J80B	B50p	s80p
A5s	B80J	B	s50 p40 B10
A4s	J80B	B	s70p
A3s	J	b	s80p
A2s	J	p90b	s60p
AKo	P90B	P90B	P70S
AQo	J90B	B	P40 S40 B20
AJo	P70 B20 J10	B50P	P80S
ATo	P90B	p90B	S
A9o	p	p	s
A8o	p	p90b	p80s
A7o	p90C	p70b	p70s
A6o	p90b	p60b	p60s
A5o	p	b50p	s80p
A4o	p60b	b70p	s50p
A3o	b50p	p70b	s80p
A2o	p90b	p90b	p80b
KQs	C	C90P	S

Equilibrium 3-Bets Depending on Opener's Position and Tournament Pressures (cont.)
(10,000 Stacks, Blinds 100/200/25)

Facing an Aggressive Button Raise

Hand	No Pressure	Medium Pressure	High Pressure
KJs	P	P	S90p
K8s	C	C	C
K7s	C	C	C
K6s	C	C	C
K5s	C	C	C
KQo	C	C	C50S
KJo	C90J	C	p70C
K2o	C	C	C90s
QJs	C	C	C
QTs	C90J	C	s80C
QJo	C	C	C
JTs	J90C	C	s60C
J9s	C	C	C
JTo	C	C70 p20 b10	p50 C40 b10
J6o	C	C	p50C
J5o	C	C	F90p
T9s	C90J	C	C
T2s	C	C	s50 p30 C20
T9o	C	C50 b30 p20	p90b
T6o	C	C	F90p
T5o	C	F90b	F
92s	C	C70p	F
98o	C	p	p90b
82s	C	C60p	F

Equilibrium 3-Bets Depending on Opener's Position and Tournament Pressures (cont.)
(10,000 Stacks, Blinds 100/200/25)
Facing an Aggressive Button Raise

Hand	No Pressure	Medium Pressure	High Pressure
87o	C	p70C	p90F
73s	C	C	F60 s30 p10
72s	C	p	F
76o	C	C	p50F
75o	C	C90p	F
63s	C	C	C90s
62s	C	p50C	F
52s	C	C	F50 s40 p10
Other calling hands	any suited, K2o+, Q2o+, J2o+, T4o+, 95o+, 85o+, 75o+, 64o+, 53o+	any suited, K2o+, Q2o+, J4o+, T6o+, 96o+, 86o+, 75o+, 65o, 54o	K2+, Q2s+, Q4o+, J2s+, J6o+, T2s+, T7o+, 93s+, 97o+, 84s+, 74s+, 63s+, 53s+, 43s

These are some massive charts with a lot of variety, so the action probabilities table will help a lot.

Equilibrium 3-Bet Action Probabilities
Depending on Opener's Position and Tournament Pressures
(10,000 Stacks, Blinds 100/200/25)

	Facing a Mid-Position Raise			Facing an Aggressive Button Raise		
	No Pressure	Medium Pressure	High Pressure	No Pressure	Medium Pressure	High Pressure
Fold	56%	80%	87%	6%	22%	34%
Call	38%	14%	6%	72%	56%	40%
Small Raise	0%	0%	0%	0%	0%	10%
Pot Raise	5%	6%	7%	15%	15%	15%
Big Raise	0%	0%	0%	0%	7%	1%
Jam	1%	0%	0%	7%	0%	0%

What can we glean from this? I see several trends here:

• The frequent calling we discussed earlier is a strong function of both bubble pressure and our opponent's range.

• We 3-bet slightly more often when the pressure is high, but it doesn't make too big a difference.

• The average raise size goes down as the pressure increases (at least with deeper stacks).

The frequent calling we discussed earlier is a strong function of both bubble pressure and our opponent's range. As the pressure goes up, implied odds go down and it's no longer profitable to call with a lot of suited junk. Not only are implied odds reduced directly due to the payout structure, but in high-pressure situations, people are less likely to overplay their one-pair hands. These two facts together move you from Gus Hansen in the no-pressure zone down to a much more selective range in high-pressure situations.

However, even with high pressure, the solution calls a lot of weak hands against the super-loose button. He has such a weak range that the solution feels safe enough to call with these great pot odds and, perhaps, take a shot at the pot later. You may have heard the advice that it's easier to set-mine against a tight EP raiser than a loose button. This is true, since his weak range implies he won't hit a good one-pair hand as often and won't stack off as often. But it also means he'll be easier to bluff, since he's less likely to hit the flop. We won't get as much value out of our sets, but we'll have a lot more bluffing success, so the solution again feels justified in calling with a lot of weak hands—even though we're out of position and the bubble factor is high.

A bit of warning: All of this liberal blind defense means playing a lot of pots post-flop and out of position. That takes a lot of skill. So make sure your post-flop skills are up to snuff before you start opening up your calling ranges. Trying to play a LAG style without the skill to back it up is a recipe for disaster. Playing out of position against hyper-LAGs isn't easy and almost always means courting higher variance. If a number of predictable players are at your table, it might be best to reduce your calling frequency against tough LAGs and hyper-LAGs to hands that flop well, such as small pairs and suited connectors, while targeting the more predictable players you can exploit with far less variance.

We 3-bet slightly more often when the pressure is high, but it doesn't make too big a difference. The bubble pressures affect both of us. While we have a bit more fold equity with our 3-bets, the penalty for being wrong is higher, so we don't overdo it. There's no magic equation for the right 3-bet frequency, but I'll talk about it at the end of this chapter. Note how often we bluff 3-bet against an aggressive button, especially with higher tournament pressure. The solution likes to bluff 3-bet with off-suit connectors (since they have a bit of play), while calling for value with suited versions.

The average raise size goes down as the pressure increases (at least with deeper stacks). The equilibrium solution makes smaller re-raises both in and out of position when the pressure is high.

When you're close to the bubble, fold equity is higher than at other times. Pushing all-in gives you the most fold equity, but it can be very risky if it's an overbet. Therefore, if pushing is too much of an overbet, it's usually best to keep the raises small. The key is that the small raises still have good fold equity, don't risk too many chips, and ensure that your opponent can't push without making an overbet as well. Extreme bubble factors create a game of chicken; you try to be the first person to go all-in without overextending yourself. If it's too dangerous to push, then it's important that your raise sizes don't make it easy for your opponent to push against you.

Now let's look at the 4-betting solution for some high-pressure situations by comparing the two high-pressure situations: when you open in mid-position and when you open on the button.

Responding to a 3-Bet Under High Pressure
(100/200/25 Blinds, Opening Raise to 500)

Mid-Position

| Hand | His 3-Bet Size | | | |
	Small	Pot	Big	Jam
AA	S60 P30 C10	C80S	C90J	C
KK	C	C	C	C
QQ	C90S	C80S	C90J	F90C
JJ	C90S	C	C80F	F90C
TT	C	C	C50F	F90C
99	C80F	C60F	F50 C40 J10	F
88	C80F	F60S	F50 C40 J10	F
77	C70F	F90s	F90J	F
66	F70C	F90s	F90J	F
55	F70C	F90s	F90J	F
44	F70C	F	F	F
33	F80C	F	F	F

Responding to a 3-Bet Under High Pressure (cont.)
(100/200/25 Blinds, Opening Raise to 500)

Mid-Position

Hand	His 3-Bet Size			
	Small	Pot	Big	Jam
22	F80C	F	F	F
AKs	C	C	C	C
AQs	C	C	F60 C30 J10	F
AJs	C80 s10 p10	F80s	F	F
ATs	C50 s30 F10 p10	F	F	F
A9s	C60F	F	F	F
A8s	C50 F30 s20	F	F	F
A7s	C60 F20 s10 b10	F	F	F
A6s	C60 F20 s10 b10	F	F	F
A5s	C60 s20 F10 b10	F	F	F
A4s	C60 s20 F10 b10	F	F	F
A3s	C60 s20 F20	F	F	F
A2s	C60 F20 s20	F	F	F
AKo	C	C	C	F
AQo	F50s	F	F	F
AJo	F90s	F	F	F
ATo	C50 s30 F10 p10	F	F	F
A9o	F	F	F	F
A8o	F90s	F	F	F
A7o	F90s	F	F	F
A6o	F90s	F	F	F
A5o	F90s	F	F	F
A4o	N/A			

Responding to a 3-Bet Under High Pressure (cont.)
(100/200/25 Blinds, Opening Raise to 500)

Mid-Position

Hand	His 3-Bet Size			
	Small	Pot	Big	Jam
A3o				
A2o				
KQs	C	C	F	F
KJs	C	F70s	F	F
KTs	C40 F40 s10 p10	F	F	F
K9s	C50F	F	F	F
K8s	F90s	F	F	F
K7s	N/A			
K6s				
K5s				
K4s				
K3s				
K2s				
KQo	C	F50C	F	F
KJo	F90C	F	F	F
KTo	C40 F40 s10 p10	F	F	F
QJs	C	F	F	F
QTs	C50F	F	F	F
Q9s	F90C	F	F	F
Q8s	F	F	F	F
Q7s	N/A			
Q6s				
Q5s				

Responding to a 3-Bet Under High Pressure (cont.)
(100/200/25 Blinds, Opening Raise to 500)

Mid-Position

Hand	His 3-Bet Size			
	Small	Pot	Big	Jam
Q4s				
Q3s				
Q2s				
QJo	F90s	F	F	F
QTo	F	F	F	F
JTs	C50 F50 s10	F	F	F
J9s	F	F	F	F
J8s	F	F	F	F
J7s	N/A			
T9s	F	F	F	F
T8s	F	F	F	F
T7s	N/A			
T9o				
98s	F	F	F	F
97s	N/A			
86s				
65s	F	F	F	F
54s	N/A			
43s				
Other calling hands	none	none	none	none

Responding to a 3-Bet Under High Pressure (cont.)
(100/200/25 Blinds, Opening Raise to 500)

Button

Hand	His 3-Bet Size			
	Small	Pot	Big	Jam
AA	S	S50 C40 J10	C90J	C
KK	S	C90S	J	C
QQ	S	S70J	J	C
JJ	S	S	J80C	C
TT	S	S70C	C50J	C
99	S	C50S	J	C
88	S	S70C	J60C	C
77	C80S	C80S	C40J	F60C
66	C90S	C	C80 J10 F10	F
55	C	C80s	C50 J40 F10	F
44	C	C70s	J60 F20 C20	F
33	C	s50C	J50F	F
22	C	s70F	F90J	F
AKs	C80S	C	C	C
AQs	C	C90S	C	C
AJs	C50S	C60S	C	C
ATs	C	C	C	F
A9s	C	C	C	F
A8s	C	C	C	F
A7s	C	C	C	F
A6s	C	C	C70F	F
A5s	C	C	C60F	F
A4s	C	C	F	F
A3s	C	C	F	F

Responding to a 3-Bet Under High Pressure (cont.)
(100/200/25 Blinds, Opening Raise to 500)

Button

Hand	His 3-Bet Size			
	Small	Pot	Big	Jam
A2s	C	C90F	F	F
AKo	S	S90J	J	C
AQo	S	S70J	J	C
AJo	S	S	J80 C10 F10	F
ATo	S80C	S60C	F60 J30 C10	F
A9o	C	F	F	F
A8o	C	F60C	F	F
A7o	F80s	F	F	F
A6o	F	F	F	F
A5o	F60s	F	F	F
A4o	s60F	F	F	F
A3o	F60s	F	F	F
A2o	F80s	F	F	F
KQs	C	C	C70J	F
KJs	C	C60s	J90C	F
KTs	s90C	J50s	J	F
K9s	s	s60J	J90F	F
K8s	F60s	s80F	F70J	F
K7s	s70F	F50s	F80J	F
K6s	s50 C40 F10	F90s	F90J	F
K5s	F80s	F80s	F	F
K4s	F70s	F	F	F
K3s	F60s	F	F	F
K2s	F90s	F	F	F

Responding to a 3-Bet Under High Pressure (cont.)
(100/200/25 Blinds, Opening Raise to 500)

Button

| Hand | His 3-Bet Size | | | |
	Small	Pot	Big	Jam
KQo	C	C90s	C50J	F
KJo	s	s	F60J	F
KTo	F60s	F70 s20 J10	F90J	F
QJs	C	C	C80J	F
QTs	C	s50J	J	F
Q9s	s	s70J	J80F	F
Q8s	s80F	s80F	F70J	F
Q7s	F60s	F	F	F
Q6s	s60F	F	F	F
Q5s	F80s	F	F	F
Q4s	F60s	F	F	F
Q3s	F60s	F	F	F
Q2s	F90s	F	F	F
QJo	C	s60 F20 J10 C10	J70F	F
QTo	C50s	F70s	F90J	F
JTs	C	C60s	F60J	F
J9s	C	F70s	F90J	F
J8s	s50 C40 F10	F	F	F
J7s	F60s	F	F	F
T9s	C	s70F	F90J	F
T8s	C80s	F	F	F
T7s	s90F	F	F	F
T9o	F90s	F	F	F
98s	C	F	F90J	F

Responding to a 3-Bet Under High Pressure (cont.)
(100/200/25 Blinds, Opening Raise to 500)

Button

Hand	His 3-Bet Size			
	Small	Pot	Big	Jam
97s	C90s	F	F	F
86s	F50 C40 s10	F	F	F
65s	C90s	F	F	F
54s	s50F	F	F	F
43s	F90s	F	F	F
Other calling hands	JTo, 87s, 76s	none	none	none

The "N/A" entries in the above table are hands that typically aren't 2-bet for that position. Here are the action percentages:

Responding to a 3-Bet Under High Pressure
(100/200/25 Blinds, Opening Raise to 500)

	Mid Position				Button			
	Small	Pot	Big	Jam	Small	Pot	Big	Jam
Fold	37%	60%	69%	11%	43%	61%	70%	12%
Call	53%	35%	29%	89%	30%	17%	11%	88%
Small Raise	8%	5%	0%	N/A	27%	19%	0%	N/A
Pot Raise	2%	0%	0%	N/A	0%	0%	0%	N/A
Big Raise	1%	0%	0%	N/A	0%	0%	0%	N/A
Jam	0%	0%	2%	N/A	0%	3%	19%	N/A

For comparison, these are the action probabilities when there is no tournament pressure:

Responding to a 3-Bet Under No Pressure
(100/200/25 Blinds, Opening Raise to 500)

	Mid Position				Button			
	Small	**Pot**	**Big**	**Jam**	**Small**	**Pot**	**Big**	**Jam**
Fold	24%	51%	64%	23%	17%	57%	65%	23%
Call	68%	40%	26%	77%	67%	22%	16%	77%
Small Raise	2%	1%	0%	N/A	8%	0%	0%	N/A
Pot Raise	1%	1%	0%	N/A	0%	0%	0%	N/A
Big Raise	1%	0%	0%	N/A	0%	0%	0%	N/A
Jam	4%	7%	10%	N/A	8%	21%	19%	N/A

Again, it seems that every time we look at an equilibrium solution, a few numbers look weird at first glance:

• In the no-pressure situation, the opener rarely makes a 4-bet that's not all-in. In the high-pressure situation, smaller 4-bets are much more common.

• The button seems to be calling a jam just as often as the mid-position raiser, even though the BB is 3-betting with a wider range against the button.

In the high-pressure situation, smaller 4-bets are much more common. This is the same thing we saw when we were looking at 3-betting. Try not to be the player who gives your opponent an easy all-in. Make sure that any all-in he makes is an overbet. Otherwise, you should be doing the pushing.

The button seems to be calling a jam just as often as the mid-position raiser, even though the BB is 3-betting with a wider range

against the button. This seems odd at first. Why are they calling the same? Actually, they *aren't* calling the same; you just have to work out the math. The aggressive button is opening 50% of the time, so if he calls a push 12% of the time, that's with a top 6% hand. The mid-position raiser opens about 10% and calls 11% of those—a top 1.1% hand. Look at the specific hands that call a push in the table above and you'll see.

Another interesting thing about the high-pressure 4-bet strategy is that the opener trap calls more often than we've seen before, especially from mid-position. Since the mid-position raiser is stronger, 3-bets against him are usually strong (but sometimes bluffs, as we've seen). So when the opener has a super-strong hand like a high pair, he flat-calls and sees a flop. Most likely, you'll get a continuation bet out of him and that gives you more value than 4-betting. However, when the opener is wide and the 3-better is wide as well, 4-betting for value makes more sense.

Notice that when the BB makes a small 3-bet against the button, the button makes frequent small value 4-bets. He knows that those 3-bets could be very light.

Bringing It All Together—
Equilibrium Solutions

As I said in the beginning of this chapter, the purpose of looking at all these equilibrium solutions is not so we can imitate them. What I'm hoping to do is illuminate some trends, so you can see which factors are important in making your 3- and 4-betting decisions. These trends will be important when we talk about exploitive play in the next section.

One of the trends I'd like to highlight is how often you can defend your blind. Next up are a series of graphs that show how often the big blind defends his blind (by either calling or raising) in

the equilibrium solutions. When considering blind defense, the four most important factors are:
- His opening range.
- Your direct pot odds.
- Your implied odds, which I express as a stack-to-pot ratio (SPR). This is your stack size (if you just call) divided by the size of the pot (if you just call).
- The tournament pressure.

For this first graph, I assume you're getting 3-to-1 pot odds and your SPR is six.

How Blind Defense Changes Based on Opener's Range
(3-to-1 Pot Odds and SPR of Six)

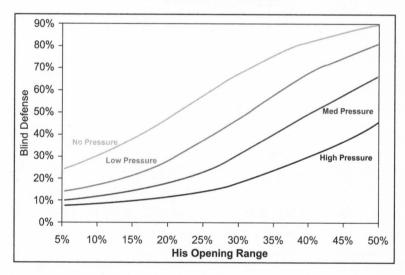

You can see how often the equilibrium solution defends his blinds (either calls or folds) depending on the opener's range. For example, if there's low tournament pressure (a bubble factor of 1.25) and the opener is raising 20%, the solution defends his blind about 30% of the time. This can rise to essentially 100% if the opener has a very wide opening range and there's no pressure. Three-to-1 pot odds is huge when there's no pressure.

Next we look at the effect of how deep the stacks are. We keep the pot odds at 3-to-1 and fix his opening range at 10%, then see how the blind defense changes as a function of SPR.

How Blind Defense Changes Based on SPR
(3-to-1 Pot Odds and Opener Raises 10%)

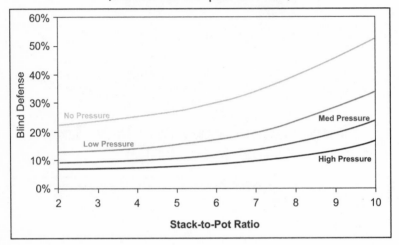

Notice how deeper stacks don't give us as much of an advantage to calling with speculative hands when there's a lot of tournament pressure. Without pressure, we can often get paid off when we hit, but people are much more selective post-flop when the pressure is high. Our implied odds shrink with pressure. Even a little bit of pressure makes a big difference. At an SPR of 10, the solution defends with 53% of hands under no pressure, but only 34% with low pressure.

Now let's see how sensitive we are to his raise size.

How Blind Defense Changes Based on Pot Odds
(SPR of Six and Opener Raises 10%)

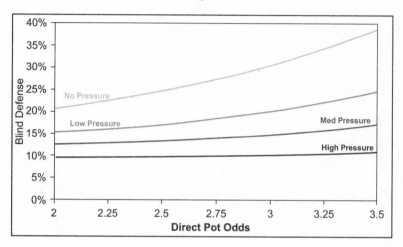

Again, we see a similar pattern where we don't care as much about pot odds when there's pressure. This chart is good support for the strategy of having a very large (3- to 4-BB) standard raise size at the beginning of a tournament, then decreasing that raise size as the tournament progresses and the pressure increases. In the beginning with no pressure, our large raise size gives poor direct odds (and cuts down SPR), keeping blind defense reasonable. Later on when the pressure increases, we have a smaller standard raise size, since it's incorrect for players to defend too often, no matter what the size.

Another thing we could look at is the implied odds that suited connectors need to call in a variety of situations. Let's first take a look at a typical suited connector, 76s, with only light tournament pressure. This graph shows the implied odds you need to call depending on how good your direct pot odds are.

Implied Odds Needed to Call from Big Blind
with 76s and Light Tournament Pressure

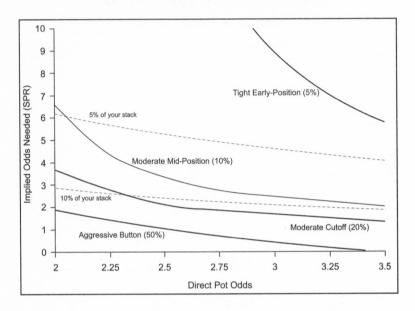

Several lines here correspond to how strong the opening raiser is. The SPR given is simply the minimum you need to make calling better than folding. For example, against a moderate mid-position raise, the equilibrium solution recommends a call if it's getting 2.5-to-1 pot odds, as long as its SPR is at least about 3.5. The dotted lines show you the range suggested by the Rule of 5 and 10, which means if it costs us 5% of our stack or less, we call; if it costs 10% of our stack or more, we fold; in between, we have a judgment call (first suggested in *Pot-Limit & No-Limit Poker*, by Stewart Ruben and Bob Ciaffone, pg. 65).

This doesn't always mean that calling is the best option; raising could be better either above or below these lines, but calling is better than folding.

As you can see, the equilibrium solution thinks that the Rule of 5 and 10 is pretty accurate facing an average raise with typical pot odds. The solution is more liberal with calling when the opener's range is very wide; it's now kind of "pre-flop floating" here and willing to bluff or semi-bluff on a lot of flops. Note that the solution won't call against a very tight player without a lot of odds. It thinks that the opener's post-flop play will be so good that it won't get paid off enough. In an equilibrium, this is probably right. However, real opponents who are this tight are usually willing to go down fighting with top pair. It will be much easier to stack them, meaning that it's probably right to call with about 5% of your stack.

What about other types of suited connectors or pocket pairs against which we typically apply the Rule of 5 and 10 (or 3 and 6)? This graph now shows the implied odds needed to call for various hand types.

Implied Odds Needed to Call from Big Blind Against a Mid-Position Raise with Various Hands and Light Tournament Pressure

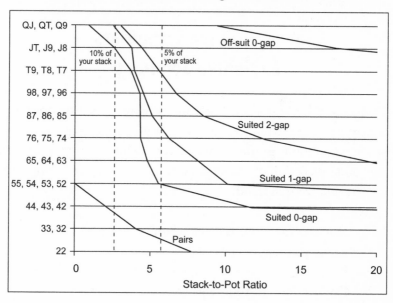

Take a look for the hand you'd like to call with on the left and find the line that corresponds to its description. For example, to call with 85s, you need an SPR of about eight. Calling with 53s needs at least 10 SPR. Again, the dotted lines show the calling range suggested by the Rule of 5 and 10.

So it looks like the equilibrium solution thinks that the Rule of 5 and 10 is pretty good for a lot of suited 0-gaps and 1-gaps; they all need about the same SPR to be profitable. The Rule was never intended for tiny connectors less than 54s; you can see how their profitability drops off dramatically. Off-suit connectors fare a lot worse than I would have expected. I probably play off-suit connectors more than most people (usually calling up to 4% to 5% of my stack), but I've been noticing lately that my results with them are less than stellar. I'll be changing my game starting today. You should be aware that the equilibrium does call or bluff 3-bet with off-suit connectors when the opener has a wider range. Against a wide range, a hand like 87o can hit top or second pair with a weak kicker and be a favorite.

Enough with the Computers— Exploitive Solutions

Finally! We can start talking about playing against that real person across the table from you, not just against perfect players. Knowing the equilibrium solutions can be very helpful and they contain many good pieces of advice. However, in real play, we suggest you keep the following in mind:

- Don't call as often as equilibrium.
- Know your opponent's style.
- Be aware of your own play and image.
- Pay attention to your raise sizes.
- Mix when appropriate.

Don't call as often as equilibrium. The equilibrium solution took every single edge it could. Many of the calls it made with weak hands were only marginally +EV. As I stated earlier, you could easily fold most of these hands and not lose a lot of value. If you give up your blinds more often, you'll greatly reduce your variance, avoid many difficult post-flop decisions, and give a bit more credibility to the hands you do call or 3-bet. All of these together probably more than make up for the lost small edges. All the authors fold more than the equilibrium suggests. Just don't fold so often that you put a target on your forehead. I know in the mid-stages of the tournament, I'm always looking for the players who fold their blinds often. Don't be one of them.

Know your opponent's style. This should go without saying. Here are the adjustments we make when facing different opponents:

Player Type	Adjustments
Aggressive, but folds often to a 3-bet	3-bet more often, with almost any two cards.
Loose donkey	Don't bluff, and make sure you make big bets with your strong hands.
Continuation bets almost 100% of the time	Call more often, both with speculative hands and monsters. Always check, no matter what the flop. If your opponent continuation bets all the time, it essentially lets you have position on the flop and he must put in more money without knowing what you have.
Tight nit	He won't often fold to a 3-bet, since his range is fairly tight to start with. You can 3-bet monsters for value, but you shouldn't bluff 3-bet. If he plays "fit or fold" on the flop, you can lead with your good hands and check when you miss. If he checks behind on the flop, you can bet the turn and pick up the pot.
Hyper-LAG	Tread lightly! If you 3-bet, be prepared for him to 4-bet on air. If your 3-bet can be all-in, then push since you have fold equity. If not, you can 3-bet good hands in an effort to trap him, or flat-call to stop the madness and see a flop. You'll have to be prepared for post-flop bluffs, but you'll have more information.
Pro	You don't want to play post-flop against a pro out of position. Rarely flat-call and make large 3-bets in an effort to take the pot down immediately. Kill Phil-style pushes of up to four or five times the size of the pot are completely reasonable.

Here's a more detailed example of playing against an aggressive opponent who folds too often to a 3-bet. We'll assume he's in late position and opens 20% of the time, but folds to a 3-bet about 10% more often than equilibrium.

Comparison of Equilibrium vs. Exploitive Play
(Light Tournament Pressure)

Hand	Equilibrium	Exploitive
AA	P80B	B
KK	P	B
QQ	B70P	B
JJ	P60B	S
TT	P90B	S
99	p	S
88	C	S
77	C	S
66	C	S
55	C	S
44	C	p
33	C	p
22	C	p
AKs	P	B
AQs	p	B
AJs	p	p
ATs	p80C	p
A9s	p	p
A8s	p	p
A7s	p90b	p
A6s	F70b	p
A5s	b60p	p

Comparison of Equilibrium vs. Exploitive Play (cont.)
(Light Tournament Pressure)

Hand	Equilibrium	Exploitive
A4s	F80b	p
A3s	F	p
A2s	F	p
AKo	P60B	B
AQo	p80b	p
AJo	C80p	p
ATo	C	p
KJo	C70p	p
QTs	C60 b30 p10	p
QJo	C60b	p
JTs	p	p
J2s	C	p
JTo	C	p
T9s	p70C	p
98o	C	p
87o	C	p
Other calling hands	any suited (except 92s, 83s, 82s, 72s, 62s), K4o+, Q6o+, J7o+, T7o+, 97o+, 86o+, 76o	none
Other pot (bluff) hands	none	any suited, A2o+, K2o+, Q2o+, J2o+, T6o+, 96o+, 85o+, 75o+, 64o+, 54o

As you can see, when an opponent folds too often, it's correct to just pounce! The equilibrium solution plays it more cautiously, calling with implied odds and mixing up its play. On the other hand, the exploitive solution never calls and raises 80% of the time, often as a pot-sized bluff.

The exploitive solution takes complete advantage of its opponent, but is vulnerable to counter-exploitation. It sometimes makes small or big 3-bets for value, but it always folds to a 4-bet after a pot-sized 3-bet. The exploitive solution never has to mix up its play, since it assumes the other guy is a sucker who won't adjust to these re-steals.

The exploitive solution gives you the highest EV possible if your assumptions about your opponent are correct. However, it doesn't protect you if you're wrong about your opponent's calling range or he notices that you're robbing him blind. It might have other unintended consequences as well, such as the other players at the table thinking you're a loose cannon, when you're only targeting a single player. A better strategy, therefore, is to take a middle-of-the-road approach: Still deviate away from equilibrium, but not 100%. You'll still be vulnerable to counter-exploitation, but you're hoping you'll be right more often than not.

We can create a semi-exploitive solution by solving a modified-equilibrium game. In this case, our opponent (wrongly) thinks he gets a small bonus for folding, so he'll fold more often. But he'll be able to react to our strategy, so we still have to be careful and mix things up. When you solve this solution, you get the following.

A More Balanced Exploitive Play
(Light Tournament Pressure)

Hand	Equilibrium	Exploitive	Balanced
AA	P80B	B	P70 B20 S10
KK	P	B	P80 B10 S10
QQ	B70P	B	P60B
JJ	P60B	S	P50B
TT	P90B	S	P70 B20 S10
99	p	S	P40 C40 s20
88	C	S	C
77	C	S	C

A More Balanced Exploitive Play (cont.)
(Light Tournament Pressure)

Hand	Equilibrium	Exploitive	Balanced
66	C	S	C
55	C	S	C
44	C	p	C
33	C	p	C
22	C	p	C
AKs	P	B	S50P
AQs	p	B	P80 B10 S10
AJs	p	p	s40 p40 C20
ATs	p80C	p	p60C
A9s	p	p	p
A8s	p	p	p
A7s	p90b	p	p90b
A6s	F70b	p	p70b
A5s	b60p	p	p60 b30 s10
A4s	F80b	p	p60b
A3s	F	p	b40 p30 F30
A2s	F	p	F70b
AKo	P60B	B	P70B
AQo	p80b	p	p90b
AJo	C80p	p	C60 p30 s10
ATo	C	p	C70 s20 p10
KJo	C70p	p	C70p
QTs	C60 b30 p10	p	C80p
QJo	C60b	p	p40 C40 b20
JTs	p	p	C50p
J2s	C	p	C90b

A More Balanced Exploitive Play (cont.)
(Light Tournament Pressure)

Hand	Equilibrium	Exploitive	Balanced
JTo	C	p	C60 p30 s10
T9s	p70C	p	C90p
98o	C	p	C90s
87o	C	p	C90s
Other calling hands	any suited (except 92s, 83s, 82s, 72s, 62s), K4o+, Q6o+, J7o+, T7o+, 97o+, 86o+, 76o	none	any suited (except 92s, 83s, 82s, 72s, 62s), K4o+, Q6o+, J7o+, T7o+, 97o+, 86o+, 76o
Other pot (bluff) hands	none	any suited, A2o+, K2o+, Q2o+, J2o+, T6o+, 96o+, 85o+, 75o+, 64o+, 54o	none

The more balanced play raises more often with weak suited aces as well as some of the better suited and off-suit connectors. But it doesn't go overboard like the fully exploitive play and continues to balance the bet sizes (i.e., with the exploitive play a big bet was always strong and a pot-sized one was weak). Notice also that the average bet size is now smaller compared to the equilibrium; since he folds more often, we can risk less, but we still have to balance that raise size with some strong hands.

The Incredible 3-Bet/4-Bet Push Charts

Pages 246, 247, and 248 contain three charts that you can use for any situation where you're considering pushing as a 3-bet from the BB or as a 4-bet: one chart for pocket pairs, one for suited hands, and another for off-suit hands. They approximate the chances you need your opponent to fold in order for the push to be profitable. No math is needed, except for calculating how big your raise is in pot-sized amounts. Note that this just compares pushing to fold-ing—calling could be superior to both, although that's unlikely if stacks are short enough that you're pushing.

Here's how you estimate how frequently you need your opponent to fold:

• Connect a line between your hand and your estimation of your opponent's opening range.

• Note where that line intersects the "pivot" line. The small bumps on the pivot line will help you keep your place; just remember how close you are to one of them.

• Connect a new line from that point on the pivot line to how big of a raise you made (in terms of how many pot-sized amounts the raise is). There are separate lines for different levels of tourna-ment pressure.

• Where this new line intersects the "Folds Needed" line is your answer.

The given answer isn't guaranteed to be 100% accurate, but this chart will give fairly close answers in a majority of situations.

Example 1

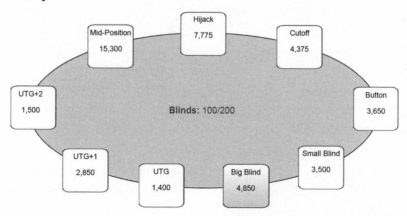

A semi-tight player open-raises to 600 from the cut-off. You're in the BB with pocket 6s. Your opponent is in late position, but he's fairly tight, so you estimate he'll raise with a top-12% hand. We'll also assume there's medium tournament pressure. How often do we need our opponent to fold for a push to be profitable?

Look at the re-steal chart for pocket pairs. Get a straight edge and make a line between pocket 6s and an opening range of 12%. Notice where this intersects the pivot line—it's about halfway between two dots, right above the "M" of Medium. Now make a new line between this point and the correct point on the medium pressure line. If you push all-in, that would be a 2.5X pot bet, so we need to guess at where 2.5X the pot is on the medium pressure line. Connect a line between these two points and see where that intersects the "Folds Needed" line. It looks like about 78% or 79%. That means if you think this opponent will fold at least 80% of the time, pushing is profitable (i.e., his calling range is tighter than JJ+, AK).

Example 2

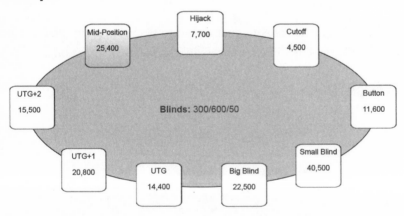

It's approaching the bubble and you raise to 1,500 from mid-position with AQo. It's folded to the small blind who 3-bets to 6,500. You can't flat-call, since that puts too much of your stack in the middle; it's push-or-fold time.

The small blind has been a bit of a bully, but not too much, so you assume he's re-raising on a top 7% hand. Use the off-suit chart and draw a line between AQ and a 7% opener. That intersects the pivot line right on the dot above the last 'e' in "No Pressure." If you push all-in, that will be about a 1.7X pot re-raise. This is high-pressure situation, because we're near the bubble and both of us are large stacks. Draw a line from the pivot point through where 1.7X is on the "High Pressure" line. That intersects around 72% on the fold line (i.e., he might fold QQ).

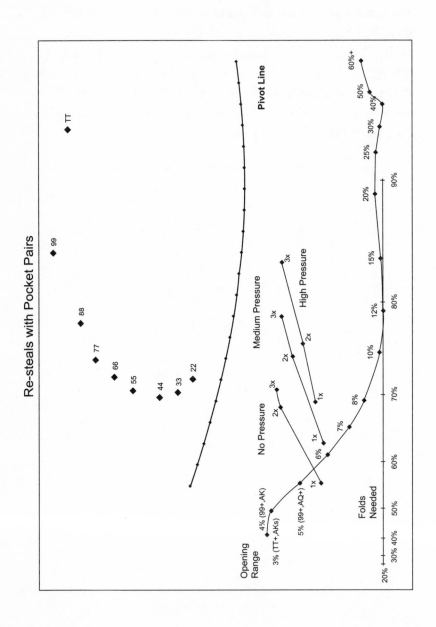

Re-steals with Pocket Pairs

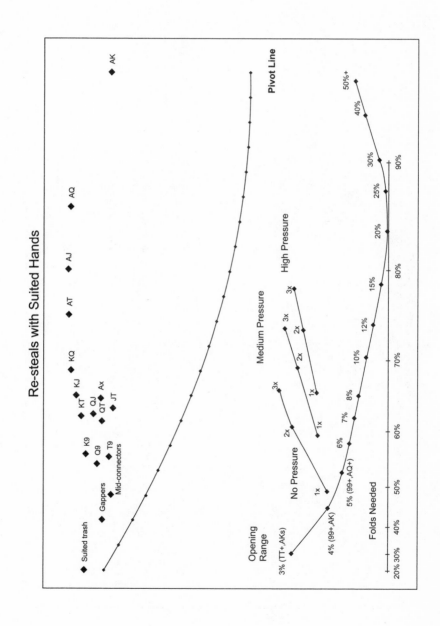

Re-steals with Suited Hands

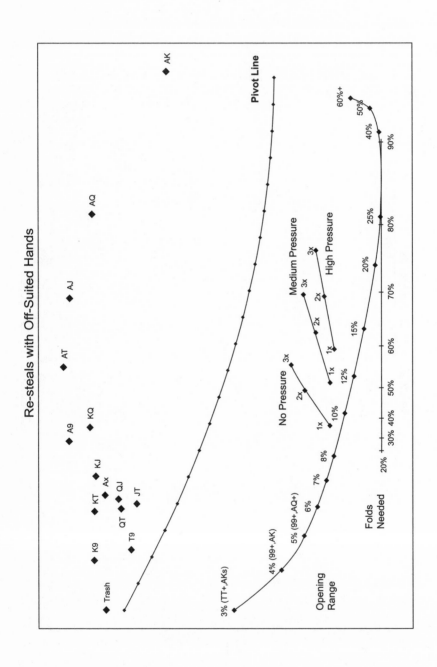

Re-steals with Off-Suited Hands

13

Advanced Tournament Concepts

RANGES TO CALL A PRE-FLOP ALL-IN DURING THE MID-STAGES

First and foremost, when determining the appropriate range with which to call an opponent's pre-flop all-in, you should have a fair idea about his shoving range. If you're completely new to the table and totally unfamiliar with the player, this can be difficult. In that case, you should make assumptions and generalizations based on physical appearance (see Chapter 4). One of the first details you should attempt to ascertain is whether your opponent is predominately a live or online player, as online players have vastly wider shoving ranges than most live players. Once you've estimated your opponent's range, the best method of calling with the optimal amount of hands is to refer to the calling charts in *Kill Everyone*.

Pot Odds When Calling a Pre-Flop All-In

Generally, if you have 2.5-to-1 odds or better in a heads-up pot, you should call with any two cards. If the player is on your left and you've seen him re-raise all-in frequently, you can make the call when getting 2-to-1 odds or better. Inversely, if you assess your opponent to be tight, don't call unless you're getting 2.3-to-1 odds or better. Whenever your odds are between 2.3- and 2.5-to-1, you should account for some parameters in your decision. Namely, consider your table image and the implications of making the call.

By calling in some situations, you're definitely sending the message that you won't be pushed off hands easily. However, you may have to show down a suboptimal hand and disclose the degree of your pre-flop aggression. This revelation may make stealing considerably more difficult. Therefore, it's sometimes better to fold, even if you're getting the marginally correct pot odds to call (such as 2.3-to-1).

Sometimes you may want to call an all-in without having the correct odds, particularly if you think that eliminating your opponent could have value as it relates to the rest of the tournament. For instance, if your opponent is a real threat to control the table and you have him well-covered, it can be OK to make a marginal call in the hopes of eliminating him. If you win the hand, you acquire a greater edge at your table. If you lose, you still have some chips left to build up a big stack again.

Lee encountered just such a situation at the Party Poker World Open in 2005. With 4 players left at the final table, a hand came up involving Tony Guoga (Tony G). Lee was the chip leader and had Tony covered by about 4-to-1; Lee raised UTG with A4-offsuit and Tony, playing pretty straightforward on a short stack, pushed all-in from the big blind. Lee was getting 2.1-to-1 to call. His read on Tony was that he had a strong hand for the following reasons: Lee was the chip leader, so he was likely to call; from a metagame perspective, Tony was aware that Lee was getting better than 2-1 to call and he knew that Lee was aware of the pot odds. All things considered, Lee thought that calling had slightly negative EV, but he also knew that if he knocked Tony out on this hand, his chances of winning the event were excellent. If he lost the hand, he'd still have a 3-to-2 chip advantage and position on Tony. In Lee's mind, this tournament consideration was the difference between calling and folding. After due consideration, Lee called. Tony tabled pocket queens. Lee spiked an ace, and went on to win the tournament.

Raising, 3-Betting, and 4-Betting Pre-Flop

Unpredictability

Based on your analysis of your opponents' ranges and profiles, the key idea to re-stealing and 4-betting is to be very unpredictable. For example, 4-betting a decent amount by coming over the top of a raise and a re-raise is a very strong move from almost any position, especially from the small blind, since late-position re-raises have a higher probability of being a re-steal themselves. However, for you to make this move profitably, you must account for all the history at your table and have your opponents identified correctly so you pick the right spot. Here's a quick example to illustrate the idea:

A weak player (A) limps from early position. Right behind him, a good and aggressive player (B) raises to isolate the limper, a move he's been making frequently. Then, in late position, another aggressive player (C) re-raises, aware of what player B is trying to do. If you 4-bet from the SB, you'll often make everyone fold pre-flop and take down a nice pot, unless, of course, one of them is actually holding a monster.

Even if player B has a big hand such as TT or JJ, it'll be extremely difficult for him to shove. Let's say he has 80 BB. Player A limps and player B isolates to 3.5 BB. Player C 3-bets to 9 BB and you 4-bet to 24 BB. Player B, with TT or JJ or even AK, now has a very difficult decision to make; should he move in, he knows he'll never get called by a worse hand, and 2 players are still left to act behind him.

Ranges to Re-Steal and 4-Bet

Versus an early-position (EP) raise, re-raising the EP raiser when both players are above 30 BB is a very strong move that you can make with a wide range of hands. Quite often, the EP raiser will fold many hands in that spot, even strong ones. We like making this play with suited connectors the best, because they have flop equity when your opponent flat-calls your 3-bet. In any case, it will put your opponent to a very tough decision, unless he has JJ+ or AK.

It's also a strong move, because a current trend is to open raise from EP with a very wide range. Therefore, you'll often get value out of a 3-bet bluff in such a situation.

Additionally, it will greatly freeze the action for the players left to act who need a truly enormous hand to play against your re-raise. For example, if the player UTG raises and you 3-bet him from UTG+2, a player in the SB will almost certainly fold TT in that spot. In the event that the EP raiser or a player behind you has a strong hand, your 3-bet will help elicit that information, since you'll likely get re-raised and get out of the hand fairly cheaply, rather than having to guess post-flop had you just called the initial raise. Make this play versus players you've seen opening UTG more frequently than expected. Avoid doing this against tight players who rarely raise UTG, such as old-school live players whose UTG opening range may be limited to 99+, AQs, and AK.

Remember, it's very important to know the initial raiser's stack size, as well as those of the players left to act behind you. With 10-20 BB, they may 4-bet all-in over your 3-bet with a much wider range than if they were making a decision with a 40 BB or greater stack. Below is an example where ElkY made just such a mistake, because he didn't pay attention to the stack sizes of the players left to act.

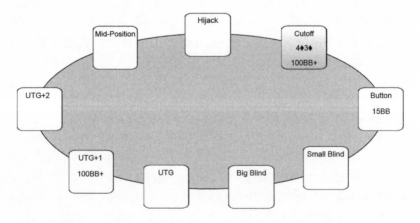

WPT Fiesta Al Lago 2008, Day 2

The effective stacks for ElkY and JC Alvarado are above 100 BB; Theo Tran has 15 BB. ElkY holds 4♦3♦ in the cutoff and has a very good table image. Opponent JC Alvarado is an aggressive young pro player. Pre-flop, UTG folds and Alvarado raises from UTG+1 to 2.5 BB. It folds to ElkY on the CO, who re-raises to 6.5 BB, and Theo Tran on the button moves-in for 15 BB. Alvarado folds and ElkY is forced to make the call due to pot odds and loses to Theo Tran's pocket tens. In addition to losing 15 BB from his stack, the move also has a negative impact on his image. After the table has seen him re-raising such cards, he now has to readjust his play very quickly in order to build up a tighter image again.

When above 100 BB effective, you can 3-bet very wide in position, everything from suited connectors to big pairs (AA, KK) and AK. The idea is to either have a speculative hand or to strongly dominate your opponent with a big pair or AK. To 3-bet correctly, you also need to consider what your position says about your hand.

For example, if the player UTG opens with a raise and you 3-bet UTG+1 with AA or KK, you're communicating a lot of information about the strength of your hand. This is why we also recommend mixing up your play by smooth-calling these spots sometimes, in order to disguise your hand and induce mistakes from your opponents. Conversely, if you smooth-call a raise in position with KK or AA and the action ends up being 3 or 4 way to the flop, you need to be ready to release your hand quickly on dangerous boards when facing substantial action.

ElkY is particularly fond of 3-betting suited connectors on the button, because his hand is hidden and deceptive when he hits the flop. It's fine to 3-bet with air if you know you'll fold to a 4-bet. However, when you have a marginal but playable hand, such as medium pairs, T♠9♠, A♠J♠, A♠Q♠, or KQo, it's often better to smooth-call; a 3-bet may make you lose the flop value in the event that your opponent re-raises and you're forced to fold, thereby wasting the value of your hand. With more marginal hands, we recommend varying your play based on your table image. If you hold ATo and haven't been active for some time, you can incorporate things like 3-betting on the button, particularly in a multi-way pot, depending on the strength of your opponents. If you face the same situation holding KQ, we recommend that you re-raise about 10%-20% of the time and smooth-call around 80%-90% of the time. This is because KQ has better potential on the flop than AT.

Let's say you 3-bet light against an aggressive raiser when stacks are 35 BB effective, and your opponent calls your re-raise in position. Your plan should be to lead out with a small bet on the vast majority of A- and K-high flops. This is because few players smooth-call with AK or any other big A, having the perfect stack size to 4-bet all-in pre-flop. Most of their calling range will be hands such as TT, 99, 88, KQ, QJs, KJs, and JTs. You can often get away with a small flop bet, in the area of a third of the pot, and you should have the intention of giving up on the turn if you're called. If you get a J-T-8 flop or something similar in the same situation, it's best just to check and fold.

When you hold TT, JJ, or QQ, 3-betting may put you in a tough spot against an early-position raiser who could 4-bet you. The raiser may come over the top with a premium hand or air (which happens surprisingly often these days), and it can be difficult to decipher which he's holding. Also, if you 3-bet and induce a fold, you may lose some value if the flop comes T high and your opponent makes top pair. For medium pairs, your decision whether to 3-bet pre-flop should depend on how often you'll be in a multi-way pot post-flop. Generally, we advise that you smooth-call more often with such holdings. If you take that route, it protects your smooth-calls when holding smaller pairs as well.

AQ can also be a tricky hand to 3-bet with in position. If you don't take the pot with your re-raise and your opponent calls, you'll be facing a range that often has you in bad shape. The open raiser is likely to fold all suited aces up to AQ, meaning that, in many cases, you're at best in a coin-flip situation, and will often be dominated by hands such as AK, KK, and AA. Therefore, even if an A comes on the flop, you'll have to be very cautious with your play, which won't enable you to win a big pot in most of these situations.

As a result, we advise that you mostly smooth-call with AQ unless, based on stack sizes or history, you feel comfortable getting that hand in against an all-in from your opponent pre-flop. This will put you in the enviable situation of having position with a disguised, relatively strong hand.

However, as previously mentioned, AQ can also be a good hand to 3-bet with when you know one of the players in the blinds is "squeeze happy," and especially when stacks are fairly deep (50+ BB), because your AQ will often be ahead of the squeezer's range. Once again, make sure the stacks are appropriate when making such a move.

One alternative to 3-betting in this spot is to try a New York Back Raise (described on page 227), but we generally don't recommend this move; it may turn out to be costly, as you'll most often be called only by hands that are either coin flips or could crush you. As always, try to be aware of the table flow and your opponents' ranges, because 3-betting with AQ should be done mainly when you think you can take the pot right there, pre-flop. Otherwise, flat-calling is the course of action we tend to recommend, as it usually spares you headaches and/or chips.

At the mid- to late-game stages of a tournament, you should re-raise 70% to 80% of the time with AK. The times you don't 3-bet are generally because the effective stacks are very deep with the opponent and he's not likely to get it in light with you pre-flop or when you're setting a trap for a small to medium stack behind you to squeeze all-in.

When you 3-bet, watch out not to put yourself in a spot where you have to give up all the equity in the hand by folding. For instance, when the EP raiser has around 50 BB, raises 2.5X BB, and you 3-bet to 6.5 BB, if he 4-bets you to 18 BB to 20 BB, you have no more fold equity left to 5-bet all-in. If you 3-bet light, you can just release your hand and move on.

However, with certain hands, you should definitely account for this parameter in your decision-making. For example, if you 3-bet with KQ or KJ and your opponent 4-bets you, you have no more fold equity to 5-bet shove and you're probably behind your opponent's range. As a result, you end up in a spot where you had a starting hand with good equity and flopping value, but had to release it PF. Therefore, you need to be careful with selecting your 3-betting range with hands that have decent equity and flopping value.

Re-Raising Out of Position

When you're out of position, we don't recommend 3-betting suited connectors while stacks are still on the deep side (roughly 70 BB or above). If you do, it's often difficult to play the hand out of position, even if you flop a draw. You can consider squeezing with them, but we think it's unnecessarily risky, unless you have a good read that your opponent is stealing.

When stacks become shallower, in the 30- to 50-BB range, you can then 3-bet suited connectors with more regularity, because you can sometimes continue in the hand with good equity on a variety of flops. In these situations, it's easier due to the stack depth to size your bets and define your lines in a more straightforward and mathematical way. You'll have options available, such as check-raising all-in on the flop or betting the flop with the intention of shoving most turns—plays not as recommendable while stacks are much deeper and getting called would result in a larger degree of loss when compared to the potential gain.

In general, 3-bets from the blinds signal very strong hands, especially against EP or MP raises. As always, your decisions should be based on how many players are involved in the hand and the history among you and your opponents.

For example, if you have AQo in the SB, it's OK to 3-bet if you know your opponents never make a move and 4-bet you with less than AK or better. In fact, some players are totally incapable of making a move pre-flop no matter what the history is between the two of you, so stay alert to identify and target these opponents. Additionally, they'll also flat-call you a lot, most of the time with a holding weaker than your AQ (often suited connectors or medium pairs), and wind up giving up too much equity when they fold to your continuation bet.

Re-Stealing

You need to be cautious with your re-stealing. It only looks believable if you do it once in a while. We advise that you re-steal mostly from the SB or BB, because no more players are left to act who might wake up with a monster. However, against smart opponents that you have some history with, it's worth considering 3-betting light from some more unexpected positions, so they don't 4-bet light on you as often, even though there's an increased risk of someone behind having a hand. Yet again, we advise that you pick opponents who open-raise a lot of pots and play aggressively. Also, we think that re-stealing is more efficient when stacks get shallower at some stages of the tournament. During the earlier stages when stacks are still deep, your opponents in position may flat-call your re-steal and put you in a difficult post-flop situation.

Big-Sized 3-Bets

Sometimes, when stacks are shallow (around 30 BB), if you're facing a raise from an aggressive opponent whom you think may 4-bet you light, it might be good to 3-bet shove (even with suited connectors occasionally), rather than going for a standard re-raise. Especially against an overaggressive raiser, you might want to really pick on him by systematically 3-betting him all-in in specific spots (when he raises your BB from the button, for instance). Of course, choose your spot carefully, especially to avoid losing equity if a player behind you wakes up with a big hand. However, if you do it at the right times, especially when the blinds are really high, you'll occasionally increase your opponent's tilt factor.

4-Betting

Over the last two years, 4-bets have become increasingly popular and frequent. Hands such as JJ or TT can easily be out-flopped. With such hands, you can often 4-bet LAG players and you'll be way ahead of their ranges a majority of the time. They'll mostly fold pre-flop and you'll take down a nice pot without the risk of further play.

For example, if you have 35 BB and are facing a LAG opponent, he may 3-bet your raise with any pair greater than 55, any two Broadway cards, and any suited ace. If you 4-bet him all-in, his calling range will likely be something in the area of ATs+, KQ+, and any pair that he has 3-bet with.

When you have even stronger hands (QQ+) and are deeper than 35 BB, there are two ways to play back at a 3-bet. First, you have to assess whether or not your opponent is making a move on you. For instance, if you hold KK and believe that your opponent has a strong hand as well (such as TT+), you might want to 4-bet small and try to induce him to move all-in. The alternative is to flat-call the 3-bet when holding a monster. Most of the time, whether your opponent has air or a strong, but dominated, hand, he'll wind up firing a continuation bet regardless of the flop, which enables you to get additional value.

3-Betting with the Intention of Calling an All-in

With some stack sizes, you should be ready to call an all-in before you 3-bet re-raise. For instance, if you start the hand with 35 BB, we believe it's suboptimal to 3-bet and fold to a 4-bet with a decent hand such as KQo. Additionally, *players sometimes give you more credit if you flat-call a LP raise from the blinds with 35 BB than if you 3-bet.* Therefore, your decision should be very player dependent and you always need to mix up your play.

Here's a quick example: Say you have 35 BB and a hyper-LAG raises 2.5 BB from LP. You 3-bet to 6.5 BB with A♠T♠ or KQo and your opponent moves all-in. In this situation, we think you can't

3-bet/fold, so you should make the call. As we stated earlier, there are spots where it's OK to 3-bet/fold 35 BB, such as when your opponent raises often and folds to 3-bets most of the time, but has a tight 4-betting range. For these opponents, you should polarize your 3-betting range; that is, 3-bet with big hands you can confidently call an all-in with, or 3-bet junk hands that can be immediately and easily folded when your opponent moves in on you.

The reason for polarizing your range is this. When you 3-bet with a decent hand and get 4-bet all-in, you have to release a lot of equity in the hand, whereas you wouldn't wind up in that spot by just flatting sometimes. For instance, if you 3-bet from the BB with a small pair and your opponent shoves, you often have to make the call and face a coin flip at best. Therefore, such a move would be suboptimal, considering how few times you'll actually flop a set. In summary, if you 3-bet in such a spot with the intention to fold to a 4-bet, you should probably just flat-call instead.

It's definitely optimal to have a plan when you 3-bet. If your opponent moves in with 35 BB, you don't necessarily have to call, but you should at least be prepared for the possibility, by having assessed his range to re-shove and the likeliness he'll make that move. Therefore, you need to account for your opponent's range and profile and the circumstances at the time the hand takes place.

For instance, the FT bubble is often a good spot to 3-bet an opponent who has 35 BB; he'll often be scared to get knocked out at this stage, even more so if two other players are short-stacked at the table (approximately 15 BB). In such a situation, your 3-bet will often make your opponent with 35 BB fold most of his range, probably up to AJ. In our opinion, that opponent will only move in with 99+ and AQ+. Therefore, even if you sometimes have to fold to a 4-bet all-in, this move is profitable in the long run.

Advantages

Obviously, the main advantage of 3-betting is that it allows you to take the lead and bully your opponents out of big pots. When you identify a weaker player who often folds to a 3-bet, you can build a good chip stack in the mid-stages of the tournament. Also, when you 3-bet pre-flop, you can take down the pot with a half-pot-size bet on the flop, which is very profitable when done in the correct spots.

Therefore, it's important to be selective in picking your spots and opponents, especially when you 3-bet for value. Good players are usually uncomfortable when facing a 3-bet and having to play OOP, even with premium holdings like AA or KK, because they're unsure how best to gain the maximum value from their hand.

Dangers

The obvious danger of a 3-bet is that it increases your variance.

For example, let's say the blinds are 50/100 and you're in the SB with AJ. There's a raise from LP to 300 by an opponent holding QTo. You then 3-bet to 800 and he calls. The flop is T-4-5 rainbow. In this spot, most of the time you'll have to lead out, around the 1,000 area. If your opponent moves all-in for another 15-20 BB, you'll have to release your hand, losing 1,800 chips in the process.

Another danger is to get 4-bet light by your opponent, especially when you're also bluffing. In general, if you're deep in chips (100 BB or more) and you have an aggressive image, we don't recommend 3-betting light OOP too often; observant players often come over the top and put you in a tough spot. Generally, we believe that 3-betting small to medium pairs, such as 88 or 99, is a mistake in most situations, since the only thing it really accomplishes is increasing variance. You'll often wind up forcing your opponents to fold all the worst hands in their range, but you'll be in a bad situation when they 4-bet all-in with a higher pairs than yours and at best, you'll be in a coin flip against the rest of their range.

An additional danger to look out for when re-stealing or 4-betting is not to commit yourself. Once in a while, based on the metagame, you may want to do so, because your fold equity is very strong when you make a 4-bet that your opponent assumes commits you. But for the most part, we see too many highly aggressive players getting caught making such a move nowadays.

In summary, the ability to 3-bet profitably lies in your capacity to identify the right spots and the right opponents for the move.

Squeeze Bets

Generally, a squeeze bet is when there's a raise and a call pre-flop, then you re-raise because you believe the flat caller is weak.

Three-bet and squeeze ranges depend on your hand's strengths and on the opponents you face, and how much respect they give to 3-bets (how they will react, how often they fold, how often they open themselves, etc).

For instance, if a weak player regularly opens from MP with bad hands and another player flat-calls, it's usually a good spot to squeeze IP, especially when the opening raiser isn't very creative and you know he's unlikely to 4-bet you as a bluff. As we discuss in the live-versus-online section, a lot of live players don't have the 4-bet bluff as a move in their repertoire. Therefore, in such situations, a squeeze is often uncontested—unless one opponent holds a premium hand, of course. We suggest making this move most often with antes; it's more profitable.

The other benefit of such a squeeze is that, should an opponent hold a strong hand behind you, you'll put him to a tough decision. For example, a weak player raises from MP, the player in the hijack flat-calls, and you 3-bet from the CO. If the player in the SB has TT or 99, he has a headache. If he 4-bets, he'll never get called or re-raised by a hand worse than his. For this move to be profitable in the long run, you must closely keep track of the stack sizes of the players behind you. If two or three opponents behind you have 30 BB, you should lower your squeeze frequency to avoid tough spots against re-shoves by short stacks.

The general factors to consider when you think about squeezing in the above situation:

• Opening range and frequency of the initial raiser.

- Calling range and frequency of flat-caller, and how tricky this player is. Some players are never tricky enough to flat-call with a monster in this situation, and that's definitely the type you should try to exploit.
- The way your opponents react to 3-bets, if you've been able to observe such situations.
- How many short stacks are left to act behind you.
- Your table image and how much credit you get from your opponents, especially as it relates to the initial raiser and the first caller.

We believe that squeeze bets have lost some of their original value, particularly during the early mid-stages. So many players are aware of them that they're increasingly less credible. Overall, most thinking players have adjusted to the squeeze bet and have developed counter strategies. However, at the later stages of tournaments, if you pick the right opponents and stack sizes, we think squeeze bets are certainly still a profitable move.

Players tend to respect squeeze bets in live play more than they do online. Some live players still don't really understand the concept of squeeze bets and fold far too often. Others may get the idea, but are still too scared to put their money in and play OOP. Nevertheless, you still need to identify opponents scared by squeeze bets and pick your spots based on that analysis.

Generally, it seems that there are fewer optimal spots to squeeze today than there were when the trend started a few years ago. An optimal spot is one where the initial raiser is somewhat loose-aggressive and not too familiar with squeezes. As to the caller, you have to assess whether he's good enough to anticipate and react to a squeeze, potentially flat-call with a monster hand waiting for you to squeeze, then come over the top with a 4-bet.

Finally, before squeezing, look at the stack sizes of the players in the blinds. If they're short (in the 15- to 25-BB area) and move all-in, you might have to call them with some very weak hands because of pot odds, which will negatively affect your table image.

Squeeze Trap

This move is definitely a new adjustment to squeeze-bet tendencies. Whereas a squeeze bet is an attempt to represent a big hand in a profitable situation, a squeeze trap is when you make a squeeze bet actually holding a premium hand. Against good players, you'll often get paid off, because they'll think you're attempting to steal a big pot with your pre-flop re-raise and won't realize the strength of your holding. This will work particularly well if you've already established a history of squeeze bets or had a highly aggressive image pre-flop, involving a lot of 3-betting.

Squeezing with a big hand is very effective against calling stations who want to see a flop no matter what. You can even size your 3-bet to be big in order to get additional value, since you expect to be called most of the time by these players.

New York Back Raise

Another method of combating regular squeeze bets—and an excellent way to maximize the value of a big hand (particularly against hyper-LAGs)—is the New York Back Raise. With this play, you flat-call a raise with a big hand when highly aggressive opponents behind you are prone to squeezing. If your plan works and they do so, you 4-bet them in a situation where they'll have difficulty folding due to the excellent pot odds. The best way to do this is to flat-call a raise with a hand such as JJ+ when effective stacks are in the 25- to 35-BB range.

Sometimes you can make a New York Back Raise with AK too. The best spots to do it with AK are when both the opener and you have big stacks and he's either a player you respect a lot or so crazy that you don't really want to start a war and ship everything pre-flop, because you believe your equity may not be the best. Calling a raise with AK is sometimes good to mix it up. However, if a shorter stack re-raises behind and the initial guy folds, back raising all-in becomes a very good option.

You have to be wary of stack sizes. Usually, you want a lot of fold equity with AK and if people behind squeeze and have less than 30 BB (unless they have air), it's unlikely they'll fold when you re-raise.

From a similar perspective, you can sometimes make the same move with 99/TT. You just need a good read! It's just not as frequent as with JJ+, because those hands are much more vulnerable. So usually you want to get it in pre-flop if neither you nor the initial raiser is over 30+ BB.

More often, a 3-bet with AK takes it down right there, making people behind you fold a lot of hands, probably even 99, whereas if you call and one of the blinds is loose, he can complete and you can easily miss and have to give up.

To sum it up, we tend to flat-call AK more in spots where the opener is also big stacked, to mix up the flat-calling hands and disguise it, because people tend to expect AK to be 3-bet all the time, so they'll c-bet almost invariably on A- or K-high flops. Sometimes OOP, we'll also flat-call against some of the best players if we both have 40+ BB, because it's an awkward stack size to 3-bet if this opponent likes to call and outplay post-flop.

Reacting to Squeeze Bets

In general, it's bad for your image to raise and fold to a squeeze bet too often. Also, you bleed away a heavy amount of chips if you attempt this regularly.

Therefore, if an opponent starts picking on you by squeeze-betting your raises, you should either fight back with a light 4-bet or tighten up your range and avoid raising with marginal hands for a while.

Advanced Moves for the Current Aggressive Game

Opponents' Styles

As always, it's important to identify your opponents' styles. Against a hyper-LAG who 3-bets light often, it's sometimes necessary to 4-bet light—even all-in—although it greatly increases variance. In general, when facing hyper-LAGs, you have one of two options: either play even more aggressively than they by 4-betting light, or tighten up your range. There's no middle ground.

The examples below assume that you are in HU situations against LAG or hyper-LAG opponents.

• You flop top pair OOP, you bet the flop and the turn, and get called twice by your opponent. What is the line on the river?

Usually, you'd check-call the river to avoid getting raised. If your opponent raises you in that spot, it greatly increases variance, which you want to avoid. This depends, however, on a variety of factors, such as the board texture, history, stack sizes, kicker, etc. Against some players, you can fire again on the river for value, especially against those who like to be heroes! On the other hand, against players who can double-float you, or perhaps with a missed draw, a check-call may be in order. Those are borderline situations that require a lot of focus in trying to enter your opponent's mind and decipher his thought process, considering different variables to make the best decision.

• You hold A♠4♠ and you call a pre-flop raise IP. The flop is: A♥-J♣-5♣. Your opponent bets and you call. The turn is the 2♦. Your opponent fires again and you call the turn bet as well. The river is the 9♣, which completes the club flush draw. Your opponent bets less than 50% of the pot.

This looks like a value or blocking bet. At this point, your opponent may have two pair, a set, a flush, an A, or he may be bluffing. If your assessment is that he's definitely a hyper-LAG and/or a good player, this might be a good spot to raise in order to represent a flush. Your opponent probably won't fold a set or AJ, but may fold most of his aces or other two-pair hands. Your move also depends on the quality of your image. If you've showed down strong hands, it will look much more credible to your opponent that you hit the flush.

Check-Raising on the River

Check-raising the river has become an increasingly popular move lately. You can mix it up and do it with the nuts, hands that have showdown value, or air!

It's a great move. It puts your opponent to a tough decision for a big pot most of the time. However, when you use that line, be aware of the opponent you're facing. The check raise on the river only works against players who can value bet. Some players don't know how to value bet and you won't be able to scare them out of the hand with this move, and you'll lose a lot of chips if they call you on a check raise bluff.

Thin Value Bets

You make a thin value bet when you hold a fairly marginal hand, second or middle pair, for instance, and bet it if you still think you're ahead against your opponent. This technique works well against calling stations and mostly against weaker players. It's also good against other professionals when they anticipate you having a polarized value betting range. Once again, unpredictability is key.

Example
ElkY, at the EPT Copenhagen 2010

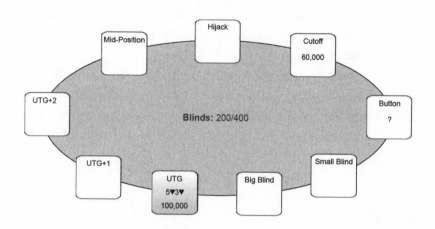

Villain 1 is in the cutoff with 60,000. Villain 2, a weak player, is on the button. I raise to 1,000 with 5♥3♥. Both villains call. The flop is K♥-K♦-4♥. It's a good flop for me to c-bet my flush draw, because my bet also allows me to gather some information on my opponents' holdings. In this spot, my c-betting range is very wide (from a K to complete air), so it's difficult for my opponents to get a read on my hand. Villain 1 calls and villain 2 folds. The turn is the 4♦. I check, with a plan to check-raise a small bet and maybe check-fold to a strong bet. Villain checks behind. The river is the 3♦. There's about 7,000 in the pot.

I check and villain bets 3,000. It looks like a weak value bet to me; very few players would check a full house in position on the turn, in my opinion. Furthermore, even if they did, they'd mostly bet big on the river to recover the foregone value of checking the turn. Therefore, my assessment is that my opponent is value betting thin in this spot. I check-raise his bet to 13,300. Villain tanks for a while and folds JJ (as he later told me).

This move keeps your opponents guessing a lot. It will be easier to thin value bet IP, because you'll have more information. It's also an effective play when your image is not so good, as your opponents will tend to call you with weaker holdings.

I really like thin value bets, because they can also protect your future bluffs when you use them adequately; when your opponents know you can value bet thin, you can bluff them relatively cheaply in similar situations down the line.

The downside of thin value bets is that you face a very difficult decision when getting check-raised on the river. Also, sometimes against the most passive and weak opponents, you can end up value betting yourself, since they play their hands in such a crazy passive manner.

Example

ElkY, at the WPT LAPC 2010

In the middle of Day 1, I'm moved to a table with Isaac Baron, a very good tournament pro, on my left. A player opens from late position. Isaac calls from the button with KJ and the BB defends (all 80+ BB deep). The flop is J-9-2 with two clubs. Both players check to Baron, who bets half the pot. The original raiser calls. The turn is A♣. Both players check. The river is Jo. The initial raiser checks, Baron bets about 80% of the pot, and the guy snap-calls with ... 99 for a full house! Whoops!

Double Floating

Here, you call bets on both the flop and the turn to try and bluff on the river. You should do this IP and when stacks are deep. It's a good move when you have one or several backdoor draws, because your hand will be well-disguised if you hit.

For instance, on a flop 8♥-5x-2x, you could float the flop with J♥T♥; a lot of turn cards give you a flush draw, a straight draw, or top pair. Floating is a good move here, because it also echoes the way we pot control a lot of our hands. Should you raise the flop, you could be in trouble if your opponent re-raises with an overpair. The idea is then to be ready to call a turn bet, whether the turn improves your hand or not, and bet the river if your opponent checks to you.

The best target for double-floating is an opponent who can double-barrel often, but doesn't like to triple-barrel. Otherwise, on a triple-barrel, you'll have to raise the river bet, which then makes the action become very expensive with high-variance. In addition, your opponent may actually have a hand, too. Therefore, as always, analyzing your opponent's profile is crucial before you decide to make the double floating move.

Floating OOP on a Paired Board in Multi-Way Pots

Below is an example of a move ElkY has been using recently on opponents who try to put him on trips.

Example

ElkY, at the 2010 WPT Commerce Hi-Roller

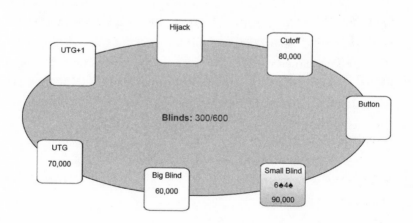

Villain 1 raises 1,700 and villain 2 calls. I have 64s. I haven't been very active for a while, so I think it's a decent hand to see a flop, as Villain 3 will likely call. It'll cost me only 1,300 more for a pot that will likely be 8,000 pre-flop. Villain 3 makes the call and the flop comes 2♥-8♠-8♦. I could lead on such a board, but I don't think it would make much sense. Any opponent with a pair would definitely call me and I'd then have to bluff on several streets. I check, a line I use with a large range of hands in a 4-way pot with a flop like this. The BB checks too, and Villain 1 bets 4,600. Villain 2 calls.

Villain 1 has been playing aggressively in such situations, so I think his range is really wide here; my assessment is that he'll c-bet 80% of the time in that spot. Villain 2 could have a pair, but maybe also A-high. I decide to set up my plan by calling too, and bluff the turn no matter what card comes out.

I'd sometimes use this line if I held an 8 or 22 as well. Check-calling the flop and leading the turn OOP with a really strong hand is a move I like; it confuses your opponents, and I think that a turn bet is sometimes scarier than a check raise on the flop. In the present case, though, I have air—but I'm trying to represent a strong hand. Surprising me, Villain 3 calls as well, which now makes me wonder whether he's actually the one holding an 8 or if he's trying to steal my move.

The turn is the 6♦, which is a good card for me, although I don't think it really matters in this situation, because I am only trying to represent an 8. I bet 14,000 and all three villains fold fairly quickly.

Like I explained earlier, the example above illustrates the counter-balancing types of lines that allow me to lead OOP against preflop 3-bettors, when I think they have missed the flop. Here is an example of that.

Example

ElkY, at the EPT Prague 2009

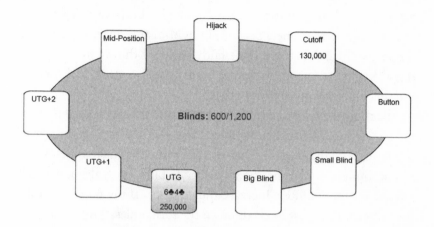

I raise to 2,800 with 6♣4♣ from UTG. The villain is a decent player who's been playing fairly straightforward to this point. He knows that my opening range is quite wide and I can make some moves. He 3-bets to 8,500. A case can be made for either calling or folding in that spot. Up to this point, I've won quite a few pots against this villain, but my table image is very strong. His 3-bet looks to me like an attempt to somehow protect his hand and get information at the same time.

I make the call and the flop is A-2-3 with one club. I lead out for 12,000. In my opinion, this bet will freeze his action on a lot of his range. Of course, he'll call if he holds AK. However, he'll likely have to fold KK or QQ right there, as I could be holding AK. If he thinks I hold a strong ace, he knows it'll be very difficult to raise me here on a bluff. Therefore, unless he holds AK or a set, his options to respond to my bet are now pretty limited and polarized. The villain folds.

What I like about this line is that it cost the same amount as a pre-flop 4-bet, so the variance is similar against players who won't often go crazy post-flop. Should I opt for a 4-bet in this situation, I think there are two things to consider: First, if I 4-bet, my opponent will get the information that my range is mostly polarized here, between hands that I'm ready to move in PF with and complete air. In this case, since I have air, my opponent can force me to fold with a 5-bet, which may still be OK if I know he'll otherwise fold most of his range to my 4-bet. Second, in light of the current metagame trends in which 4-bets are done fairly lightly, I think I'm representing a very strong hand by simply calling the 3-bet OOP. I tend to use this line with most of my range.

Back to the way I played the hand. Should my opponent raise me on the flop, I'd usually fold right there—depending on the size of the raise, though, because that raise still wouldn't make much sense to me. I might sometimes float and try to bluff later, although such a move would definitely increase the variance. If my opponent calls my flop bet, I'm most likely done on the turn, unless I hit a club or a straight. Indeed, should he hold an A, he'll most likely check behind on the turn, then have a fairly easy call on the river. He'll probably use the same line with all the big pairs as well. All in all, since I don't believe my play is much more high-variance than 4-betting, as it represents about the same amount of chips risked, I think it's correct and allows me to mix up my moves a bit.

Additionally, I think players should watch out not to 4-bet too often, especially against opponents with deep stacks. If those opponents are good enough to identify that you 4-bet with a polarized range, they might start playing back at you with tricky 5-bets.

Also along the same lines, some players like to see a flop no matter what, as long as they've already put money in the pot. They tend to ignore a lot of parameters, such as position and hand ranges, when they're 4-bet. They call most of the time. Against such opponents, even though it wasn't the case in the hand above, 4-betting light is definitely not recommended.

Leading the Flop OOP against a PF 3-Bet

If I feel an opponent tends to 3-bet too much, I sometimes flat-call the 3-bet OOP and then lead out on the flop, bluffing. I've found this move freezes my opponents most of the time. If you do this with a good image, you usually get a lot of respect. Obviously, I counterbalance this move by sometimes leading on a dry board when I flop a set.

Example

ElkY, at the WSOP Main Event 2009

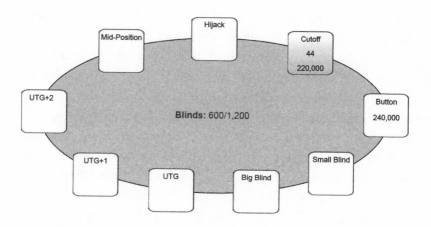

I raise to 2,700 from the CO and the villain 3-bets to 8,500 from the button; I call. The flop is A-4-3 rainbow, and I lead for 11,000. The villain raises me to 25,000. In this situation, I think his range is polarized to AK or air. I don't believe he has AA, because I think he'd rather call the flop and try to trap me. He may have a set or a straight, but I believe he'd slow play such holdings. Finally, I really don't think he'd fold AK in this spot.

Also, even though there's always a chance I may be holding two pair or AA, it looks like a good spot for me to make a move, since I disguised my flopped set by leading out. I believe that re-raising here could look like I'm actually making a move. Therefore, I re-raise to 66,000 and the villain calls. The turn is a K, which is a great card for me. Indeed, if the villain holds AK, he'll never get rid of it in this spot. Based on the line he used so far, I don't think Villain has

KK. Therefore, I fire again for 45,000, and the villain moves all-in. I obviously snap-call, and he shows J9o!

The bet sizing is also important in this example. My bet size on the turn gave the villain room to come over the top with the right amount of chips left.

Raising the Turn

Raising the turn in the right situation can be highly profitable. Of course, you can always raise for value on the turn, but this probably doesn't require too much explanation. An obvious situation would be if you check behind the flop for pot control and turn a very strong hand. For example, you raise with 87 from mid-position and the big blind defends. The flop, Q-7-3, is checked through. The turn is an 8 and he leads into you. Raising for value here is probably the best choice, especially if his play is straightforward and you figure him for holding a queen. If the board has an open flush draw, it's even better; he could put you on it and 3-bet the turn with his queen, or check/call big on the river, or have it himself.

Here are some other situations for raising the turn.

Against weak or timid players who often check the flop and try to bluff on the turn, bluff-raising the turn is a very strong line. In a multi-way pot especially, when an opponent makes a bet that screams weakness, whether your hand has showdown value or not, you're in a great situation to raise and take down the pot right there.

Another situation for raising the turn is when the turn card opens some good draws to your hand. Be aware that your opponents might not give your turn raise too much credit, though, often because they'll read your move too well. Let's say you have A♥8♥ and your opponent holds KxQx. On a flop of K♣-T♥-2♦, you both check. The turn is J♥ and your opponent bets. If you raise there, your opponent will seldom fold, and you'll have to bet the river really big if you miss your draw in order to take down the pot. In addition, your opponent could re-raise you and it's not very profitable to have to fold a good draw in such a situation. That said, raising the turn can be a good move against opponents who lead a lot on the turn, or when your move may represent a very strong hand.

The more you check the flop behind, especially when playing HU, the more credible your turn raises will be on a broad range of turn cards. For instance, let's say a player always bets on an open-ender or gutshot on the flop. On a K-Q-2 flop, this player checks behind. Then the turn is a 9 and the player raises a bet from his opponent. In this spot, I don't think the raise is very credible. We know the player will always bet with JT on the flop. Therefore, the best hand he might have in this situation is 99 or similar.

Smooth-Calling with Big Hands

You need to be aware of this new trend, so you can avoid getting trapped by a player who smooth-calls your raise or 3-bets with a premium hand! Smooth-calling with a monster can be very profitable, depending on how often the players behind are likely to squeeze. Also, if your opponents know you're capable of smooth-calling big hands in such spots, they'll likely c-bet a little less, letting you see more free cards. Of course, the danger of this practice is that you may sometimes get outflopped by garbage hands when you simply called the pre-flop raise, but the risk is worth the reward in the long run.

In the modern game with all its recent evolutions, a smooth-call IP by a good player to an EP raise is often more suspicious than a pre-flop 3-bet, especially when stacks are somewhat shallow. If a hyper-LAG flat-calls an EP raise from the button with 30 BB or less, a siren should go off in your mind. Danger!

Regular squeeze moves are becoming less and less popular, possibly because of the new trends of flat-calling with a big hand and 4-betting light. However, it's important to mix up your range when defending against squeeze moves. For instance, when you call a squeeze, your opponents should know that when the flop is A- or K-high, you might actually have AK or AA once in a while; otherwise, you'll lose credibility, getting pushed off a lot of A- or K-high boards.

When you smooth-call with a big hand, you should also consider other factors, mainly how many players will be involved in the hand. Obviously, when you hold KK or AA, you don't really want to get involved in a 5-way pot, so you may have to re-raise instead of flat-calling. Perhaps the best trap to set with AA or KK is to smooth-call behind when there's already a raise and a call. Indeed, if one of the players left to act is squeeze happy, he'll rarely believe you when the action comes back to you and you 4-bet him. However, you need to assess the situation well, as always. For example, if you think the initial raiser has a big hand and will go with it, you probably want to 3-bet PF and try to get all the money in right there.

One move ElkY likes to make is to smooth-call from the BB with KK or AA, especially when it's HU action, in order to mix up his game. Then he either leads or check-raises the flop, depending on his opponent's tendencies. Here is an example where he ended up getting lucky in the hand. He believes his reasoning was correct.

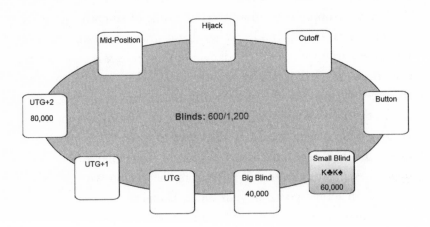

In the last two orbits, I've seen the villain raise flop bets from his opponent twice on unconnected boards, then bet the turn and take down the pot. He's a good player. Even though he could have held hands, I think he was mostly bullying his opponents. Villain 1 raises 3,000 from UTG+2 and I flat-call with KK from the SB. I like this spot too, because the player in the BB is weak, often calling in that spot as well, making the pot even bigger. The BB calls.

The flop is Q♣-T♥-3♣. I lead for 5,200. Villain 1 often raises me with hands that have no value (unless the BB calls), and sometimes with drawing hands. Villain 1 may also raise me with any Q or T in that spot, in my opinion, in which case I would also get instant value.

The BB folds and Villain 1 raises me to 15,000. At this point, I think calling is the optimal move. I believe he's the type to continue the aggression, even on a bluff, and the strength of my hand is well-disguised. I call.

The turn is the 9♠, which gives me a gutshot straight draw. I check and Villain 1 puts me all-in for about 45,000 more. This puts me to a tough decision. I'm not so sure he is still bluffing in this spot. However, he can be holding a number of combo draws, such as A♣T♣, A♣J♣, AQ or KQ, in which case I'm still ahead. I go for it and call the all-in.

As it turns out, my opponent is holding AA. I hit a J on the river to complete my gutshot! Regardless of the outcome, I think it's an interesting example of how to mix up one's play with premium hands.

14

Final Table

Studying Your Opponents Before the Final Table

Online

Before the final table begins, when play is down to three to four tables, close all the cash games you're possibly playing and study your opponents at the other tables (raising, 3-betting frequencies, 4-betting, and showdowns). If you're using tracking software, study their stats; if not, observe their tables closely and try to identify tendencies and weaknesses, as previously discussed in this book. This way, you'll have an idea of your opponents' styles when you face them at the final table. ElkY did this at the WCOOP tournaments he won in 2009.

Live

Try to study here as well, maybe by watching live reporting during the breaks from sites such as pokernews.com from your phone, or from your room if you're staying at the same venue. You can sometimes retrieve valuable information that could help you make more educated decisions later.

For instance, at the EPT Deauville 2010, one player who made the final table accumulated almost all his chips by 5-betting all-in with T4o. Knowing that he was capable of this level of aggression and multi-level thinking was useful to ElkY, who was also at that final table.

Another way to study your potential final-table opponents is to check their profiles: Are they pros, amateurs, or online players? Of course, keep in mind that the more recent the information on a player, the more relevant it will be for your purposes.

Identifying Opponents' Ambitions

In our experience, most of the live-oriented or amateur players who haven't been at a final table before are less likely to be creative or bluff a lot during final-table play. Contributing to the generally straightforward play by these players may be the fact that, at the final table, stacks usually aren't very deep. Play usually slows down a lot at the final-table bubble, especially when it's televised. Therefore, against these players, you shouldn't expect too much 3-betting light. Rather, you may see more big folds than usual.

Payout Structure

Depending on the payout structure, play at the final table might slow down. Again, it also relates to the profiles of your opponents. The less experienced are likely to play tighter than usual, while the pros are likely to abuse the aforementioned trend and open up their game against these weak-tight opponents.

How Stack Sizes Influence Strategy

In general, try to avoid confrontations with bigger stacks, especially if you're still fairly deep. Of course, clashing might be inevitable, especially with fewer players left (five or six, for instance).

Usually, as stacks get shallower and fewer players remain, play tends to become tighter.

Pay close attention to the stack sizes at the table, so you can avoid opponents making moves on you. For instance, if the short-stacked player at the table has 15 BB and the second short stack has 40 BB, the first player will likely shove a fairly wide range in an attempt to double up. Raising this player's blind should therefore be done judiciously.

When you have chips, your focus should be to put pressure on the middle stacks. Let's say play is 5-handed, two players have 20 BB, and one player is middle-stacked with 35 BB. If the middle stack raises from mid-position and has been playing fairly tight, your 3-betting range from the blinds should be very wide. A move like this will put that player in a tough spot—facing a decision to push or fold—and he might not necessarily want to gamble on exiting the tournament before the short stacks. He could easily fold up to 88 or 99 and AJs and AQo in that situation.

Protecting your stack is crucial at the final table; it lets you put pressure on your opponents. Therefore, you should use all the concepts discussed in this book to protect your chips efficiently. The final table is one of the situations where you can consider avoiding marginal +EV spots against big stacks. However, the validity of this approach can change, depending on the composition of the table. If you're facing only top pros with a lot of experience, you'll probably have to clash at some point anyway, so you should take advantage of any +EV opportunities.

Table Flow

The table flow is probably more important at the final table than any other time during the tournament. At the beginning of play, there are lots of uncontested pots. Therefore, assuming you've done your homework, studied your opponents, and you have a decent stack, the beginning of the final table is a strategic time to be very active with raises and 3-bets, since your opponents generally spend some time observing one another.

•   **With six players left at final table.** At six players, the aggression usually kicks into a higher gear. The top money is in sight and stacks are getting shorter relative to the blinds. At this stage, picking your opponents is based as much on stack sizes as on playing styles, since decisions for large portions or all of a stack are obviously extra crucial at the final table.

Here, we break down what your plan and targets should be, based on your stack size and opponents.

• **When you have a short stack in the 15-BB area.** Naturally, you don't have many moves available to you outside of moving all-in. The important thing is that you pick on players who are apt not to call you, either because they're conservative with their calling ranges or forced to be cautious due to their stack size. Your ideal targets based on stack size should be players open-raising with a 20- to 35-BB stack. They'll be risking a high portion of their stack to try and bust you. Reduce your shoving range if big stacks are in the blinds behind you, particularly if they're apt to call light. When medium stacks are in the blinds, push a wide range; in general, they're your targets.

• **When you have a stack in the 15-25 area.** With this size, you need to pick your spots against stacks in the 20- to 35-BB range. Do what you can to avoid big stacks; you have substantially less fold equity against them, unless they're the type that have a wide open-raising range, but a tight calling range—this exists, but it's fairly rare; it's a leak that most aggressive players identify. A perfect target to 3-bet re-steal all-in is a similar-sized stack, as he basically risks his tournament life to call you at a stage when there's maximum pressure to do so. You should open-raise with any ace, suited kings, suited queens down to Q8s, suited jacks down to J7s, suited connectors, suited one-gappers, and good suited two-gappers. Reduce your opening frequency if your opponents move in on you frequently.

• **When you have a stack in the 35-BB area.** At this stack size, you have much greater flexibility. Your aggression now becomes much more open-raise-oriented than 3-bets; losing your open-raise has very little effect on your overall stack size, whereas a failed 3-bet puts you into an entirely different area. That's not to say you should completely remove light 3-betting from your arsenal (that would make you unbalanced), but you should be much more selective about it than at other stages of the tournament.

Your targets at this stage are stacks in the 20- to 30-BB area. They're a bit too deep to move in on you light with much consistency, but not deep enough to call a lot of your open-raises and get difficult post-flop. Conversely, you should actually look to avoid stacks in the 15-BB area who'll move in on your open-raises very often, unless your opponent is clearly concerned with moving up the money ladder and unwilling to gamble his tournament life without a major hand.

• **When you have a big stack, 50 BB or above**. Naturally, you have the full variety of options open to you with this stack size. At certain final tables, having more chips allows you to completely dominate, meaning that the times a player forces you to a decision for a significant amount of them, you should back down if you feel losing those chips would prevent you from bullying your table. We generally advise that you avoid major confrontations with other big stacks, particularly in the form of light 4-bets, but in many situations you can abuse them with light 3-bets. If you're fortunate enough to land one or two to the left of another aggressive big stack on the table, you can use small 3-bets in position to make his life very hard; he'll have to take an enormous gamble in order to play back at you without a legitimate hand. Many are entirely incapable of making a light 4-bet in such a situation. With this stack size, you can also look to set up the aggressive smaller or medium stacks, potentially by running a small and obvious bluff. If you've got a highly overaggressive player on the table, you can manipulate the dynamic without risking much of your overall stack, then wait for him to attempt a move against one of your open-raises when you've got a hand you can happily call with. You should aim to open-raise the blinds of players with 25- to 35-BB stacks, since they'll be slightly too shallow to flat-call without good hands, but slightly too deep to 3-bet you without a hand that can play for all their chips as well.

When you have a commanding chip lead, your main efforts should go toward putting a lot of pressure on medium stacks, who will tend to play too tight. However, you may encounter situations where some aggressive players won't hesitate to 3-bet you all-in. If that scenario arises, especially when your opponents all have similar stacks, you might want to refrain from opening with some marginally +EV hands.

Let's say play is four-handed, you have 60 BB, and everyone else has 15-20 BB. In this case, you might want to keep a low profile until one of your opponents gets knocked out. As a result, you'll have one opponent with 15-20 BB and the other with 30-40 BB, and you can put pressure on both of them. The short stack won't be able to move all-in all the time anymore; he could get called by either of you. In addition, the medium stack is still a good target to pick on; he'll likely try to protect his chips in light of the pay jump between third and second place, assuming he doesn't want to bust before the short stack.

As long as your opponents keep folding to you when you have a big stack, you can keep raising every hand; it's greatly profitable. Furthermore, once in a while, you'll actually hold a hand. If by chance this is the spot an opponent picks to move all-in and you call, your image will benefit greatly, with the fear factor even more enhanced. The psychological factor here is crucial.

When ElkY won the WPT Festa Al Lago at Bellagio in 2008, after eliminating the sixth-place finisher, he had a huge chip lead and he proceeded to open 70% of the hands. In one hand, he opened with QQ from UTG+1 with 150+ BB and Adam Levy shoved 22 BB from the button with A9o. Of course, he snap-called. His hand held, and he had another 22 BB. After that, he opened close to 100% of the pots, often uncontested.

Nowadays, most final tables are eight-handed (e.g., EPT) or six-handed (e.g., WPT, Aussie Millions, etc.), whereas final tables are nine-handed at the WSOP. For final tables that are less than nine-handed, you should definitely account for more pre-final-table play (for instance, from nine to six players), during which you can bully your opponents a lot with a big stack. Indeed, during the pre-final-table play, especially if the final table is televised, many players fold their way onto the silver screen, hoping some opponents will bust before they do.

• **Handling pressure**. At no stage of the tournament are you likely to feel more under pressure than the final table. This is obvious, since it's when your decisions and the variance of the cards have the highest impact on your potential rewards. First and foremost, you'll want to make sure you're well-rested leading up to it. Try to get a good night's sleep and, if possible, some exercise in the morning in order to get your blood flowing. We recommend you take extra time to think through your decisions. If you don't make a point of taking your time, the pressure can cause you to be impulsive instead of contemplative.

If there's any stage of the tournament where you should do what you can to stifle your emotions, it's the final table, where the quantity of equity on the line naturally causes a greater emotional investment in outcomes beyond your control. There's nothing wrong with feeling disgusted when you're unlucky or elated when you win a big pot at this stage, but if you can tell that you're becoming emotionally unbalanced, you should aim to take a few hands off (if they're not obviously playable) and spend a moment to focus and center yourself. If need be, step away from the table for a minute after you've folded and just take a moment to calm yourself, so you can accomplish the job at hand.

• **How to alter your play if you are inexperienced compared to your opponents.** If you get the sense that your final-table opponents have a substantial edge in skill and experience over you, your goal should be to fold marginal hands and move up the pay ladder. You don't want to tighten up to the point that your opponents clearly single you out as a nit and an easy bullying target, but when you're at a skill disadvantage, it pays not to try and force action in situations that opponents are more accustomed to than you are.

For example, the runner-up to Lee Nelson in the 2006 Aussie Millions was a young American named Robert Neely, who more or less folded all the way to second place and a massive payout for someone of his experience level.

The Final Table Prize Pool

Kill Everyone introduced the concept of the "bubble factor," a quantitative indicator of how strongly the prize structure penalizes coin flips. It's a measure of the tournament pressure that the players feel in order to make it to a higher pay level. Bubble factors are highest when the tournament is close to a big jump in prize money. When the jump is fairly small or far in the future, pressure is lower.

MTTs typically have two periods of intense pressure: right before the money bubble and the final-table bubble. Each tournament has a different prize structure, so sometimes the money bubble has more pressure, while sometimes it's the final table. The tournament pressure isn't the same for everyone—medium stacks have the highest pressure when they face off against anyone with more chips. Big-stack versus big-stack clashes also involve high bubble factors. High tournament pressure puts a premium on survival, which is a fact that aggressive players can take advantage of.

Any bubble is the perfect opportunity for big stacks to play the bully; any raise from the big stack is frequently followed by folds from the rest of the table. The big-stack's bubble factor is low against anyone smaller, but the other stacks have high bubble factors, so they have to get out of the way.

Personal considerations may also increase the bubble factor beyond what the math of the payouts indicates. For example, if you're approaching the final table of a major tournament with TV coverage, you can expect an extra "premium" for reaching the final table. That TV exposure is worth something that could arguably be measured in dollars, although it's worth different amounts to different people. This essentially raises the bubble factor for everyone, as some players will sacrifice some dollar EV in order to ensure they get some face time.

You also see the same thing approaching the money in any major tournament—both live and online. Many players who either satellited in or are playing above their normal level may be just looking to get to the cash. They'll increase their own bubble factor with self-induced tightness.

Your best play approaching any bubble (either money or final table) is not to fall victim to this way of thinking. Instead, you should be analyzing your opponents and finding out who has tightened up. These players should be your targets and you should frequently raise their blinds, no matter what your position. However, if you're accurate on your read, watch out if they ever 3-bet you. They're looking to survive, so they'll let you take blind after blind away from them. Most players will wait until they have a premium hand before playing back; you won't see much bluffing.

Things change after the bubble bursts and you're into the final table proper. Again, depending on the pay structure, bubble factors could drop significantly once you reach the final table. Those players who let themselves be blinded away to get this far will now turn around and think this is the time to make a stand. With low bubble factors, short stacks will now push all-in with pleasure, so you won't be able to steal blinds like you did before the final table.

During the final table, bubble factors will usually remain moderately high, since each elimination is a step up in prize money. Readers wanting to practice MTT final-table play should play online single-table tournaments (STTs), which contain many elements of a MTT final table.

15

Heads-Up (HU)

Playing HU obviously doesn't happen very often in a tournament. For this reason, most players don't get much experience with this dynamic. However, it's the last hurdle to clear on your way to a giant payday and the bragging rights that come with winning (second place doesn't qualify). If you absorb all the information in this book and incorporate it into your play, chances are you will find yourself heads-up at a final tournament table, and it's an eventuality for which you need to prepare yourself.

A good way to practice is to play some HU Sit-n-Go's (SNGs) on the Internet. To mix it up, you can also play some HU cash games once in a while, in order to get familiar with the dynamics of play.

The metagame in HU is probably not as important as it may be throughout the tournament. Indeed, it's very rare to reach HU in a tournament against an opponent you've previously faced for a tournament title. Even if you do, the game evolves so fast that your styles may have changed since your past encounter(s). There are, however, a few metagame considerations. If your opponent is short (15-20 BB) and shoves twice in a row to your button min-raise, you'll probably want to re-adjust the third time around, by limping for instance, and not giving him another opportunity to move-in.

Overall, optimal play in HU matters more than metagame considerations. Having a plan is critical in HU play, arguably even more so than during regular tournament play. Obviously, there's a lot of guessing involved HU, due to the lack of information on your opponent's style and strategy. The best way to counterbalance that is to look for the most correct mathematical play.

Example

ElkY, at the PCA 2009 Hi-Roller HU

I'm facing Will Molson with a 3-to-1 chip lead. Will has been pretty tight, folding his way into HU. He's short-stacked (15 BB). I know he's likely to readjust his strategy and become more aggressive as soon as the HU begins in an attempt to double up. Since I've been opening a lot of hands, I know he'll take advantage of the first opportunity to shove. So, my strategy is to fold all the worst holdings in my range, make a standard min-raise with any holding I'm ready to call his all-in with, and shove all suited aces, kings, and suited connectors higher than 65.

The strategy works like a dream. On the very first hand, I min-raise AJ and Will shoves KTo—actually the right play in my opinion, as that holding is often ahead of my opening range. Of course, I instantly call, and my hand holds to win the tournament!

In HU play, the most important factor is to adapt really quickly and not let your opponent ever manipulate you.

Calling for information in HU play is suboptimal, in my opinion. You should never sacrifice any EV, because the dynamics of HU change too rapidly for you to afford it.

Relative Stack Sizes

Relative stack sizes can change quickly and, to be effective, you need to adjust your strategy to these sudden fluctuations. If your opponent doubles up from 15 BB to 30 BB, for example, you have to instantly re-adjust your strategy to the new stack sizes (refer to playing different stack sizes later in this chapter). Experience in adjusting quickly is a key parameter for your HU skills. And again, you should probably spend some time playing Internet HU to acquire such experience.

As is the case generally at the final table as well, inexperienced players, especially at a TV table, tend to play tighter than usual.

Ranges, Bet Sizing, and When To Shove

There's definitely an equilibrium strategy for HU play, as discussed in detail in *Kill Everyone*. However, ranges are very much player-dependent. In HU play, 88+ and AT+ can be considered premium hands, which ElkY is always ready to play all-in for 30 BB to 40 BB.

In sizing your bets, the most important thing to keep in mind is to make sure you never commit yourself with marginal holdings. Also, size them so you always leave room for your opponent to make mistakes, and for him to think he has fold equity when you hold a strong hand.

From the button, we usually don't mix up raise sizes, with a few exceptions. For example, when stacks are getting shallow and your short-stacked opponent is given the opportunity to 3-bet all-in too often to a standard raise (2.5 BB), we might start limping or min-raising more often. Another situation is when you face a weak opponent who tends to call too frequently. In position with a big hand, ElkY makes a larger than normal raise if confident his opponent will call anyway, because it's +EV in the long run to play big pots IP with big hands. However, whenever possible, he tries to keep his raise size consistent, in an effort to control variance and disguise the strength of his hand.

Ranges

The hand range from the button is really opponent-dependent. If you face a weak opponent who folds too much PF or on the flop, you should probably min-raise 100% of your hands, folding 72o once in a while. In general, you should raise more often when you think you can outplay a weak opponent post-flop.

Against hyper-LAGs and maniacs, the situation is always more difficult, because they invariably keep you guessing. As usual, against such aggressive opponents, you'll be forced to play a higher-variance style, with limited time and information to adjust to their creative moves. Hyper-LAGs and maniacs use any scare card to their advantage, and since the blinds typically increase quickly, you have to be competent at reading hands and ready to make tough decisions!

When you're OOP against hyper-aggressive opponents, you should tighten up your range to hands that flop really well, such as high Broadway cards. Ace-high hands can be problematic when you're OOP. We think you should mostly 3-bet your better A-high holdings, such as AT+, or hands with which you're ready to move in. Sometimes, for deception value, you might want to flat-call and try to trap with these same holdings. When an A hits the flop, your hyper-aggressive opponent will tend not to believe you have top pair and such a strong kicker, but you didn't 3-bet PF. When you flat-call PF, with AQ for example, even if you miss the flop (let's say a J-T-2 board), you should be ready to check-call the flop, since your hand will often be ahead in that spot.

Generally, *against hyper-LAGs and maniacs, you need to be ready to make big calls.* You just don't have enough time in HU play to control the variance much.

From the BB, the 3-betting range is somewhat difficult to determine, because stacks are rarely deep and the overall dynamics of HU play are quite different from the rest of the tournament. Therefore, even if you've been playing with your HU opponent for a while, his HU range and strategy will likely be different from what you've observed up to that point. A good rule when the HU session has been going awhile and you haven't 3-bet yet is to 3-bet with a fairly wide range. On the other hand, if you have 3-bet several times, you should tighten up the 3-betting range or be ready to 5-bet all-in (even with air) if stack depths allow you to do so (35-50 BB), even though this opportunity seldom arises. In 3-betting light, also consider stack sizes, so you can fold to a 4-bet shove without committing yourself with the 3-bet. Keep in mind that when your opponent has 25 BB, a 3-bet from the BB is almost always a pot-committing move. Whenever you 3-bet from the BB, it's best to evaluate and anticipate the way your opponent is likely to react to 3-bets in given situations.

When in the BB against maniacs and/or hyper-LAGs, we don't recommend 3-betting with less than premium hands. First, you know your opponent will 4-bet you a decent percentage of the time, therefore forcing you to release your marginal hands PF. Second, in the event you 3-bet and get called, you're playing a pot that is already bloated pre-flop and you're out of position against a very unpredictable opponent, who could be holding any two cards. Not good! So, for you to 3-bet a hyper-aggressive opponent, you should hold a strong hand most of the time (all the better Broadways, KJ+, etc.). The size of the 3-bet is very much player dependent, as some people fold a lot more to bigger raises. In that case, we should obviously increase our fold equity, whereas some people call no matter what the amount is. Then we should raise big, but only our very best hand (AJs+, 99+). Try to get a feel for which group of player he belongs to. Other players also fold the same no matter what the 3-bet is; then we should definitely 3-bet smaller to reduce variance and get info at a cheaper price.

Effective Stacks Less than 10 BB

In position, you should simply open shove, considering that most opponents' calling ranges will generally be too tight. Don't even consider limping or making a smaller-than-all-in raise. Out of position, it's the same playing style: all-in or fold pre-flop all your hands.

Effective Stacks 10-20 BB

In position, min-raises are efficient. Your opponent will fold all of his trash holdings most of the time. If he defends too much, it's actually profitable for the short stack in the long run. Therefore, *whether he's playing too tight or too loose, min-raises are the exploitive strategy at this stack size.*

One adjustment your opponent might make is to widen his 3-betting range, which then puts the short stack in tough spots. If you're the short stack and your opponent starts 3-betting light after your min-raises, you should start limping most of your range with 10-20 BB and see how your opponent adapts. If he continues to shove as frequently when you limp, adjust by min-raising with monsters and open shoving hands with which you were min-raising or limping previously. If your opponent adjusts, limping to see the flop more frequently, limp with hands that have potential in position post-flop, such as 76o, 97o, 85s, etc. For balance, sometimes trap by limping with 88+, AT+, or even KQ versus aggressive foes. With hands such as Axo, K9o, etc., open shoving is ElkY's preference.

We'll also see in the next chapter that equilibrium solutions for these effective stacks also prefer starting out with limps on the button, since the BB can be so aggressive over opening raises.

Out of position, it's best to 3-bet shove most of the time, as you'll likely force an aggressive opponent to fold most of his range. We recommend mixing up your play with a balance of marginal holdings and strong hands to keep him constantly guessing as to your hand range.

Effective Stacks 20-40 BB

Once again, min-raises in position work wonders. Stacks are too deep for your opponent to just 3-bet shove. Also, they give him lots of trouble, because he has the odds, but he'll be out of position the whole hand and stacks aren't so deep that he can just wait to hit a big flop. Depending of his folding frequency and how often he 3-bets, you might want to fold the absolute worst hands (bottom 10%).

Guidelines for post-flop play are to keep your opponent in the dark as much as possible. Sometimes you might check back 100% on the flop and raise the turn; this puts him in a difficult situation. Or be ready to 3-barrel, or just play passively. Limping in with a few hands is also good; it can confuse some opponents and force them to make a mistake if they aren't used to it. It all depends which style you think your opponent is playing. If you assess that you're a better player, you can counter it. As usual, if you think you have an edge, try not to increase the variance, while mixing it up as much as possible.

Out of position, 3-betting is often suboptimal. Your opponent has the best stack size to 4-bet shove a wide range, so you should try to see more flops. Leading OOP on many flops is good against weaker opponents, but balance your range so you're leading OOP with air, or top pair and good draws that you intend to 3-bet shove if your opponent raises your bet on the flop. Against predictable players that c-bet with air, check-raising is a good response. But if he's passive on the flop, leading is the most powerful move. We don't recommend 3-betting hands you're not ready to go all-in with, though you can try it with 20% of your 3-bets; that way he can't fold correctly on your 3-bets all the time. Obviously, be ready to adapt your strategy and change everything all at once. One small pot can tip the scales and change stack sizes really easily in HU.

Effective Stacks More Than 40 BB

In position, as stacks get bigger, we believe it's correct to increase the open-raising frequency from the button. Stacks are now too deep for your opponent to 3-bet you all-in. Even if you get 3-bet, you still have enough fold equity to 4-bet all-in. Of course, you still need to be cautious and ready to adjust quickly.

Out of position, your 3-betting range should be fairly mixed, depending on your opponent's min-raising frequency from the button. ElkY prefers not to overuse 3-bets, because his re-raises then become more credible when he makes the move. If his image is good and his 3-bets are credible, his range to 3-bet extends from trash to very strong hands, and he tries to pick his spots appropriately. This comes down to his assessment of his opponent's strategy. If he open-raises with too wide a range, ElkY 3-bets more frequently. If he's 4-bet happy, ElkY 3-bets to give him the opportunity to make a move when he has a strong hand.

As for defending, the range should depend on the flow of the game and your opponent's style on the flop and the turn.

Playing the Flop

It's difficult to set guidelines on how to play the flop HU. It depends greatly on the board texture and your opponent. For example, holding bottom pair on a J-T-5 board is fairly marginal, compared to holding KJ on a board of A-K-2. Along the same lines, holding bottom pair on some boards is sometimes less dangerous than holding top pair on drawy boards.

Check-Raising

Whenever you decide to check raise in HU play, you must have a definite plan. Sometimes you check raise with the intention of calling an all-in. Other times you're ready to fold to a shove.

However, it's safe to say that check-raising for information in HU might be one of the most -EV moves, especially against LAGs, hyper-LAGs, and maniacs, because they come over the top too often for your move to be profitable. Therefore, as always, you need to mix up your check raise range among monsters, hands with good showdown value, and complete air. It's worth noting that raising for information should generally be avoided in nearly all scenarios, as there are often better options.

When you check raise with air, make sure your move actually makes sense. This won't always be the case on some boards or in some betting sequences. For example, if the board is A-2-3 and you check raise, your range is polarized to very few possible hands (AA, A2, A3, two pair, small sets, and 54) or complete air. If your opponent is observant and picks up on your move, he could call you down with K-high or come over the top.

To determine your patterns of check-raising, you should account for ranges and frequencies, the flow of the game, your opponent's profile, and the level of metagame he's capable of playing. If you check-raise on a bluff, you have to make sure your move is consistent with your pre-flop action and calling range. Going back to the example above, a check raise on a 7-8-9 board is usually much more credible than the same move on the A-2-3 board, as you might have many more combinations (two pair, upper or lower straight, sets, straight draws, etc.). As a result, it will be much more difficult for your opponent to re-raise you, even with a decent hand.

Check-raises with air should be used with caution, depending on your opponent's profile and how frequently he takes stabs at the pot.

Draws

When you hold a big drawing hand, such as a gutshot and a flush draw, or an ace-high flush draw, it's OK to play very aggressively by check-raising and being ready to call an all-in, especially against hyper-aggressive opponents. They also have inferior drawing hands in their pushing range, in which case you'll strongly dominate them.

With weaker drawing hands, you need to use more caution and adjust your lines depending on your opponent's profile.

Second Pair, Bottom Pair, Ace-High

These are arguably the most difficult hands to play, because most of the time you have to use good judgment and play the entire hand under pressure. *It's important to note that a three-barrel in HU play is usually all-in.*

A line we find effective with A-high is to check-call the flop and check raise the turn, especially with some kind of draw. This betting line represents great strength and often forces your opponent to fold many future holdings. Let's say you have A5 and the flop is J-2-3. You check, then call his bet on the flop; the turn is a 7 (board is rainbow). If you check-raise now (most of the time all-in, unless you're extremely deep), he'll have to fold a lot of hands, even most of his Jx holdings. Even if he does call, you still have between four and seven outs most of the time. This line is effective against a more aggressive opponent.

Against a passive player in the same situation, it seems fine to check-call the flop and be ready to check-fold the turn, since he's less likely to double-barrel without a decent hand. If a passive opponent bets the flop and checks the turn, it's likely that A-high will often be good at showdown. Still, against a passive opponent, check-raising the turn often forces him to fold his better A-high holdings and a lot of drawing hands right there.

Let's say your opponent has raised with A9o from the button and you've called with A5o from the BB. On the same J-2-3 board, your opponent will often take a shot at the pot if you check to him on the flop. However, he'll have to release his A9 to a check-raise on the turn most of the time.

16

Heads-Up Equilibrium Solutions with 20 BB and 15 BB

The following equilibrium solutions show an unexploitable strategy in heads-up play with 20 BB and 15 BB effective stacks. Since we generally recommend a push/fold strategy only with less than 10 BB or 12 BB, these additional solutions allow you to take advantage of further actions, such as limping or making standard raises.

In all of these solutions, the button was allowed to initially fold, limp, raise to 2 BB, 2.5 BB, 3 BB, or push all-in. After the initial action, both players are allowed to make 0.5x-pot, 1.0x-pot, or 1.5x-pot raises, in addition to being able to jam at any time.

Button's Initial Strategy (20 BB stacks)

Suited

	A	K	Q	J	T	9	8	7	6	5	4	3	2
A	S	S	S70C	C	C	C	S	C	C	C	S	S	S60C
K	C90S	S	S	C60S	C	C	C	C80S	S	S	S	S	C
Q	C	S	C	S	S50C	C	C	C	S	S	C60S	C	C
J	C	C	C	C	S	S70C	C	C	C	S	S	C	C
T	C	C	C	C80S	C	C70S	C	C	C	C	C	C	C
9	C90J	C	C	C	C	C60S	C	C	C	C	C	C	C
8	C	C	C	C	C	C	C80S	C	C	C	C	C	C
7	C	C	C	C	C	C	C	C	C	C	C	C	C
6	C	S	S90C	C	C	C	C	C	C	C	C	C	C
5	C	S	S	C	C	C	C	C	C	C70S	C	C	C
4	C	S	C	C	C	C	C	C	C	C	C90S	C	C
3	C	C	C	C	C	C	C	F	F	F	F	C80S	C90F
2	C	C	C	C	C	C	C	F	F	F	F	F	C70J

*(Left axis label: **Offsuit**)*

F	Fold
C	Call
S	Make a small (2BB) raise, then use a later table for follow-ups
J	Jam

These tables use the same notation as in Chapter 13: For example, A9o says C90J, which means call 90% of the time and jam 10%. Later on, we'll see more complicated entries, like F40 B30 p30, which means fold 40%, make a big (1.5x-pot) raise, and be willing to get it all-in 30%, and finally make a pot-sized raise, but fold to a re-raise the final 30%.

The equilibrium solution doesn't open-raise as often as the authors usually do. We open-raise on the button at least 40% of the time, and maybe up to 100% if our opponent is tight. The equilibrium prefers to limp re-raise with several of its strong hands in an effort to better protect its weak limps. Although the solution was allowed to open raise to 2.5 BB or 3 BB, it always elects to min-raise, except for the rare cases where it open jams. Why does the equilibrium solution limp so often? I think there are a couple reasons:

• If you limp with some weak hands, you have to limp with strong hands too, which is part of balancing and protecting your limps. So your decision is, do you limp a lot or raise a lot with both?

• If you raise, how big? We'll see later that the BB never folds to a min-raise. Raising to 2.5 BB is a bit more effective, but risks more if you're raising with trash. The computer abandons the larger raise and goes with 2 BB consistently. But that means no fold equity, which means playing a bigger pot with all the weak hands if you raise a lot. The computer would rather not raise as much, but it limp-raises a bunch to make up for it.

• When your stack is 15-20 BB, raising on the button cuts a lot of your positional advantage. He can push over your raise and eliminate your position. Or if he flat-calls, stacks aren't that deep, so your position counts less. If you limp with a good hand and he checks behind, you still have 3 streets to play in position with a deeper stack. Plus, limping makes it overkill for him to push. If you solved the equilibrium strategy for much deeper stacks (say 50 BB), I think you would see a lot more button raising, since it builds a pot in position and doesn't cut down the deep stacks as much. But those deeper-stack solutions are very difficult to solve[4].

---

[4] The top bot in the 2009 AAAI poker competition based on equilibrium strategies raised on the button about 65% of the time with 200 BB stacks.

Button: You limp, he makes it 2 BB (20 BB stacks)

Suited

	A	K	Q	J	T	9	8	7	6	5	4	3	2
A	-	-	P	P	P	P	-	C	C	C	-	-	C
K	P	-	-	C	P	P90J	C80p	C	-	-	-	-	C
Q	P	-	P	-	C	C	C	C	-	-	C	C	C
J	J	P70J	C	P	-	C	C	C	C	-	-	C	C
T	J	p	C	C	P	J	J	J70C	J70C	C	C	C	C
9	J	C90p	C	C	C	P	C90J	C	C	C	C	C	C
8	P	C	C	C	C	C	P50C	C	C	C	C	C	C
7	p70J	C	C	C	C	C	C	C	C	C	C	C	C
6	J50p	-	C	C	C	C	C	C	C	C	C	C	C
5	J	-	-	C	C80p	C	C	C	C	C	C	C	C
4	J80p	-	C	C	C	C	C	C	C	C	C	C	C
3	J	C	C	C	C	C	C	-	-	-	-	C	C
2	J70p	C	C	C	p80C	C70p	C	-	-	-	-	-	C

Offsuit (row axis label)

F	Fold
C	Call
P	Make a pot-sized raise, and be willing to get it all in
p	Make a pot-sized raise, but fold to a re-raise
J	Jam
-	Not limped

Here's the situation where we just limped and the BB makes a min-raise. We never fold, since we're in position and getting 3-to-1 pot odds. Notice that there are limp re-raise bluffs, such as T2o.

Button: You limp, he makes it 3 BB (20 BB stacks)

Suited

Offsuit

	A	K	Q	J	T	9	8	7	6	5	4	3	2
A	-	-	C90S	J90S	S90J	C90J	-	C	C	C	-	-	C
K	S	-	-	C	C80S	C	C	C	-	-	-	-	C
Q	J	-	S60J	-	C70J	J70C	C	C	-	-	C	C	C70s
J	J	C80 J10 S10	J50C	J	-	J90C	C90J	C	C	-	-	F90C	F80 s10 C10
T	J	C	C	C	J90S	C90J	C	C	C60F	F	F	F	F
9	J	C	C	C	C	J	J90C	C90J	C	F90C	F	F	F
8	J80s	C	C	C80F	F	C90F	J80 S10 C10	J80C	C60J	C	F	F	F
7	C	C	C80F	F	F	F	C	C90S	C	C	F80C	F	F
6	C	-	F60C	F	F	F	F	C	C	C90J	C	F90C	F
5	J80C	-	F	F	F	F	F	F	C	C	C80J	C	C
4	C	-	F	F	F	F	F	F	F	F	C	C80F	F
3	C50 s30 J20	C	F	F	F	F	F	-	-	-	-	J90C	F
2	J80s	C	F	F	F	F	F	-	-	-	-	-	J

F	Fold
C	Call
S	Make a small (0.5X pot) raise, and be willing to get it all-in
s	Make a small (0.5X pot) raise, but fold to a re-raise
J	Jam
-	Not limped

Button: You limp, he makes it 4 BB (20 BB stacks)

Suited

	A	K	Q	J	T	9	8	7	6	5	4	3	2
A	-	-	J	J	J	J	-	C	C	C	-	-	C
K	J	-	-	C70J	J	J	J80C	C	-	-	-	-	F
Q	J	-	J	J	-	J	C	C	-	-	C	F	F
J	J	J	C	J	-	J80C	C90J	C60F	F	-	-	F	F
T	J	C60J	C	C	J	J	J	J90F	F	F	F	F	F
9	J	C	C	F50C	F	J	J	C	F	F	F	F	F
8	C60J	F	F	F	F	F	J	C90J	F90C	F	F	F	F
7	C	F	F	F	F	F	F	J	C	F	F	F	F
6	C	-	F	F	F	F	F	F	J	C70J	F90C	F	F
5	C	-	-	F	F	F	F	F	F	J	J90C	J90C	F
4	C	-	F	F	F	F	F	F	F	F	J	F	F
3	C	F	F	F	F	F	F	-	-	-	-	J	F
2	F40 C40 J20	F	F	F	F	F	F	-	-	-	-	-	J

Offsuit (row axis)

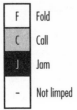

F	Fold
C	Call
J	Jam
-	Not limped

Button: You limp, he jams (20 BB stacks)

Suited

	A	K	Q	J	T	9	8	7	6	5	4	3	2
A	-	-	C	C	C	C	-	C	C	C	-	-	F
K	C	-	-	C	C	C	F	F	-	-	-	-	F
Q	C	-	C	-	C	F	F	F	-	-	F	F	F
J	C	C	F80C	C	-	F	F	F	F	-	-	F	F
T	C	C90F	F	F	C	F	F	F	F	F	F	F	F
9	C	F	F	F	F	C	F	F	F	F	F	F	F
8	C	F	F	F	F	F	C	F	F	F	F	F	F
7	C	F	F	F	F	F	F	C	F	F	F	F	F
6	F	-	F	F	F	F	F	F	C	F	F	F	F
5	F	-	-	F	F	F	F	F	F	C	F	F	F
4	F	-	F	F	F	F	F	F	F	F	C	F	F
3	F	F	F	F	F	F	F	-	-	-	-	C	F
2	F	F	F	F	F	F	F	-	-	-	-	-	F

Offsuit

F	Fold
C	Call
-	Not limped

We clearly call less often the bigger he raises, due to the shrinking pot odds.

Button: You make it 2 BB, he makes it 4 BB (20 BB stacks)

Suited

	A	K	Q	J	T	9	8	7	6	5	4	3	2
A	J	C	C	–	–	–	C90J	–	–	–	C	C	J90C
K	C60J	C80J	C	C80J	–	–	–	J	C90J	C70J	C70J	C90J	–
Q	–	C	–	C	C	–	–	–	C90F	C	C	–	–
J	–	–	–	–	C	C70J	–	–	–	C	C90F	–	–
T	–	–	–	C	–	J80C	–	–	–	–	–	–	–
9	J	–	–	–	–	C70J	–	–	–	–	–	–	–
8	–	–	–	–	–	–	J60C	–	–	–	–	–	–
7	–	–	–	–	–	–	–	–	–	–	–	–	–
6	–	F	F	–	–	–	–	–	–	–	–	–	–
5	–	F80C	F	–	–	–	–	–	–	C	–	–	–
4	–	F	–	–	–	–	–	–	–	–	C	–	–
3	–	–	–	–	–	–	–	–	–	–	–	C	F
2	–	–	–	–	–	–	–	–	–	–	–	–	F80C

Offsuit (row axis)

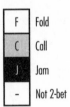

F	Fold
C	Call
J	Jam
–	Not 2-bet

Button: You make it 2 BB, he makes it 6 BB (20 BB stacks)

Suited

	A	K	Q	J	T	9	8	7	6	5	4	3	2
A	J	J	C	–	–	–	C	–	–	–	C	C50F	F
K	J	J60C	C	C	–	–	–	F	F	F60J	F	F	–
Q	–	C	–	C	C60J	–	–	–	F	F	F	–	–
J	–	–	–	–	J50C	J50C	–	–	–	F	F	–	–
T	–	–	–	C	–	J80C	–	–	–	–	–	–	–
9	C90F	–	–	–	–	C80J	–	–	–	–	–	–	–
8	–	–	–	–	–	–	J90C	–	–	–	–	–	–
7	–	–	–	–	–	–	–	–	–	–	–	–	–
6	–	F	F	–	–	–	–	–	–	–	–	–	–
5	–	F	F	–	–	–	–	–	–	J50C	–	–	–
4	–	F	–	–	–	–	–	–	–	–	C60J	–	–
3	–	–	–	–	–	–	–	–	–	–	–	J50C	F
2	–	–	–	–	–	–	–	–	–	–	–	–	J

Offsuit (row axis label)

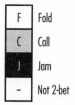

F	Fold
C	Call
J	Jam
–	Not 2-bet

Button: You make it 2 BB, he jams (20 BB stacks)

Suited

	A	K	Q	J	T	9	8	7	6	5	4	3	2
A	C	C	C	–	–	–	C	–	–	–	F	F	F
K	C	C	C	C	–	–	–	F	F	F	F	F	–
Q	–	F	–	C	C	–	–	–	F	F	F	–	–
J	–	–	–	–	C	F	–	–	–	F	F	–	–
T	–	–	–	F	–	F	–	–	–	–	–	–	–
9	C	–	–	–	–	C	–	–	–	–	–	–	–
8	–	–	–	–	–	–	C	–	–	–	–	–	–
7	–	–	–	–	–	–	–	–	–	–	–	–	–
6	–	F	F	–	–	–	–	–	–	–	–	–	–
5	–	F	F	–	–	–	–	–	–	C	–	–	–
4	–	F	–	–	–	–	–	–	–	–	C	–	–
3	–	–	–	–	–	–	–	–	–	–	–	C	F
2	–	–	–	–	–	–	–	–	–	–	–	–	C

Offsuit (row label)

F	Fold
C	Call
–	Not 2-bet

If we open with a raise and he 3-bets, there are very few bluff 4-bets. That's because stacks are fairly short and we don't have too much fold equity over a 3-bet. If we make it 2 BB and he makes it 4 BB, there are a few bluffs, mostly with weak suited aces and kings.

Big Blind: He limps (20 BB stacks)

Suited

	A	K	Q	J	T	9	8	7	6	5	4	3	2
A	S	S	P70B	B	B	B	B	B	B80J	J	J	J	J
K	P70S	S	S	B	S80P	S*	s*	s*	K60s*	s*	p*60s*	p	K
Q	J	S*60B	P	S	P60S	S	S*	S*	S*	S*	S*	s*	s*80 p10 K10
J	J70B	J	J90B	S90B	J	S	S*	S*	s*	s*	s*	K	K
T	J70B	P	J90p*	J	B70S	J	S*	s*	s*80 K10 p*10	K90p*	K	K	K
9	J	p	s*	s*	J	S70P	J	K	K	K	K	K	K
8	J	K80p	s*	s*	K	K	B30 S30 P20 J20	K	K	K	K	K	K
7	J	K	s*	s*90K	K	K	K	J	K	K	K	K	K
6	b70p	K	s*	K60s*	K	K	K	K	J80S	K	K	K	K
5	J	K	s*	b50 K30 p20	K	K	K	K	K	S60J	K	K	K
4	J	K	p90s*	K90b	K	K	K	K	K	K	J90P	K	K
3	b80J	K	b60K	K	K	K	K	K	K	K	K	J	K
2	b	K	K	K	K	K	K	K	K	K	K	K	J

Offsuit (row labels, left side)

K	Check
J	Jam
P	Make it 3 BB, and be willing to get it all-in
p*	Make it 3 BB, then call up to a 6 BB 3-bet
p	Make it 3 BB, but fold to 3-bet
B	Make it 4 BB, and be willing to get it all-in
b	Make it 4 BB, but fold to 3-bet
S	Make a small (2 BB) raise, and be willing to get it all-in
S*	Make a small (2 BB) 2-bet, then call up to a pot-sized 3-bet
s*	Make a small (2 BB) 2-bet, then call up to a 4 BB 3-bet

Now we're looking at the strategy from the BB after the button just limped. There are a few complicated entries, because the follow-ups don't always fit nicely into a compact table like this. The most complicated example is probably T6s. With T6s, the solution makes it 2 BB 80% of the time, checks 10% of the time, and makes it 3 BB 10%. After both of those raises, it's willing to call a half-pot 3-bet, but nothing bigger. A lower-case "p" without an asterisk means that it will fold to any sized 3-bet.

Most weak hands are simply checked behind. The bluffs tend to be hands with one high card that could potentially hit a top pair and take the lead. Suited connectors are less valuable due to the short stacks (smaller implied odds), as well as the fact that he's less likely to flop a big hand. If *you* flop a big hand, you're less likely to be paid off by ace-high and the like.

Big Blind: He makes it 2 BB (20 BB stacks)

Suited

	A	K	Q	J	T	9	8	7	6	5	4	3	2
A	P90S	P	P	J90P	J90P	P70J	J	P90J	J	J	J	J	J
K	P	P70S	C	C	C	C	C	C	C	C	C	C	C
Q	P80J	C	J70P	C	C	C	C	C	C	C	C	C	C
J	J	C90J	C90J	J	J	C80s	C	C	C	C	C	C	C
T	J	C	C	J	J	J	C	C	C	C	C	C	C
9	J70P	C	C	C	J50C	J	C90J	C	C	C	C	C	C
8	J	C	C	C	C	C	J	C	C	C	C	C	C
7	P80J	C	C	C	C	C	C	J70S	C	C	C	C	C
6	J50 p40 s10	C	C	C	C	C	C	C	C	C	C	C	C
5	J	C	C	C	C	C	C	C	C	C	C	C	C
4	J	C	C	C	C	C	C	C	C	C	C90J	C	C
3	J90p	C	C	C	C90p	C	C	C	C	C	C	p50 C20 s20 J10	C
2	p60J	C	C	C	C70p	C90p	C	C	C	C	C	C	p70C

Offsuit (row labels)

Legend:

| C | Call | | **J** | Jam | | **S** | Make a small (0.5X pot) 3-bet, and be willing to go all-in |

| **P** | Make a pot-sized 3-bet, and be willing to go all-in | | **s** | Make a small (0.5X pot) 3-bet, but fold to 4-bet |

| **p** | Make a pot-sized 3-bet, but fold to 4-bet |

The big blind never folds when the button min-raises. Aces always 3-bet and there are also a few bluffs thrown in for balance (good suited and offsuit connectors, plus some garbage hands like T2o).

Big Blind: He makes it 2.5 BB (20 BB stacks)

Suited

	A	K	Q	J	T	9	8	7	6	5	4	3	2
A	J	J	J	J	J	J	J	J	J	J	J	J	J
K	J	J	C	C90J	C	C	C	C	C	C	C	C	C
Q	J	C	J	C50J	J	C	C	C	C	C	C	C	C
J	J	C90J	J	J	J	J60C	C	C	C	C	C	C	C
T	J	C	J	J	J	J	J60C	C	C	C	C	C	C
9	J	C	C	C	J60C	J	J	C	C	C	C	C	C
8	J80C	C	C	C	C	F90C	J	C	C	C	C	F90C	F
7	J70C	C	C70F	C	C70F	F90C	F	J	C	C	C	C	F
6	J80C	C90F	C	F90C	F	F	F	F	J	C	C	C	C
5	J	F80C	F60C	F70C	F	F	F	F	C	J90C	C	C	C
4	J	F	F	F	F	F	F	F	F	C	J90C	C	C
3	J	F	F	F	F	F	F	F	F	F	F	J50C	C
2	J	F	F	F	F	F	F	F	F	F	F	F	C70J

Offsuit (rows)

Legend: F Fold | C Call | J Jam

Big Blind: He makes it 3 BB (20 BB stacks)

Suited

	A	K	Q	J	T	9	8	7	6	5	4	3	2
A	J	J	J	J	J	J	J	J	J	J	J	J	J
K	J	J	C	J	C	C	C	C	C	C	C	C	C
Q	J	C	J	C	J	C	C	C	C	C	C	C	C
J	J	J	J90C	J	J	C	C	C	C	C	C	C	C
T	J	C	J80C	J80C	J	J	C	C	C	C	C	C	F
9	J	C	C	C	J60C	J	C	C	C	C	C	C	F
8	J	C	C90F	C	C	F	J	C	C	C	C70F	F	F
7	C	C	F70C	C90F	F	F	F	J	C	C	C	F	F
6	C	F	F	F	F	F	F	F	J	C	C	C	F
5	J	F	F	F	F	F	F	F	F	J	C	C	F
4	J	F	F	F	F	F	F	F	F	F	J	C	F
3	J	F	F	F	F	F	F	F	F	F	F	J	F
2	J80F	F	F	F	F	F	F	F	F	F	F	F	J

Offsuit

| F | Fold | C | Call | J | Jam |

Big Blind: He open jams (20 BB stacks)

Suited

	A	K	Q	J	T	9	8	7	6	5	4	3	2
A	C	C	C	C	C	C	C	C	C	C	C	C	F
K	C	C	C	C	C	F	F	F	F	F	F	F	F
Q	C	C	C	C	C	F	F	F	F	F	F	F	F
J	C	C	F50C	C	C	F70C	F80C	F	F	F	F	F	F
T	C	F60C	C70F	F60C	C	C	C90F	F	F	F	F	F	F
9	C	F	F	F	F	C	F70C	F	F	F	F	F	F
8	C	F	F	F	F	F	C	C70F	F	F	F	F	F
7	F50C	F	F	F	F	F	F	C	F60C	F	F	F	F
6	F	F	F	F	F	F	F	F	C	F	F	F	F
5	F	F	F	F	F	F	F	F	F	C	F	F	F
4	F	F	F	F	F	F	F	F	F	F	C	F	F
3	F	F	F	F	F	F	F	F	F	F	F	C	F
2	F	F	F	F	F	F	F	F	F	F	F	F	C

Offsuit (row labels)

| F | Fold | | C | Call |

Notice that the solution for calling an open jam for 20 BB here isn't the same as you might find in a Nash equilibrium solution on the web or in another book. That's because that other solution is calling a push when the button was forced to only push or fold. In this case, our button has many other options besides push/fold, so his pushing distribution is different. Our button pushes occasionally with 22 and A9o, plus a few other hands that push less than 5%, so they don't show up on the table. So our push-calling strategy is heavily weighted to counter those hands, which is why you see odd strategies, like preferring to call with QTo over QJo (QT actually does better against those hands!). In practice, calling or folding with both of those hands is equally fine and you shouldn't worry about little nuances like this.

Now we'll repeat all the same tables, but with 15 BB effective stacks.

Button's Inital Strategy (15 BB stacks)

Suited (columns) / Offsuit (rows)

	A	K	Q	J	T	9	8	7	6	5	4	3	2
A	C	C70S	C	C	C	C	C	C	C	C	C	C	C
K	C	C50S	S	C	C	C	J	J	C80S	C	C	C	C
Q	J	C	C	C90S	C90S	S40 C40 J20	C70S	C	S	C	C	C	C
J	J	J	C	C	C90S	J	C80J	C	C	C80S	C	C	C
T	J80C	C90J	C70J	C90S	C	J	J	C	C	C	C	C	C
9	J	C80S	C	C	C	C90S	J	J	C	C	C	C	C
8	C	C	C	C	C	C	C	J	J	C	C	C	C
7	C	S90C	C	C	C	C	C	C90S	J	J	C	C	C
6	J	C	C70S	C	C	C	C	C	C80S	J	C70J	C90F	F
5	J	C	C	C	C	C	C	C	C	C	J	C	F
4	J	C	C	C	C	C	F	F	F	F	C	C	F
3	C60J	C	C	C	C	C	F	F	F	F	F	J90C	F
2	C	C	C	C	C	C	F	F	F	F	F	F	J

F Fold C Call S Make a small (2 BB) raise, then use a later table for follow-ups J Jam

Open pushing is more common at this shorter effective stack; in fact, we rarely make the smaller raise. Limping is still prevalent for the reasons outlined earlier and pocket aces now join the list of limp-trappers.

Button: You limp, he makes it 2 BB (15 BB stacks)

Suited

	A	K	Q	J	T	9	8	7	6	5	4	3	2
A	P	P	P	P80J	J70P	P	P	C80P	P	P	P	P	P
K	P	P	-	C70P	P	P	-	-	C	C	C	C	C
Q	-	C	P	C	P90C	C	C	C	-	C	C	C	C
J	-	-	C90J	P	P60J	-	C	C	C	C	C	C	C60p
T	J	P	C	C90p	P	-	-	p50C	C60p	p60C	C	C	p80C
9	-	C50p	C	C	C	P	-	-	C	C	C	C	C
8	P	C	C	C	C	C	C	-	-	C	C	C	C
7	P	C	C	C	C	C	C	C	-	-	C	C	C
6	-	C	C	C	C	C	C	C	C	-	C	C	-
5	-	C	C	C	C	C	C	C	C	C	-	C	-
4	-	C	C	C	C	C	-	-	-	-	C60p	C	-
3	J	C	C	C	C80p	C	-	-	-	-	-	p	-
2	J70p	C	C	C90p	p	C90F	-	-	-	-	-	-	-

(Offsuit — row labels down the left side)

F Fold	**C** Call	**P**	Make a pot-sized raise, and be willing to get it all-in
J Jam	**–** Not limped	**p**	Make a pot-sized raise, but fold to a re-raise

The key below refers to the chart on the following page.

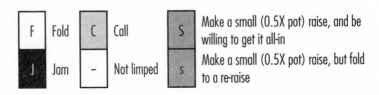

F Fold	**C** Call	**S**	Make a small (0.5X pot) raise, and be willing to get it all-in
J Jam	**–** Not limped	**s**	Make a small (0.5X pot) raise, but fold to a re-raise

Button: You limp, he makes it 2.5 BB (15 BB stacks)

Suited

	A	K	Q	J	T	9	8	7	6	5	4	3	2
A	S90J	C60S	C80S	J90S	J70S	S60 C20 J20	C80S	C	C	C	C	C	C90S
K	S60J	S80J	–	C	C	C	–	–	C	C	C	C	C
Q	–	C	J	C	S70J	C50 J40 S10	C60 J20 S20	C60 J20 S20	–	C90J	F	J40 F30 C20 S10	J50 C20 F20 S10
J	–	–	C70 J20 S10	J	C80 S10 J10	–	C	C	F	C80F	F	F	F
T	J	C	C	C	S60J	–	–	C50 J30 S20	F60 C20 J20	F	F	F	F
9	–	C	C	C90F	C	S80J	–	–	C90J	C80F	F	F	F
8	J60S	C	C70F	F80C	F	C	C50 S40 J10	–	–	C80J	F	F	F
7	C60 J30 S10	C	F90C	F	F	F	C	C70 S20 J10	–	–	F	F	F
6	–	C	F90C	F	F	F	F	C80F	C90S	–	F	F	–
5	–	C	F80C	F	F	F	F	F	C50F	C70 S20 J10	–	J50 S40 C10	–
4	–	C	F	F	F	F	–	–	–	–	C	F	–
3	J40 C40 S20	C70F	F	F	F	F	–	–	–	–	–	J80S	–
2	J60 S30 C10	F60C	F	F	F	F	–	–	–	–	–	–	–

Offsuit

Button: You limp, he makes it 3 BB (15 BB stacks)

Suited

	A	K	Q	J	T	9	8	7	6	5	4	3	2
A	J	J	J	J	J	J	J	C90J	C	C	C	C	C
K	J	J	-	C60J	C	C	-	-	C	C	C	C	C90F
Q	-	C	J	C	J	C80J	C90J	C	-	C60F	F	F	F
J	-	-	J70C	J	J70C	-	J80C	F80C	F	F	F	F	F
T	J	C	C90J	C	J	-	-	C50 F40 J10	F	F	F	F	F
9	-	C	C90F	F	F60C	J	-	-	F	F	F	F	F
8	J	C	F	F	F	F70C	J	-	-	F	F	F	F
7	J90C	C	F	F	F	F	F	J	-	-	F	F	F
6	-	C	F	F	F	F	F	F	C60J	-	F	F	-
5	-	C70F	F	F	F	F	F	F	F	J90C	-	F	-
4	-	F	F	F	F	F	-	-	-	-	J70C	F	-
3	J	F	F	F	F	F	-	-	-	-	-	J	-
2	J80C	F	F	F	F	F	-	-	-	-	-	-	-

Offsuit (row labels)

| F | Fold | C | Call | J | Jam | - | Not limped |

Button: You limp, he jams (15 BB stacks)

Suited

	A	K	Q	J	T	9	8	7	6	5	4	3	2
A	C	C	C	C	C	C	C	C	C	C	C	C	F80C
K	C	C	-	C	C	C	-	-	F	F	F	F	F
Q	-	C	C	C	C	C	F	F	-	F	F	F	F
J	-	-	C	C	C	-	F	F	F	F	F	F	F
T	C	C	C	F	C	-	-	F	F	F	F	F	F
9	-	F	F	F	F	C	-	-	F	F	F	F	F
8	C	F	F	F	F	F	C	-	-	F	F	F	F
7	C	F	F	F	F	F	F	C	-	-	F	F	F
6	-	F	F	F	F	F	F	F	C	-	F	F	-
5	-	F	F	F	F	F	F	F	F	C	-	F	-
4	-	F	F	F	F	F	-	-	-	-	C	F	-
3	F	F	F	F	F	F	-	-	-	-	-	C	-
2	F	F	F	F	F	F	-	-	-	-	-	-	-

Offsuit

| F | Fold | C | Call | - | Not limped |

Button: You make it 2 BB, he makes it 4 BB (15 BB stacks)

Suited

	A	K	Q	J	T	9	8	7	6	5	4	3	2
A	–	J	–	–	–	–	–	–	–	–	–	–	–
K	–	J90C	C	–	–	–	–	–	C	–	–	–	–
Q	–	–	–	C	C80J	C60J	J70C	–	F	–	–	–	–
J	–	–	–	–	C90J	–	–	–	–	–	–	–	–
T	–	–	–	–	–	–	–	–	–	–	–	–	–
9	–	C70F	–	–	–	C90J	–	–	–	–	–	–	–
8	–	–	–	–	–	–	–	–	–	–	–	–	–
7	–	–	–	–	–	–	–	C60J	–	–	–	–	–
6	–	–	–	–	–	–	–	–	C80J	–	–	–	–
5	–	–	–	–	–	–	–	–	–	–	–	–	–
4	–	–	–	–	–	–	–	–	–	–	–	–	–
3	–	–	–	–	–	–	–	–	–	–	–	–	–
2	–	–	–	–	–	–	–	–	–	–	–	–	–

Offsuit (row axis)

F	Fold	C	Call	J	Jam	–	Not2-bet

Button: You make it 2 BB, he makes it 6 BB (15 BB stacks)

Suited

	A	K	Q	J	T	9	8	7	6	5	4	3	2
A	–	J	–	–	–	–	–	–	–	–	–	–	–
K	–	J60C	C	–	–	–	–	–	C	–	–	–	–
Q	–	–	–	C	C	C50J	C	–	C70 F20 J10	–	–	–	–
J	–	–	–	–	C	–	–	–	–	–	–	–	–
T	–	–	–	–	–	–	–	–	–	–	–	–	–
9	–	C	–	–	–	J	–	–	–	–	–	–	–
8	–	–	–	–	–	–	–	–	–	–	–	–	–
7	–	–	–	–	–	–	–	C50J	–	–	–	–	–
6	–	–	–	–	–	–	–	–	C90J	–	–	–	–
5	–	–	–	–	–	–	–	–	–	–	–	–	–
4	–	–	–	–	–	–	–	–	–	–	–	–	–
3	–	–	–	–	–	–	–	–	–	–	–	–	–
2	–	–	–	–	–	–	–	–	–	–	–	–	–

Offsuit

F	Fold	C	Call	J	Jam	–	Not 2-bet

Button: You make it 2 BB, he jams (15 BB stacks)

Suited

Offsuit	A	K	Q	J	T	9	8	7	6	5	4	3	2
A	–	C	–	–	–	–	–	–	–	–	–	–	–
K	–	C	C	–	–	–	–	–	F	–	–	–	–
Q	–	–	–	C	C	C	F	–	F	–	–	–	–
J	–	–	–	–	C	–	–	–	–	–	–	–	–
T	–	–	–	–	–	–	–	–	–	–	–	–	–
9	–	F	–	–	–	C	–	–	–	–	–	–	–
8	–	–	–	–	–	–	–	–	–	–	–	–	–
7	–	–	–	–	–	–	–	C	–	–	–	–	–
6	–	–	–	–	–	–	–	–	C	–	–	–	–
5	–	–	–	–	–	–	–	–	–	–	–	–	–
4	–	–	–	–	–	–	–	–	–	–	–	–	–
3	–	–	–	–	–	–	–	–	–	–	–	–	–
2	–	–	–	–	–	–	–	–	–	–	–	–	–

F — Fold	C — Call	– — Not 2-bet

The types of play for 15 BB are similar to those for 20 BB, but are more likely to push, just like you would expect for shorter stacks.

Big Blind: He limps (15 BB stacks)

Suited

	A	K	Q	J	T	9	8	7	6	5	4	3	2
A	S	S	J60B	B	B60J	B	J70B	J	J	J	J	J	J
K	P60B	S	S	P60 B30 S10	S	S	s*	S*	S*	S*	s*	s*90p*	J90K
Q	J	S	S70P	S	S	S	S	s*	S	S*	s*	s*	K
J	J	B70J	J	S	S	S	S*	s*	s*	K90s*	K	K	K
T	J	B80P	J50 B40 P10	J	S80P	J	K80J	J70K	K90J	K	K	K	K
9	J90B	K90p*	s*	J90s*	J	S80 P10 B10	J	J90K	J70K	K	K	K	K
8	J	K	s*	s*90K	K	K90J	B	J	K90J	K	K	K	K
7	J	s*80K	s*	s*90K	K	K	K	K80B	J	K	K	K	K
6	J	s*90K	s*	K70 b20 p10	K	K	K	b70 K20 J10	J60B	K	K	K	K
5	J	s*90K	s*	K	K	K	K	K	K	J	K	K	K
4	J	p80 K10 b10	K70 b20 p10	K	K	K	K	K	K	K	J	K	K
3	J	K60b	K90b	K	K	K	K	K	K	K	K	J	K
2	J	b80K	K80b	K	K	K	K	K	K	K	K	K	J

(Row label: Offsuit)

Legend:

- **K** — Check
- **J** — Jam
- **P** — Make it 3 BB, and be willing to get it all in
- **p*** — Make it 3 BB, then call up to a 6 BB 3-bet
- **p** — Make it 3 BB, but fold to 3-bet
- **B** — Make it 4 BB, and be willing to get it all-in
- **b** — Make it 4 BB, but fold to 3-bet
- **S** — Make a small (2 BB) raise, and be willing to get it all-in
- **S*** — Make a small (2 BB) 2-bet, then call up to a pot-sized 3-bet
- **s*** — Make a small (2 BB) 2-bet, then call up to a 4 BB 3-bet

The 15 BB solution after the button limps is very similar to the 20 BB solution. There is still a variety of bet sizes—the solution freely uses all of the bet-size options it was given (2 BB, 3 BB, 4 BB, and jamming to 15 BB).

The key below refers to the chart on the following page.

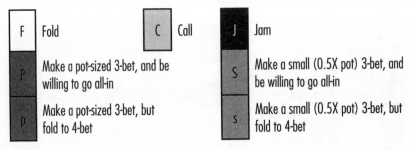

F	Fold
P	Make a pot-sized 3-bet, and be willing to go all-in
p	Make a pot-sized 3-bet, but fold to 4-bet

C	Call
J	Jam
S	Make a small (0.5X pot) 3-bet, and be willing to go all-in
s	Make a small (0.5X pot) 3-bet, but fold to 4-bet

Big Blind: He makes it 2 BB (15 BB stacks)

Suited

	A	K	Q	J	T	9	8	7	6	5	4	3	2
A	S70P	P	J	J	J	J	J	J	J90P	J	J	J	J
K	J80P	S	C	S	S	C	C	C	C	C	C90J	C60 J20 s20	C40 s30 J30
Q	J	C70S	J50P	C	S70P	C	C	C	C	C	C	C	C
J	J	S	J60 C20 s10 P10	P60J	J	C	C	C	C	C	C	C	C
T	J	S70C	C70s	J90p	P50 J40 S10	J	C	C	C	C	C	C	C
9	J90P	C	C	C	C70 J20 s10	S60J	J	C	C	C	C	C	C
8	J	C	C	C	C	J40 C30 s30	J	C80J	C	C	C	C	C
7	J	C	C	C	C	C	C	J80S	C	C	C	C	C
6	J80P	C	C	F	F	C	C	C	C50 J30 P10 S10	C	C	C	C
5	J	C	C	C80F	F	C	C	C	C	J80P	C	C	C
4	J	C	C	F50 C40 p10	C50 p30 F20	F	C	F80C	C	C	J90P	C	C
3	J	C90s	C50F	F	F	F	F	F	F	C	C	J	C
2	J	C50 s30 p20	F90C	F	F	F	F	F	F	F	F80C	F	J90S

Offsuit (row axis label)

Here's a difference from the 20 BB solution: The BB will occasionally fold to a min-raise at 15 BB stacks. A shorter stack is an overall advantage to the BB, since on average he'll be out of position for fewer betting decisions. But this advantage mostly helps his strong hands. Weak hands are actually worse with shorter stacks; you have worse implied odds and you can't bluff as much post-flop (less fold equity). So while over all hands the BB is happier with a short stack, his weak hands are less desirable, so they fold despite getting the 3-to-1 pot odds.

Big Blind: He makes it 2.5 BB (15 BB stacks)

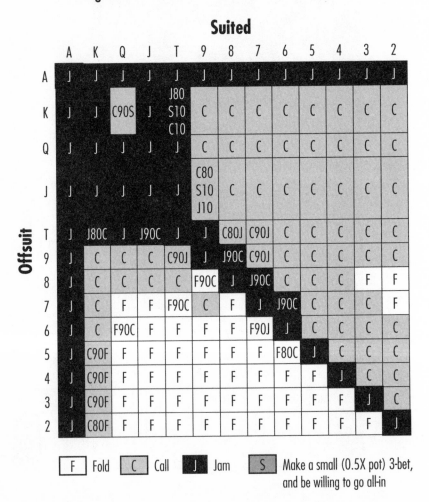

Big Blind: He makes it 3 BB (15 BB stacks)

Suited

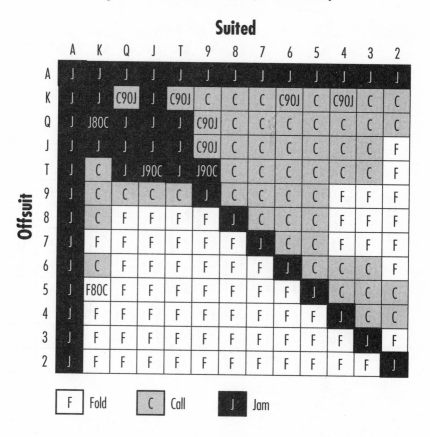

	A	K	Q	J	T	9	8	7	6	5	4	3	2
A	J	J	J	J	J	J	J	J	J	J	J	J	J
K	J	J	C90J	J	C90J	C	C	C	C90J	C	C90J	C	C
Q	J	J80C	J	J	J	C90J	C	C	C	C	C	C	C
J	J	J	J	J	J	C90J	C	C	C	C	C	C	F
T	J	C	J	J90C	J	J90C	C	C	C	C	C	C	F
9	J	C	C	C	C	J	C	C	C	C	F	F	F
8	J	C	F	F	F	F	J	C	C	C	F	F	F
7	J	F	F	F	F	F	F	J	C	C	F	F	F
6	J	C	F	F	F	F	F	F	J	C	C	C	F
5	J	F80C	F	F	F	F	F	F	F	J	C	C	C
4	J	F	F	F	F	F	F	F	F	F	J	C	C
3	J	F	F	F	F	F	F	F	F	F	F	J	F
2	J	F	F	F	F	F	F	F	F	F	F	F	J

Offsuit

F	Fold	C	Call	J	Jam

Big Blind: He open jams (15 BB stacks)

Suited

		A	K	Q	J	T	9	8	7	6	5	4	3	2
	A	C	C	C	C	C	C	C	C	C	C	C	C	C
	K	C	C	C	C	C	C	C	C	F	F	F	F	F
	Q	C	C	C	C	C	C	C	F	F	F	F	F	F
	J	C	C	C80F	C	C	C	F70C	F	F	F	F	F	F
	T	C	C	C70F	C50F	C	C	F60C	F	F	F	F	F	F
Offsuit	9	C	F	F	F	F	C	F	F	F	F	F	F	F
	8	C	F	F	F	F	F	C	F	F	F	F	F	F
	7	C	F	F	F	F	F	F	C	F	F	F	F	F
	6	C	F	F	F	F	F	F	F	C	F	F	F	F
	5	C	F	F	F	F	F	F	F	F	C	F	F	F
	4	F60C	F	F	F	F	F	F	F	F	F	C	F	F
	3	F	F	F	F	F	F	F	F	F	F	F	C	F
	2	F	F	F	F	F	F	F	F	F	F	F	F	C

F	Fold	C	Call

Again, this solution of calling an open jam isn't the same as an equilibrium solution when the button is forced to jam or fold.

Although these solutions don't take advantage of weaknesses in your opponent's play, they're very strong and sound strategies to use without deviation. These strategies have been field-tested in actual play and have proved to be extremely profitable. You can't really go wrong to play "by the book" in these cases.

Part Three

Considerations

17

Live Versus Online:
Live Players' Weaknesses

Many online players seem to have difficulty adjusting to the live arena. Generally, we believe that a very successful online player in high-stakes tournaments is likely a +EV player in the majority of live tournaments he chooses to enter. However, we also think that many of them aren't winning at near the rate they ought to be, due to a failure to modify their game to live conditions.

When referring to live players in live tournaments, let's make some assumptions:

• The villains in the hand are unknown live players or known live pros who play badly and/or have bad fundamentals.
• The villains in the hand aren't established or successful Internet players.

Those are perhaps a fairly cumbersome set of generalizations, but discussing how we'd play against other Internet pros in a live setting seems more appropriate for a book about online poker. Although there are added variables, it's a comparable situation. Table compositions vary, but in most live tournaments, you won't run into Internet players anywhere near as much as you will unknown live players. Additionally, you won't always know when a player is successful online, as no one wears a name tag in a tournament.

Also, the language in these lists might sound absolutist, but please don't think we mean that 100% of live players play like this; it's just that if you play people as unknowns instead of making at least *some* generalizations, you're throwing money away. Some of these lists will overlap.

First, some tendencies that are more standard for live players:

Early in the tournament, they call raises or limp too loosely. In $100-or-above freeze-outs online, it's becoming increasingly rare to see limping, particularly once the antes kick in. This isn't necessarily true in live tournaments, even at some of the higher buy-ins and especially at the mid-buy-ins. Additionally, many live players flat-call raises in spots that most online players either fold or re-raise.

As ElkY views it, live players can flat-call in some spots that look ludicrous for online guys and not only early in a tournament! He describes this example: "In the Deauville EPT 2010 with about 15 left, on my feature table action is 7-handed with Freddy Deeb just busting. I've been playing super tight all day, showing down jacks twice, and that's about it. Also, a big stack is sitting out in the SB and a French girl who plays quite straightforward just sat down in the big blind. I open UTG with T6o, because I think I'll win the blinds and ante very often. The French live pro calls on the button; the flop is A-T-8. I c-bet 40%, he calls, then we check down on an 8 turn and a 2 river. He had A9o. We were both 40 BB+ deep in that spot."

Live players have a weak understanding of pot odds. They may not understand when they *must* (in order to make the optimal decision) make a decision solely based on odds. It's not uncommon to watch live players fold pre-flop when getting more than 2.5-to-1, and even much higher in some instances. They might also not be aware of when the equity of a draw makes calling your bet, raise, or all-in +EV, and instead fold to protect their tournament lives.

Their open-raising standards are often too tight. Very few live players realize that they can open with a wide range from early positions and be given a huge amount of respect. Thus, many still have too-tight open-raising ranges in all positions, particularly on the cutoff and button. Even though many of them have loosened up their opening ranges in these spots over the last few years, they rarely open as wide as is optimal.

They re-steal infrequently. Some live players simply aren't capable of making a light 3-bet. Some are capable, but extremely picky about their spots. Some do it with hands with good flat-calling equity, because they don't have a plan, for example, AJ or 88.

They're highly concerned with their tournament lives. In many areas, they often only get to play one major tournament and a few medium ones throughout the year. If they might not get another opportunity at such big money for months, or even a year, players are especially cautious about busting. Additionally, a lot of the older poker literature places an inordinate amount of value on the concept of tournament life, leading those who follow outdated advice to believe that they're making correct folds.

They call raises out of position too lightly and defend their blinds too loosely. Many live players aren't aware of what a major disadvantage it is to play a hand out of position. They often believe that they can consistently outplay their opponent to compensate for the lost advantage, or they aren't aware of what a major loss the advantage of position is. Many live players believe that the discount they're getting in the blinds makes up for the fact that they're out of position and without the lead, and they don't realize what a huge percentage of the time they'll be forced to check-fold the flop.

However, it should be pointed out that there are two schools of thought about calling small pre-flop raises from the BB. Tysen's equilibrium strategy calls for a high calling frequency from the BB when getting odds of 3-to-1+. Gus Hansen also believes too much equity is lost in folding many hands from the BB and he liberally defends, with good results. The caution above about playing OOP, however, is shared by most online pros.

So what's the optimal approach? The best approach lies somewhere in between. ElkY thinks this is a spot where math alone doesn't provide the complete answer, because even though the direct odds can be great, the reverse odds of playing a hand OOP versus a good player often offset them.

We think you should play your opponent and not rely purely on odds. As Tysen said in his equilibrium analysis, you must be highly skilled in post-flop play (à la Gus Hansen) to play as many hands from the BB as his solution calls for and modulate your calling frequency against tough opponents. Against straightforward opponents, calling small raises from the BB when getting good odds and outplaying them post-flop makes sense. Against online regulars, however, all the authors think it's fraught with difficulty and is probably negative EV.

They don't understand what kinds of actions their stack size should limit them to. Plenty of live players are completely unconcerned with stack sizes as a whole, and plenty aren't aware of the concept of effective stack sizes whatsoever. They often call raises at 15-25 BB stacks with much wider ranges than an online player would.

They tend to play large draws more weakly than online players (less big semi-bluff raises, more calling). This goes back to their risk aversion and overvaluing their tournament lives. Most online players are aware that a big draw has serious equity and that combined with fold equity, raising or shoving makes aggressive play preferable. Conversely, plenty of live players are by no means happy to get their entire stack in with a draw, even if it's one with excellent equity.

They tend to bluff less, especially in terms of extended multi-street or large elaborate bluffs. The double- and triple-barrel bluffs that look so reasonable and sensible in the earlier portions of this book are often unthinkable moves to many of your opponents in a live tournament.

They don't think about ranges very well, if at all. Many live players have an idea that you can hold a number of different hands, but odds are they wouldn't call it a range (though that's changing in some locations) and they certainly aren't as calibrated as online players in anticipating what your range could be. Live players don't sit around using software like Pokerstove and Pokertracker, and their perception of ranges is much more likely to be based on how they think they themselves would behave, or how their fellow live players would behave, than having legitimate insight into how online players function.

If they're capable of adjusting their play, they often react to a

loose-aggressive style too quickly. The vast majority of online players at high-stakes tournaments are capable of making adjustments and often do so by mildly or moderately tightening up their ranges. However, a number of live players will attempt to adjust too hard, too fast, particularly if you create an aggressive history with them.

They don't make thin value bets very often. The thin value bet is a fairly complex play, since it requires a combination of reading hands, understanding ranges, and anticipating your opponents' perception of your betting frequencies. Many live players have fairly polarized betting ranges and are incapable of the thin value bet, often opting to check and evaluate instead. They're also afraid of getting check-raised on the river if they value bet thinly.

They slow-play much more than they do online. Because online players are used to people attempting bluff raises, floats, and light call downs, they often fast-play their big hands, particularly when it helps balance their range with bluffs. This isn't the case live, where many players are completely unaware that they should balance their ranges or protect certain hands from draw possibilities. If a player has only been calling, then all of a sudden makes a monster check-raise on the turn or river, you can usually feel pretty confident about folding all but your strongest hands.

They mostly read all-ins as strong, or at least stronger than nominal bets, especially early in a tournament. As mentioned earlier, live players often overvalue their tournament lives, and as a result they treat the all-in bet extremely seriously, particularly during the early stages of the tournament. The best way to get value from them in the early stages is to use nominal bets. Even if you think your strategy may be transparent, remember that they're not as aware of ranges as online players.

They may seem highly inconsistent. That is, you'll see some players play very weak-tight for a long time, then suddenly do something loose and reckless. This can sometimes be the result of having a very limited sample size against them (one hour is only worth about 30 hands) or the result of a fast-changing metagame. Some players open up in this way because they've seen something about you (be it in your play or physicality) that they interpret as a key indicator that they should make a move.

They bet and raise for information and don't necessarily have a clear motivation of value bet/bluff behind their actions. Earlier in the book, we preached that you must have a plan for your actions. Most online players are used to working with a limited amount of time, especially those who play multiple tables, so they normally know what they'll do against the majority of potential variables in the hand. However, many live players still make raises for information, unaware that they're potentially taking a hand with excellent showdown value and turning it into a bluff against your range. If you can identify the players who do this, you can re-raise them off their hands until they realize what you're doing.

ElkY gave an excellent example earlier in the book when he re-raised AJ on a board of K-x-x against an opponent he knew liked to slow-play and would likely raise for information with top-pair-type hands. Those opponents are also the perfect ones to 4-bet pre-flop, because a lot of their 3-bets are for info with hands such as 99 or TT. They know have to be way ahead of your range, but they'll never be ready to play for stacks with hands such as these, especially if you're deep.

They may aggressively commit a large percentage of their stack, yet fold to more aggression. This is a slightly redundant point about not being aware of pot odds, yet there are slight alterations. For example, a live player may attempt a bet or bluff that commits the majority of his stack, but folds to further aggression, even when you're almost certain that your bet will get called. If a live player bets half his remaining stack on the river, although he normally wouldn't fold, don't think he's nearly as committed to that pot as his online counterpart.

Here's an example from ElkY at Bellagio Festa Al Lago: "I start the hand with 500k at 3k/6k. Jennifer Tilly covers. She opens middle position for 15k and I call from the cutoff with A♥T♥; the big blind calls also.

"The flop is 8-7-3 with two hearts. She c-bets 30k; I call. The turn is K♥, making me the nuts. She checks. I bet 88k. She makes it 250k, a *huge* check/raise. I probably make a mistake by moving all-in at that time, because I don't expect her to ever be bluffing in that spot, nor folding a real hand, getting 4-to-1 on the call. To my great surprise, she eventually folds!"

They perceive a pre-flop 3-bet range to be much tighter than it normally is, unless you are 3-betting very often. At this point, almost everyone live is aware of regular light 3-betting. However, they often treat the first couple of 3-bets with an enormous amount of respect, and likely won't play back until you've displayed an extremely aggressive image or had to table a weak holding after making a pre-flop 3-bet. They're also apt to perceive your 3-bet shoving range to be much tighter than it actually is, and will sometimes make folds that are incomprehensible to an online player.

They may search for tells or visual cues of intent. Online players aren't used to concealing their thoughts and emotions while they play, and even though almost all of them are smart enough to be self-aware at the table, they aren't necessarily practiced at making their motions, actions, and verbal declarations entirely devoid of tells or clues. Experienced live players often put heavy emphasis on the importance of tells, and if they pick something up on you, they'll give it considerable credence in their decision making.

They make decisions based on specific reads. As we mentioned earlier, live players don't often think about ranges and seem to prefer to put people on a specific holding or two. The idea of making an impressive soul read is quite appealing to them, and they might hero call or hero fold to you based entirely on putting you on a single holding.

They won't isolate limpers in position nearly as often as they should or could. In fact, many live players are incapable of isolating limpers and vastly prefer to limp behind. Some aren't aware of the play as a whole, and those who are rarely call it "isolating"; they'd probably label it "stealing."

They squeeze at a much lower frequency. Many are incapable of this, although Dan Harrington's books have made many players increasingly aware of this tricky play. Online, the squeeze is all but dead, because players now frequently flat-call with big pairs or move in over the top of your squeeze with a wide range, but plenty of opportunities for it still exist in the live arena. The effectiveness and credibility of squeeze bets online have dramatically decreased over the last 18 months; they've been overused and discussed at length on training sites and poker forums. The current trend seems to be the squeeze trap, which we discuss at length in mid-stakes play.

There's basically no such thing as a pre-flop 4-bet all-in as a bluff in their arsenal. This play simply hasn't developed in the repertoire of the majority of live players yet. To them, it seems like an enormous risk for a relatively small gain, particularly if it's a re-raise that puts their tournament life at risk.

Their shoving ranges with a short stack tend to be much tighter than online. Open shoving 14-20 BB stacks has become all the rage online recently, and it's something that live players will almost never do, particularly above 15 BB. They often raise-fold instead, opening themselves up to frequent re-stealing.

Again, these are some massive generalizations, but when devoid of a specific read, they're often useful.

Live-Tournament Adjustments for Online Players

Now let's elaborate on specific adjustments that online players can make to take advantage of the differences in play that we've identified in the previous list.

Online players should call down tighter. Live villains are less likely to bluff, especially in multi-way pots. You can feel confident giving villains more credit than you're used to online. Take spots that seem like marginal/close call downs and weight them toward folds. The kinds of bluffs you should call down are the more obvious ones in pot-controlled situations when a draw misses and you've checked on the turn. Live players often make the mistake of betting rivers in those spots, because they're desperate to win the pot and aren't anticipating you pot controlling the turn so much. This is a thought that ElkY echoes in the mid-stage-play section. When you check for pot control on the turn or a flop that has a notable draw, then that draw misses, consider calling down the villain's bet more often than you would online, especially if he's shown any ability to bluff. Live players don't expect you to read their hands well. As far as making hero calls, you need a much stronger suspicion that your opponent is bluffing to make big calls than you do online; they just aren't bluffing as frequently as online players.

You should call in position a bit looser pre-flop, when stack appropriate. Since many players play a bit more weakly and straight-forward post-flop, as well as slow-play and give you more free cards, you can call a bit lighter than normal in position, especially with the decreased chance of being squeezed (though obviously you need to be aware of who's behind you). Also, calling a looser range is especially effective, since they often won't give you credit for many hands in your range if you haven't established that kind of loose image yet, and they tend to call too many value bets on the river, assuming it doesn't get to the all-in stage. Again, your opponents don't read hands as well as you're used to, so if you hit the type of hand that most online players expect to be in your range, live players will give you credit for it less often and pay you off accordingly.

You should value bet nominal amounts in favor of all-in when appropriate. If the all-in gets treated seriously and players aren't often aware of stack-size considerations, you're missing value by moving all-in in spots where you could make a clear value bet and get a call much of the time. If you think the player is unlikely to adjust to this and start shoving over your bets as an all-in bluff (unlikely with most live players), then betting for value intending to fold to a shove might be the best alternative.

Obviously, if all-in on the river is only a half-pot bet, you should never bet the nominal amount. Because live players are overly concerned with their tournament lives, you can make a bet for most of their stack that technically leaves them alive, but extracts value more frequently than the all-in would. Conversely, bluffs that put your opponent all-in should be used more than online, because most live players won't risk their tournament life without a very strong hand.

They can use plays that have become somewhat outdated online. These plays include things such as the go-n-go and the squeeze. Live players are expecting these less, and few put in enough volume to become overly familiar with these plays. The squeeze is especially effective, since many live players simply flat-call open raises too wide (as well as flat-call re-raises too wide), giving you the opportunity to bluff them out on the flop as well.

Limp more, especially behind other limpers. This is an issue where the opinions of the authors diverge somewhat. It's extremely table-dependent and should only be done very early on, if at all. In terms of stack sizes, you should have enough implied odds to call a raise from an isolater in position (Tony Dunst knows of two players whose game he really respects, Alan Sass and William Thorsson, who do a fair bit of open limping with considerable success). The concept is to limp behind limpers loosely, since it's less likely to get isolated and people play pretty poorly in limped pots. You can get away with open-limping more often, since you'll get isolated less frequently and raise sizes might be too small to correctly price you out of seeing a flop.

Tony and Tysen wouldn't go crazy with this, but they think you should open limp some small pairs and suited connectors with which you'll easily have pot odds if there's a raise. This can be quite profitable on passive tables.

ElkY and Lee think it should be done more when isolating doesn't work well and you don't have such strong hands, yet still have decent flopping value. If, when you try to isolate, three or four players call your raises each time because they have no clue about position or hand strength, it'll be hard to take down the pot on the flop. In these spots with hands that have good flopping value, such as 33 or 98o, limping in after only one or two players is fine.

You should increase your 3-bet frequency with antes. Increase your frequency even more so than you do online. But there's a catch: You can increase your 3-betting frequency to a point, but finding the line is very important, since eventually live players might just smooth-call you much wider.

Tony was talking to a successful Australian live player, David Saab, who called this the "vindictiveness factor." Tony thought that was a good term, since basically, you can pummel your table with re-raises for only so long until suddenly they just kind of snap and start spite-calling you down with a very wide range. To reduce the vindictiveness factor, consider being friendly and chatty with your table, complimenting people on the way they play a hand (even if you don't mean it), and whatever else to get people to shy away from fighting back.

You should be much more aggressive on the bubble on most tables. Unless your table is packed with pros who don't care about cashing, we think you can go all out on a live-cash and final-table bubble much more than you can online. People normally play for multiple days to reach these points and going out at that stage is a pretty gross feeling for most (even plenty of online players, when you consider the time investment involved). We think you should be willing to break rules in terms of stack sizes needed to 3-bet or open raise (to a reasonable degree). You should consider putting people all-in with an almost reckless abandon at certain tables and times. Against other deep stacks, you should flat-call pre-flop when a 3-bet isn't appropriate and aim to make their lives miserable post-flop by getting tricky.

When you have a tight image, consider making bigger or more elaborate bluffs. Whether they're multiple-street or 3- and 4-bet moves, live players will make some surprisingly tight folds if your image isn't particularly loose. Many talented online players rarely bother with creative or multi-street bluffs, and while we certainly don't think you should go crazy with them, it's more possible to make these work live than online. However, make sure not to out-think yourself, since some players have a skewed perception of what the nuts are. Some still stack off with KQ on a K-7-5 flop for 200 BB, so be sure not to bluff those types. ElkY discusses this type of aggression line at length in the section on early-stage play.

Consider the inverse of the "Gigabet Dilemma." The theory behind the Gigabet Dilemma is that there are occasional spots in tournaments where it's acceptable to take a -EV situation in order to open up the potential for future +EV situations. You might be in a position to completely dominate a table if you get enough chips to do so, or take advantage of especially bad players, but don't have those options available to you unless somehow you gain additional chips. This is one reason people often justify taking a big risk with an edge early in the tournament, even when the edge is small. The question is, though, should we be thinking about the inverse of this and avoiding high-variance spots early?

ElkY elaborates on the idea. "In some situations, I believe it's OK to give up on slightly +EV spots if you're controlling the table really well and you think you have a big edge. A good example is the big fold I made with TT at the EPT Deauville, as referenced in the section on big folds.

"Here's another quick example. At the WSOP Main Event, I probably won't take a big coin flip early on with QQ against AK, because I think I have a good shot at building a stack throughout the tournament without having to gamble quite so fast. The structure is deep and long, so I believe I'll be able to exploit my opponents' mistakes over time. Also, in general, if I'm facing amateur players, I don't mind passing on some +EV spots early on, because I like to take the time to study and analyze my opponents. The more time I spend at the table, the more I can identify and exploit their weaknesses. Of course, the same is hardly true of an online tournament where the average stack is 30 BB!

"In deep tournaments, the decision to pass on +EV hands also depends on how strong your table is. For instance, at the NAPT 2010 Hi-Roller Shootout in Las Vegas, I was at a really tough table, with Scott Seiver, Brian Rast, Chau Giang, Esfandiari, Mizzi, and Barry Greenstein. At such a table, the opposition is so strong that you know you won't be able to exploit mistakes and weaknesses as much as you would against amateur players. Therefore, you probably want to take the +EV situation there.

"Of course, it's always nice to have a massive stack and use it to control your table. However, like I explained earlier, I also believe in thresholds regarding stack sizes. For instance, let's say the average is 40 BB. You have 50 BB, and you're facing a decision to flip a coin for a 25-BB pot. You need to weigh the pros and cons of the two outcomes, because in one of them, you'd be left with only 25 BB and a lot of work to do, whereas having 75 BB may not be so different than 50 BB after all, since you should control your table in both cases.

"Unfortunately, you can never see your opponents' cards before the play. Therefore, you need to consider all the above parameters in order to make the best decision possible. In some instances, however, I never pass on +EV play, such as in the example of the EPT Warsaw 2009.

"The villain is Kevin McPhee, eventual winner of EPT Berlin 2010. He has 35 BB in the hijack; I've got 50 BB in the SB. The villain opens for 2.5 BB with 66. I look at AK and I 3-bet to 6.5 BB. He re-shoves and I instantly call.

"Despite the fact that many live tournament players consider AK a 'drawing hand,' I never fold it in that spot. Of course, I'm often on a coin flip. However, I also often dominate my opponent's AQ, AJ, KQ, all definitely in his 3-bet shoving range."

Call short-stack and 3-bet all-ins tighter until the player proves he's capable of moving in light. Live-tournament players don't seem to shove very light with a short stack, even with less than 10 BB and high antes. It's hard to say how tight you should go, and obviously the villain in the hand is the pertinent detail here, but you should definitely tighten up in this spot. Again, people seem to be overly concerned with their tournament life, and even some recognizable pros have seriously misguided ideas about shoving ranges, so consider making some folds that would be unheard of online against live players who haven't been moving in much. This concept obviously carries over to when a player moves all-in over the top of you and, if anything, should be applied even more thoroughly. Some people have learned about pre-flop all-in ranges, but fewer know the correct ranges to move-in over the top of a raise, which they also feel is a riskier play, because an opponent has already shown aggression and intent on staying in the hand.

Be really image conscious. Since you're only getting around 30 hands an hour in a live tournament, everyone can (if they want and bother to) watch most hands pretty attentively. People seem a bit less observant in the early stages than mid/late stages where every pot is so important, but they often sit around talking about the way other people at the table play, and if you play as loose/aggressive as most of us do (especially compared to them), they eventually start calling you a lot wider, even if their calls are very bad in relation to their stack or your range. The difficulties of image and metagame in live poker are hard to quantify for someone with a predominately online background, but adjusting to this factor is really important in dominating the live scene. You can often feel what kind of tipping point your table is on based on table talk, people's physical reactions to your raises, and how often they start calling and 3-betting you.

You should do more obvious things and take more obvious lines to accomplish what you want. In the simplest of terms, we think that your ranges don't need to be anywhere near as balanced live as they are online. You can take betting lines that anyone capable of doing a moment of logical thinking would realize the obvious about what you're representing, yet they continue to work time after time, because many live players stop their thought process at, "What am I holding and how many chips out of my stack is it to call?"

For example, many people know that online, if they get check-min-raised on the turn in a large pot, their opponent is rarely bluffing, because they're being laid excellent odds and will be facing a large river bet. However, this same line still works consistently in some live scenarios, because people are too preoccupied with their own holdings. Although we discuss this concept elsewhere, it's worth reiterating here that *balancing betting lines is much less important live than online.* Beside the fact that people won't realize what your line means, a lot of situations in live tournaments don't come around that often with similar players, positions, and stacks.

Online tournaments seem to have a smaller community (perhaps due to multi-tabling) and you find yourself in some spots versus thinking players a lot more often, so it's important to keep your ranges balanced as to not be exploitable. However, live tournaments are now so big that the odds of facing the same players in similar spots are quite small. Even if you wind up facing some of them again, playing the first few levels with some guy on your left, or playing on the bubble when he's chip leader on your right, or making the final table when you're both short are completely different situations. There's absolutely no point in mixing your ranges in these spots, since you won't be giving up any EV.

You should learn to slow down and be more patient. Many online players are used to the constant stimulation of playing anything between four and 24 tables at any given time. They play literally hundreds if not thousands of hands an hour, which can make the roughly 30 an hour you'll get at a live table excruciatingly boring. To make a successful transition, you need to slow down in two different regards. First, slow down your thought process and try not to do things so quickly, since a different kind of information is available to you at the table and your expectations for ranges and patterns need to be thoroughly adjusted and contemplated. Second, learn to tame your aggression at certain junctures. Online aggressors often become so used to playing a 20- to 30-BB stack that they forget they have much more time to pick their spots live when working with deeper stacks.

Lack of patience and failure to adjust to deep stacks are probably the main reasons why some online players aren't seeing the same success live; most of the online tournaments play with an average stack much smaller than live ones, and it takes longer to adapt to deeper stacks. It's much harder to play live tournaments, because they're so time-consuming.

Keep constant track of the chip stacks on the table. Many online players give the table a once over, but aren't particularly worried about stacks; they anticipate asking someone what theirs is when they get in a hand with them. The problem here is that when you ask your opponent for a stack count, he may deceive you, miscount, or get a small yet useful insight into your thought process (namely, that you're smart enough to care about details like that). Online players are used to having the stack sizes constantly displayed for them and even though almost all of them recognize the importance of knowing the amount, many still fail to carry that focus with them over to the live arena.

Stop talking about your thought process at the table. For some reason, many online players feel the necessity to demonstrate at the table just how smart and knowledgeable about poker they are. Tony generally talks more than most players at the table and he's chatted about strategy before, but he doesn't go out of his way to comment on other people's play, offer advice on what they should have done, or give any unnecessary insight into the way he thinks about how poker should be played. ElkY, Lee, and Tysen rarely talk at all!

At the table, completely drop the habit of criticizing people's play. It's not only rude and socially inappropriate, but you may end up causing your opponent to up his aggression against you out of spite. Instead, try to become friends with everyone on the table, which you'll often find decreases aggression and deception in their play. If someone asks for your thoughts on the hand, we recommend giving a polite but bland reply that doesn't give anything away. A simple line such as, "You made a good fold," will do. To accomplish your goals, it's better to be complimentary than hostile. ElkY agrees with this approach about 95% of the time, but sometimes he spots players who look way too emotional, and if he can tilt them by showing them a bluff in some spots where they show him that they made a ridiculous fold, it can be worth it.

Stop anticipating that people will play push or fold against their 3-bets. The online-tournament game has evolved in such a way that the majority of 3-bets are met with either an all-in or a fold. The stacks are often too shallow to smooth-call with most hands and the majority of profitable players are aware of this. However, live players still often flat-call 3-bets in incorrect spots, which online players are used to playing as push or fold. As a result, be aware that when you 3-bet, you'll be facing more post-flop action than you're used to. This means that when you do 3-bet light, make sure that if your opponent is the type to flat-call, you're 3-betting with hands that have the potential to flop well, so you can continue with your aggression and still have equity in the hand.

Work on not being distracted, losing focus, or getting bored. This is easier said than done, of course. As previously mentioned, online players simply aren't used to the pace of live events, particularly when they first make the transition. The end result is often a lot of boredom or getting distracted by anything that's put in front of them. Nothing forces you to pay close attention and we all need a break from time to time. But when you mentally check out from the table, you're costing yourself money in the long run.

If you know that boredom is a problem, bringing an iPod isn't a bad idea. Even though you'll miss some value in what people say, if the music helps keep you focused on the action, it's almost certainly a +EV decision. Simple and obvious tips include making sure you log enough sleep before you play, getting even a small amount of exercise before you play to get your blood flowing, and having a coffee or energy drink if need be. It's also not a bad idea to chat with people at your table, since this helps prevent boredom and gives you insight into their thinking level, as well as potentially getting them to tone down aggression against you.

Be extremely selective about the situations you 4-bet light. Online players are used to being 3-bet quite often. However, as previously mentioned, many live players rarely 3-bet light, or at least as frequently as their online counterparts. As a result, greatly cut down the times you attempt to 4-bet light and make sure you have sound reasoning and a developed read if and when you decide to make that risky play.

Online-Tournament Adjustments for Live Players

Now let's take a look at the other side of the coin and see how live players should adjust when making the transition to online tournaments.

Tighten your calling ranges for open raises and re-raises. Online tournaments are played predominately as a raise-or-fold style of poker and for the most part, if you regularly flat-call raises or re-raise, you're making a serious mistake, especially considering that people behind you with smaller stacks have a wider shoving range over the top of your flat. Additionally, your opponents play better post-flop, meaning the implied odds of calling with your hands are decreased.

Learn to use tools like *Pokertracker* and *Hold 'em Poker Manager*. These tools track not only your play, but also the play of everyone else at the table. You can use them to review your own play and locate your leaks, or analyze your opponents' play and get a sense of their style. These programs actually overlay your opponents' statistics on the tables for you, so at any given time you can know at what rate your opponents have been open-raising, seeing the flop, re-raising, and many other options.

Widen your calling range against pre-flop all-ins. Live players are used to their opponents moving in with a much tighter range than happens online. Just how wide you should adjust is difficult to describe, but live players generally call with 5% to 10% less of their range than they should for an online scenario. Use a program like *Pokerstove* to discover which hands you should fit into your calling range.

Learn to multi-task. At the beginning of your online poker career, you will probably be playing only one table, which is fine. However, the money to be made online (if you reach the point where you are a winning player) is through playing many tables at once. Serious tournament grinders will play up to 20 tables at a time, and the majority are usually playing at least 10 during the peak hours of their session. This will cause you to learn a sort of auto-pilot form of play early in your tournaments, then adjust more and more based on reads as the tournaments you go deep in continue.

Learn to 4-bet light. The light 4-bet simply isn't in the arsenal of most live players, but it's something you need online. If players sense that you fold to too many 3-bets, they'll pound you with them. Even players unaware of your tendencies and statistics will 3-bet you to a much higher degree than you're used to, so you need to learn the effective spots to make that move.

Lower your open-raise and 3-bet sizes. Most live players open in the full 3X area, sometimes a bit smaller. Most online players open somewhere between 2X and 2.5X these days. Three-bet sizes have come down online as well. Much less flat-calling goes on, so if you're to get folds or 3-bets, you might as well risk fewer chips finding out.

Finally, begin posting strategy on poker forums. A huge wealth of information about poker is available for free on the Internet and poker forums like twoplustwo.com are an excellent source. The attitude and vernacular used can be somewhat intimidating at the start, but if you plow through and become a regular poster, you'll find that you get excellent advice from some very experienced players. These forums are on the front line of the evolution of tournament poker and the players who frequent them are generally winners or aspiring winners.

Stop the Presses:
The Latest in Online Poker Trends

Here are the latest developments in online poker trends, compiled just before this book was sent to press!

Opening to 2X BB has become the new "standard" pre-flop raise at all stages of the tournament, replacing the old standard of 3X BB.

Minimum re-raises IP for the amount of the BB are becoming increasingly more common with a wide range of hands. This allows the re-raiser to take control of the hand post-flop. The wide range also leads to opportunities when done with a big pair. Check out this hand from a recent online tournament:

Blinds are 60/120. Hijack raises to 240 off a stack of 5,200; cutoff calls off a stack of 4,800; button 3-bets to 360 off a stack of 7,800. Big blind 4-bet squeezes to 850 off a stack of 6,900; hijack & cutoff fold, and button calls.

Flop: Q♥-5♠-3♦
BB bets 1,200; button calls
Turn: 3♥
BB bets 1,800; button calls
River: 8♠
BB all in; button calls
BB has AQ; button has KK.

Shoving pre-flop with 20 BB stacks in late position is being done more frequently. This is in response to the trend for opponents in the blinds to 3-bet all-in over a standard raise.

Note that the above changes are trends that we see currently and are not necessarily our recommendations. The reason for most of these changes revolves around small-ball evolutions to take control of hands in position while maintaining control of pot size, and providing the raiser with more fluidity. The effective 20 BB pushes later in the tournament result directly from the frequency of getting re-raised all-in by the blinds after a standard late-position raise and being forced to make a tough decision. By pushing with 20 BB, your opponent is forced to guess the strength of your hand. Of course, this does increase variance.

How do the authors think you should respond to these trends? Your response should be player dependent. For example, if you are playing with an effective stack of 20 BB with aggressive players in the blinds with a high frequency of 3-betting, you can either push with a 20-BB stack pre-flop or tighten up your 2-bet range and be prepared to call an all-in 3-bet.

In response to the trend of min-raising more frequently pre-flop, 3-betting IP with a fairly wide range may be effective. Against stronger players capable of 4-betting light, tighten your 3-bet range, but call more often IP with hands with good flop value.

Appendix I

Tells

NOTE: This bonus chapter was written by Steven Van Aperen, a.k.a the "Human Lie Detector," with comments by Lee Nelson.

Cunning is the art of concealing our own defects,
and discovering the weaknesses of others.

—William Hazlitt

In 1996, I was a police officer with the Victoria Police, having served a total of 14 years in both the Victoria and South Australian police departments in Australia. That year, I was fortunate to visit the Behavioral Sciences Unit at the FBI academy in Quantico, Virginia, where I was struck by the effort spent on teaching agents effective interviewing and observation techniques. I'd conducted thousands of criminal interviews over the years, but quickly realized that I'd received little formal training in how to accurately analyze body language and detect deception.

I was constantly amazed that some detectives I worked with were masterful at eliciting information, picking off liars, and making accurate observations, whereas others were able to obtain very little information at all. I wanted to be an expert at reading body language and detecting deception. Human behavior and understanding what motivates people continue to fascinate me to this day.

I now speak to dozens of agencies throughout the world, teaching police, customs and military personnel, interviewers, investigators, intelligence agencies, and government departments how to detect deception, analyze behavior, and read body language. Although my skills and services were initially limited to the criminal-investigation world, I'm now consulted by the media, large corporations, and police departments to look for deception by analyzing body language and spoken language. Over the years, I've been referred to by the media as the "Human Lie Detector," the "Truth Doctor," and the "Truth Sleuth"—tags I'm not terribly fond of, but they do accurately describe what I do.

My foray into the world of poker is a recent phenomenon. I was approached by the 2005 World Series of Poker Champion Joe Hachem and the 2006 Aussie Millions Main Event Champion Lee "Final Table" Nelson to assist in a reality-television program called "The Poker Star," which attracted a staggering 18,000 contestants, hoping to take part in a series looking for the next Australian poker champion. In my role, I was asked to interview and analyze the "tells" that each of the final 11 contestants exhibited during several interviews that I conducted. During the filming of this program, I realized that good poker players need skills—not only in bluffing, but also in reading other players' tells.

I immediately saw the similarities between the suspected criminals I'd analyzed and the players. Criminals bluff and lie to cover their past indiscretions, whereas poker players bluff their opponents to be financially rewarded. Having watched several poker tournaments on television, I was amazed at how much information many of the professional players were giving away to their opponents. If the professionals were giving away information unwittingly through their body language, I could only imagine what amateurs players were giving away at the tables!

The Basics of Lying and Bluffing

Often we have an innate gut feeling that we're being lied to. We rely on our instincts and perceptions based on our observations. However, just as often, we listen to what people are saying, but don't pay close attention to what people are doing while they're talking. People may lie with words, but their body language often betrays the spoken word. And what people *don't* say is often more important than what they *do*.

Take former President Bill Clinton's response when giving evidence relating to a sexual tryst with a young intern named Monica Lewinski:

"As you know, in a deposition in January," he stated, "I was asked questions about my relationship with Monica Lewinsky. While my answers were legally accurate, *I did not volunteer information.*"

Here we can see the selective editing process that comes into play. People often tell you what they want you to know. Even by Clinton's own admission, he didn't volunteer information. By omitting crucial information, he minimized the risk of being caught in a lie. As you well know, deceptive people often hedge, omit crucial facts, feign forgetfulness, and pretend ignorance. Fortunately, they also engage in body language at a subconscious level. *Having the skills to read body language in any poker game is not only essential, it can also be financially rewarding.* Very rewarding.

I'm often asked when speaking at various functions, "How do you spot a liar or someone who is bluffing?" The answer lies in watching for various behaviors and understanding how human beings communicate with one another. Often, we listen to the person conveying the story and try to find fault with the *content* of the story. Holistically, we need to be aware of much more than the words spoken by a poker player or deceiver. We need to pay attention to the process of communication itself. We need to analyze content, structure, and delivery. In addition, we need to look for conflict or contradiction between what a person is saying and what his or her body language is telling us. We also need to scrutinize verbal, non-verbal, and paralinguistic styles of delivery.

In reality, it's very difficult for the average person to hide his emotions and control his involuntary responses. For every lie a person tells us, he's required to invent two or three further lies to protect himself from the first lie. Thus, the deceptive person has to think,

"What have I said previously that could contradict me now?"

Neurologically, a truthful person relies on memory to recall smells, conversations, events, times, dates, places, names, feelings, and emotions, whereas a deceptive person has to fabricate these factors when bluffing or lying. A good poker player can fabricate and embellish his behavior to convince his opponents that he has an exceptional hand even when he may not. This is one of the characteristics that helps differentiate a good player from a chump. *A top player is able to read his opponent's behavior, while disguising his own tells.*

A good poker player with a bad hand needs to convince his opponents that he has the winning hand when he may have only a pair of 2s. This requires a combination of effective technical skills, confidence, and an understanding of body language. It is here that we often see changes in language, tenses, the use of pronouns, body language, and micro-expressions associated with the fear of being caught during a bluff. Often we don't even look for these changes, much less pay attention to them! This is especially true of online players making the transition to live tournaments.

There is no single telltale sign that indicates bluffing, but there are often several clues.

Looking for clusters of signals that contradict what a person is saying is a great start. For example, a flush card comes, my opponent moves all-in, and I ask, "Did you really make a flush?" If he says, "Yep," while shaking his head as if to say no, breaking eye contact, sitting back in the chair with his arms crossed tightly against his chest, changing his frontal alignment, shuffling in the chair and scratching his

Lee's comment: It's critical to observe players when you're not involved in a hand. Match their actions and verbal cues with their betting patterns and the cards they show down, and try to identify any consistent pattern of behavior. Once identified, these can sometimes be as consistent as having an opponent turn over his hole cards!

eye, ear, or nose, and covering his mouth with his hand or a finger, then we clearly have conflict and contradiction between what he's saying and what his body language is conveying. The combination of several of these actions is indicative of concealment and stress.

Words alone and how a person responds to a question can sometimes either exonerate the innocent or implicate the guilty. One recent high-profile case reported widely throughout Australia related to the disappearance of Anna Kemp, 37, who was five months pregnant with her second child, and her 19-month-old daughter Gracie Sharp. Anna's husband, John Myles Sharpe, reported their disappearance to police and subsequently took part in a number of media interviews. In one interview, the visibly distressed Sharpe, when asked if had killed his wife and daughter, replied, "No, I haven't harmed my wife or my daughter. I haven't harmed either of them."

On closer analysis we can see that John Sharpe didn't answer the question. In fact, he avoided the question altogether. The question was clear and unambiguous. He was asked if he had *killed* his wife and daughter, not whether he had *harmed* them. During a subsequent police interview, John Sharpe admitted to police that he killed his wife and daughter. Although this represents an extreme case of deception, the signs and signals are always present; we simply have to look for them and identify them.

To be a champion, you need to be an analyst of human behavior, rather than just a poker player. Anyone can learn the rules of Texas hold 'em, but money-making skills in live poker can be significantly enhanced by reading your opponent,

---

Lee's comment: Steve has an uncanny talent for reading signs and signals, both verbal and non-verbal. I think it would be hard to deceive him. If you're acting, he'll see through it. More significantly, he'll also pick up on any involuntary signals you give off that might reveal the strength or weakness of your hand.

while controlling and manipulating your own behavior. I can often tell when you have a great hand just by the way you react to your cards, how you hold them, how you sit in your chair, and what you do with your hands, and that's even before you start talking! Although I've written books on the subject of reading body language and detecting deception, this chapter provides you with a condensed version of what to look for.

Facial Expressions

In his 1872 book, *The Expression of the Emotions in Man and Animals*, Charles Darwin argued that all mammals show emotion reliably in their faces. Much research has been done since Darwin's book, but one thing is certain: *Our body language often shows our real emotions even when we try to conceal our feelings!* These displays can happen very quickly and are difficult for some people to identify, but they *are* visible and present; you just have to look for them and know what you're seeing.

Professor Paul Ekman, an emeritus psychology professor at the University of California Medical School in San Francisco, is an expert on facial expressions. He's been described as being the most astute analyst of human emotions since Charles Darwin. In fact, the character Dr. Carl Lightman in the television series "Lie to Me" was based on research by Prof. Paul Ekman.

Paul Ekman has spent much of the past 30 years looking very closely at people's faces and he identified a crucial scientific breakthrough: *Facial expressions aren't culturally specific behaviors; they're universal products of evolution.*

For seven years Ekman worked tirelessly with fellow psychologist Wallace Firesen pinpointing every single twitch, scowl, frown, and smile—in short, the full range of facial expressions—a person's face could perform by learning all there was to know about the anatomy of our most visible feature. The pair poured through medical textbooks and journals and finally identified each and every one of the face's 43 distinct muscular movements, which they called "action units." The pair also discovered almost 90 individual muscles in the face, with as many as five muscles combining at one time to produce an expression, meaning that, astonishingly, a person's face is capable of well over 10,000 visible facial configurations, around 3,000 of which give a very clear pointer to the truth of what somebody is saying or feeling.

As important as all of this was, Ekman discovered something even more stunning about the human face. In reviewing his videotapes of the expressions and observing videotaped interviews with a range of honest, calm, deceitful, and even angry individuals, Ekman found that whenever a person experiences a basic emotion, a corresponding message is automatically sent to the muscles of the face. This message-sending system is involuntary, and while we can attempt to use our voluntary muscular system to try to suppress it or hide it from view—for example, we fake a smile, even though we might be feeling miserable—a small part of that suppressed emotion leaks out. Ekman calls these telltale emotional signals "micro-expressions" and to the well-trained eye, they're dynamite when it comes to playing poker.

Ekman's classification of the range of facial expressions has meant that a once-seemingly innocent face can now be looked at more closely and minutely, as if under a microscope. A furrowing of the brow, a down-turned lip, a well-hidden smirk, even a slightly raised eyebrow can all give the game away. His research and its findings have brought a whole new meaning to "taking things at face value." There's more to the face than meets the eye.

> **Lee's comment:**
> Although people have differing inherent aptitudes for reading micro-expressions, we can all improve our recognition with practice. Professor Ekman has some DVDs available that can help train you to read them.

Body Language

Not only do micro-expressions betray a person's spoken word, but so do a person's body language. *Body language is the non-verbal component of communication.* It's an outward reflection of a person's emotional condition. Put another way, body language is an unconscious outward reflection of inner feeling. Recognizing what body language signals mean and correctly interpreting them will give any player a distinct advantage over his or her opponents.

Although it's impossible in one chapter to cover every indicator of body language, I can cover the most obvious and crucial tells to look for at the table.

Benchmarking a Player's Baseline Behaviors

To competently read and understand body language with a high degree of accuracy, a good poker player first and foremost needs to be a good observer. Some of the best poker players aren't just proficient at the technical skills of the game, but are astute analysts of human behavior.

Often people aren't very observant. Research conducted at Harvard University found that women are far more alert to body language cues and signals than men are. To illustrate this point, they showed short films of a man and woman communicating with the sound turned off. The participants were asked to decode what was happening by reading the couple's expressions. The research showed that women read the situation accurately 87% of the time, while the men scored only 42% accuracy.

Furthermore, thanks to Magnetic Resonance Imaging (MRI), we know that women have a far greater capacity for evaluating people than men. Women use 14 to 16 areas of the brain when evaluating, compared to men who use four to six areas. The result of this research showed that those who rely on hard visual face-to-face evidence about the behavior of another person are likely to make more accurate judgments about that person than someone who relies solely on a gut feeling or instinct.

This being the case, it's imperative that your observational skills are finely tuned right from the beginning, and I'm not talking about when you first take your seat at the table. You need to make specific and relevant observations about your fellow poker players right from the first meeting. Indicators of which to be aware include confidence levels and manner of speech. Do they stutter, display nervous behaviors, such as picking imaginary lint off their sleeve, play with or manipulate their jewelry, look down when communicating, talk into their hand, or avoid eye contact? Are they loud and obnoxious in an attempt to attract attention to themselves by telling you how good they are or how many tournaments they've won?

When interviewing people, I often make a number of observations about their behavior from the first minute that I meet them, then look for deviations from their normative behaviors thereafter. Quite simply, if I don't take the time to create a baseline, I won't have anything to compare any changes of behavior against later on. This is a crucial point. *If you don't benchmark a player's behavior, you have nothing to compare it to later on.*

From the start, I observe how a person introduces himself to me and others around him. When he shakes my hand, is he confident, aggressive, direct, or shy? Does he lack confidence or avert his gaze when talking to me? Is the handshake firm, domineering, overpowering, or weak and loose?

I also ask questions that require them to recall a memory, then watch to see which way their eyes dart when recalling information. I might ask, "What year did you finish studying at university?" Or, "Do you remember what the registration number of your very first car was?" The reason for these types of questions is that a person has to access his memory to recall information. When this occurs, most (but not all) people look left while genuinely attempting to recall. This is when I will first benchmark a behavior, because later on, if I ask further questions and the person then starts looking to his right, he's probably fabricating or embellishing, using the side of his brain responsible for creative thinking. This is extremely useful information at the poker table.

A simple question could be, "Where are you from?" Watch the reaction and listen to the words. If he's direct and responsive and says something like, "I'm from Darlinghurst, New South Wales. I've lived there my whole life," while looking you in the eye with no facial distortions, micro-expressions, or hand-to-face gestures such as nose pulling, eye rubbing, or ear scratching, umms or ahhs, then it can be interpreted as a direct and concise response. The question hasn't been perceived as threatening and the person didn't attempt to conceal information.

Now compare that response to asking this question: "That's a big bet. Do you really like your hand that much?" and watch the reaction. Has your question become the threatening stimulus that induces a change in demeanor? Does he even answer your question? If he does,

Lee's comment: It's critical to get a baseline reading on all players, especially under normal non-stressful conditions, if possible. Deviations from the norm are what I look for. However, remember that some players are good actors and will give you false or reverse tells designed to purposely lead you to the wrong conclusion. It's important not to buy into gross acts of disappointment or uncertainty. A player may be "Hollywooding"—acting to portray an emotion that he or she doesn't feel. I'm much more likely to make a decision based on a fleeting micro-expression or inadvertent hand or mouth gesture than an elaborate poorly acted deception. Elaborate acts are usually easy to see through anyway. Be careful with observed tells from live-tournament professionals. They often mix these up as part of the metagame. It's probably best to just ignore them, unless you pick up a discernable pattern of behavior.

are the answer and facial expressions congruent? Is he looking right now rather than left? Does he seem confident or ill at ease?

Gestures of Confidence and Insecurity

Some of the following categories are unique to human beings and are displayed in many situations, not just at the poker table. Learning to recognize these non-verbal signals is paramount to success in poker.

Personal Space

Research shows that when we're interested or like something or someone, we sit up and pay attention. In fact, if we're excited, we often move closer to the person.

Take several courting gestures both men and women engage in. When a man is attracted to a woman and vice versa, they move closer to each other. Compare this to when we're threatened or approached in a hostile manner, where we tend to separate by moving back to create a protective space. Watch when a poker player really likes the cards he's dealt. You'll often notice a change in demeanor, such as sitting up, moving closer to the table, and even slightly hunching over the cards in an effort to protect the hand. Pay particular attention to what your opponent's hands are doing in this situation. Are they moving toward, touching, or counting their chips as a display of high-level confidence?

You should pay attention to every part of your opponent's body, including his feet, if possible. I know this is hard to do at a poker table. Still, over many years of interviewing, I've found that a person's feet are great indicators of confidence levels. In one sexual-assault interview I conducted, I noticed that the interviewee started, ever so slightly, to kick the edge of the table with his right foot when I was discussing his possible involvement. When I changed the subject, he stopped kicking the table, then started again when I returned to the subject. When a person makes a conscious effort to conceal information, he often experiences internal conflicts that create increased tension and anxiety, which leads to certain behaviors. Good analysts of human behavior observe when these actions are occurring. In some cases you'll see a poker player push away from the table and cross his legs at his ankles and move them beneath his seat as a sign of defensive behavior.

Lee's comment: Leaning slightly forward is usually a reliable indication of interest in playing a hand. In a WPT tournament a few years ago, Gus Hansen, who has a reputation of not liking to fold, made an unexpected big laydown. When asked about it, he said, "He leaned forward slightly and I thought I was beat, so I folded." Sometimes, pros say they "intuitively" know when a player is bluffing. In my view, this "intuition" equates to their ability to read micro-expressions.

The crossed arms indicate defensiveness. Also notice that the fingers are tightly gripping the upper arms. This is an indication of concern. This player is probably bluffing.

Be aware of when a player pushes away from the table or cards to create distance. Most players, immediately before folding, push away from the table before mucking their hand. In the image above, notice the crossed arms that reinforce the negative and defensive gesture. His legs might also be crossed at the ankles in a supporting defensive posture. It's amazing to watch how many people either push themselves away from the table or slump back into their chairs when they're unhappy with their cards, and how often players move forward when they hold good cards.

Universal Gestures

Lee's comment:

Although Steve is correct that a shoulder shrug can indicate indecisiveness, I think you need to be a bit careful in interpreting this. Especially when combined with a sigh from an amateur player, a shoulder shrug may indicate a strong hand. The player may be feigning indecisiveness. A sigh or deep exhalation accompanying this gesture is often the tipoff.

The Shoulder Shrug

The shoulder shrug is a gesture associated with doubt or lack of understanding. Watch someone when you ask him a question to which he doesn't know the answer. Invariably, he'll shrug his shoulders. Ultimately, this gesture involves three main parts: exposed hands or palms to show nothing is being concealed, hunched shoulders that protect the throat from attack, and a raised brow. The gestures of doubt can show the technical skills or lack thereof of a poker player.

Open-Hand/Clasped-Hand Gestures

When people are open and honest, they often hold one or both palms open and pointing outward, which indicates they have nothing to hide. Compare this with someone crossing his arms, sitting on his hands, or putting his hands in his pockets. The opposite of an open-hand gesture is what I call "lockdown," where a person tries to hide his uncertainty by clasping his hands tightly together, while gently stroking or rubbing his hands with a finger. This is a gesture meant to comfort or reassure himself.

Watch for self-assurance or reassuring gestures such as the thumb gently rubbing or stroking the hand. This is a subconscious behavior to alleviate concern and provide reassurance if the person is harboring doubt. This is what a mother does to reassure a child, by rubbing the child's hand or back, while offering words of encouragement.

The Smile

Studies conducted by Paul Ekman and French scientist Guillaume Duchenne de Boulogne showed a significant difference between a genuine smile and a fake smile. They found that when a person invokes a genuine smile, two sets of facial muscles, the zygomatic major and the orbicularis oculi, act together to produce the expression. Together, these muscles pull back the eyes and mouth to expose the teeth and enlarge the cheeks, while the orbicularis oculi make the eyes narrow and cause the "crow's-feet" effect around the corners of the eyes. This is considered to be a genuine and truthful smile.

Insincere people, on the other hand, smile with their mouth only, a deliberate behavior rather than a natural occurrence. This is important to understand, because the zygomatic majors are consciously controlled when a person engages in a deceptive smile.

> **Lee's comment:** This is often a reliable tell. Genuine smiling is hard to mimic when a player is under stress. When you see a relaxed smile that involves the eyes, the player is usually happy with his hand; a forced smile, on the other hand, is often associated with a bluff.

The first place to check for a genuine smile is around the eyes. A real smile involves the majority of the face (eyes, cheeks, and mouth), where a fake smile only involves the lips. This information is particularly useful at the poker table when someone is engaging in a bluff with substandard cards. He could be engaging in a fake smile to convince you that he's happy with his hand, when his eyes are telling you another story.

Arm Signals and Barrier Positions

Hiding behind a barrier is a normal response we learn at an early age to protect ourselves. Both arms folded together across the chest can be an attempt to put a barrier between yourself and someone or something you don't like. Don't confuse this gesture with being cold. Often when people are cold, they place their hands under their armpits to retain warmth.

When decoded, most variations of the crossed-arm positions mean a defensive or negative attitude.

Reinforced Arm Crossing

This is where a person has his arms crossed and fists clenched. This indicates hostility as well as defensiveness.

Arm Gripping

This is where a person's hands tightly grip his upper arms to reinforce himself. It's almost like a self-hug, a comforting and reassuring gesture.

Lee's comment:
Arms folded tightly across the chest is a tell that I frequently observe in players on a bluff. Look for this tell, especially in inexperienced players. If you're on the fence about calling or folding, lean toward calling.

Good poker players notice similar crossing gestures during a tournament. A player lacking confidence due to an average hand might cross his arms in front of him on the table itself.

Insecurity Gestures

When a human being is feeling insecure or lacks confidence, a number of subtle signals reveal the feeling or mood. One of these indicators is lack of eye contact. Confident people will look you in the eye, whereas those who lack confidence and security may look elsewhere. You should pay attention to loss of eye contact (excluding Asian cultures, where lack of eye contact is more a sign of respect than avoidance). Poker players wearing dark glasses while playing don't have to worry about where they're looking, blink frequency, and other eye tells. This has the added advantage of preventing players from observing you while you observe them.

When a player tries to remain cool under pressure, his anxiety or apprehension often leaks out. Be on the lookout for unnecessary adjustments of clothing or jewelry. This takes the form of winding

Lee's comment:
Although lack of eye contact in interpersonal relations is a sign of insecurity, at the poker table, opponents often stare you down when they're weak and feigning strength, and look away when they're strong and feigning weakness. This is often a classic strong-is-weak/weak-is-strong tell. Players vary greatly in this regard, but if you can pick up a pattern, it can be remarkably revealing. Close observation of hands shown down compared with stare-downs should give you the necessary clue.

watches and rotating rings, necklaces, chains, earrings, etc. Does he engage in this behavior only when concerned or is it a constant mannerism?

Also watch for unnecessary activities that indicate insecurity, such as checking the contents of a wallet (several times), clasping hands together, rubbing the back of the hand, playing with buttons,

Lee's comment: Steve's point about the importance of identifying a pattern is well-taken. Many players fondle chips incessantly, whereas others only do so when they feel insecure, such as when they're bluffing. One pro player I know well plays with chips as a kind of reverse tell. When he has a strong hand and an opponent is in the tank, considering whether or not to call a river bet, this pro rhythmically shuffles a stack of chips for a while, then suddenly stops and freezes. Opponents often interpret this sudden cessation of all motion as fear, then make a bad call.

zippers, chips, or holding something in front of himself that acts as a security blanket. Once again, it's the pattern that reveals the tell. Does the player use security gestures all the time, or only when under increased stress?

Another strong indicator to look for is frustration. Watch for rubbing the back of the neck, throat, or shoulders, or gently slapping the forehead (which can often be construed as a bad play or frustration with the cards dealt).

In this picture, the player indicates frustration as he exhales, rubs the back of his neck, and moves away from the cards.

Hand and Thumb Gestures

Scientists have noted that there are more connections between the hands and the brain than between any other parts of the body. Because our hands, like our faces, are easily visible, signals are easily detected if we pay attention to them.

Rubbing the palms together is a way in which people subconsciously communicate positive expectation. Pay particular attention to the speed in which a person rubs his palms together. The quicker the speed, the greater the excitement. Not long ago, I observed a celebrity poker match in which one player, holding AKs pre-flop, rubbed his palms together while engaging in an authentic smile. His body language told me he was holding strong cards and this impression was reinforced by a lift in his mood, sitting closer to his cards and looking at his chips, pondering his bet. The shuffle in the seat by moving forward indicated high-level confidence. This behavior was totally different from the last hand dealt to him. His behavior told me what was going on, not the cards.

Rubbing palms together is an example of positive expectation. Usually, when people talk about winning the lottery or coming into money, they rub their palms together. This could illustrate a strong hand and high confidence.

Lee's comment: These are reliable tells that most players are not aware of. When I observe two or more high-confidence gestures in an amateur player, I proceed with great caution. Moving slightly forward in the chair, combined with a glance down at his chips, usually indicates strength, as does briefly rubbing the palms together.

A variation of positive expectation is rubbing the open palms together. This is a high-confidence gesture indicating positive thoughts. This is usually accompanied by a smile, also exhibiting positive expectation. The player in the above image is very confident and self-assured.

Hand Clenching

This is an interesting behavior to identify; it's often confused with a steeple gesture, which indicates confidence. The typical hand-clenching gesture is where the hands are cupped into each other in front of the person. A variation on hand-clenching is where the fingers are interlaced. I saw a player do this while watching a televised tournament recently. The problem was that it looked like his hands were fused or glued together. More visible was that his hands were turning white from the pressure (lack of blood circulation). This was a masking behavior. Generally, hand-clenching indicates a restrained, anxious, or negative attitude. It's also accompanied with a false smile, which belies a person's real feelings.

Generally, the hands are clenched in front of the face, resting on the poker table, or resting in the lap. It's been discovered that there is a correlation between the height at which the hands are held and the degree of the person's frustration. A person is often more difficult to deal with when his hands are held high in front of him. A good way to open him up is to hand him something or offer him a drink.

The Steeple

This is where the fingers of one hand lightly press against those of the other hand to form a church steeple. The steeple gesture is frequently used to display confidence and a self-assured attitude, and is often associated with smugness or arrogance. The higher the steeple, the more confident the person. This is particularly useful when playing poker. I remember watching a woman player smile during the flop, move forward, then engage in a high-steeple gesture (indicating confidence) during a tournament. All this should have been obvious to the other players, but no one noticed. Not surprisingly, the woman won the pot.

Steepling is an indication of confidence. The higher the steeple, the more confident the person. This could indicate a strong hand.

It's important here not to confuse the steeple gesture with a praying gesture. Steepling indicates confidence, while the praying gesture often indicates hope or wishing for something. Pay attention to when a person places his clasped hands in front of his mouth or when his fingers or hands are placed across his mouth, especially if he's talking to you. This indicates either deception, or he doesn't believe what he's saying. Most children, when they lie, place their hands over their mouth, or cover their mouth altogether. In adulthood, we often engage in a hand-to-face gesture when we lie and at the

> **Lee's comment:** This is a remarkably reliable tell. At the 2010 Aussie Millions, a player assumed this steepling pose every time he had a big hand. I went out of my way to play hands heads-up with him. When he steepled, I folded; when he didn't, I bet or raised. This tell was 100% reliable. The player never called a bet or raise when he didn't steeple. Not once!

last moment perform a diversion, such as a cursory rubbing of the nose or touching the face or ear. So be on the lookout for nose tugging, ear pulling, or eye rubbing. These often indicate anxiety and deception.

Be aware of blocking gestures, especially when someone places either his hands or fingers across the lips or mouth. When someone is engaging in blocking gestures while talking, you should pay particular attention. Blocking gestures are associated with doubt, uncertainty, or exaggeration. This was the position that Bill Clinton adopted when responding to questions about Monica Lewinski.

This position is also indicative of withholding information.

In one poker tournament, I noticed one of the better players place his head in his cupped palms and look down at the table. His palms were also covering his mouth and by looking at the table, other players couldn't see his eyes. He engaged in this position every time like clockwork, but when he was confident, his blink rate increased threefold! Even though he tried to conceal and disguise his excitement, his body language gave him away every time. One astute player, noticing the pattern, realized that this was very valuable information indeed.

The Most Common Lying Gestures

Blinking

It's interesting to note that many people believe when a person engages in deception or bluffing, that person's blink rate increases. In fact, the opposite is true. Dr. Sharon Leal, co-author of a study conducted at Portsmouth University, found that liars blink less frequently than normal during the lie, then speed up to around eight times faster than usual *after* the delivery of the lie. The researchers studied a group of volunteers as they went about their normal business for 10 minutes. A second group was asked to steal an exam paper from an office, then deny having taken it. The groups were then asked to recall exactly what they'd been doing.

During the interview, their blink rates, which had all been the same at the start, were monitored with electrodes placed above, below, and at the sides of the eyes to monitor all movements. Results showed that when the questions were asked and the answers were given, the blink rate in the liars went down. Afterwards, the blink rate of the liars increased rapidly, while that of the truth tellers remained the same.

Researchers believe the increased effort involved in telling fibs could be the reason why liars don't blink during the act of lying.

To use this tell at the poker table, observe the blink frequency of the player when he makes a bet, then make him sweat for a few minutes by staring him down. If he hardly blinks while preparing his bet, then starts blinking rapidly when you're staring him down, there's a good chance he's bluffing.

The Mouth Cover

This is where the hand covers the mouth as the brain subconsciously instructs it to try to suppress the deceitful words that are being spoken.

Be on the lookout for masking and concealment gestures. This behavior can indicate doubt, uncertainty, and concern.

The Nose Touch

This can be a cursory touch, a rub, or several quick rubs, and is often observed with a loss of eye contact and upper-body movement.

The Eye Rub

The eye rub is also a telling factor. When an adult doesn't want to look at something, he often masks his behavior by covering his eyes or by rubbing his eyes. Watch here for prolonged eye closure, which also indicates avoidance. The eye rub is the brain's attempt to block out the deceit or distasteful things it sees, or to avoid having to look at the face of the person being lied to.

Lee's comment: This tell, combined with several others, was exhibited by Tom "Durrrr" Dwan in a classic hand against Phil Ivey in "High Stakes Poker 2010." Watch this clip if you can find it (it was recently removed from YouTube for copyright concerns) and carefully observe Dwan, unquestionably one of the best players around. With a pot of $408,700 (real money, not tournament chips), Dwan bets $268,200 on the river with complete air! Ivey tanks for forever, sweating Durrrr. When Ivey asks Dwan how much he has left, Dwan's voice is a little shaky when he answers, "About two hundred and eighty-thousand dollars." Dwan looks nervous and gulps and this appearance increases when Ivey announces, "This could be the sickest call ever." (Ivey has a pair of 6s with three Broadway cards on the board.)

Ivey continues to ponder and sweat Durrrr, who then rubs his right eye! All the information that Dwan is bluffing is evident. Of course, from Ivey's perspective, it's possible that Dwan, a pro (but with countless more hours online than live), is faking these tells with a monster hand to induce a call from Ivey. In this case, however, the nervousness and the tells associated with it were real. I won't spoil the clip for you if you haven't seen it, but it's worth several close looks!

The Ear Grab and Tug

The ear grab is a symbolic attempt by the listener to "hear no evil." Watch out for people talking to you while covering their own ears. This may illustrate that they themselves don't believe what they're saying or hearing.

Fingers in or Covering the Mouth

Any time the hand or fingers cover the mouth while a person is speaking, it's an outward sign of an inner need for reassurance.

Fingers in the mouth provide comfort and security for a baby. It indicates doubt and concern in an adult.

The Neck Scratch

This signal is an indication of doubt or uncertainty. It's characteristic of the person who says, "I'm not sure if I agree." Watch for when a player tries to indicate confidence, while at the same time scratching his neck. This behavior is contradictory to what he may be saying or representing. Watch for the type of scratch as well. Is it a real scratch to soothe an irritation or simply a touch? It's obvious when someone is relieving an itch as opposed to simply touching a spot on their neck.

The Collar Pull

This is an interesting gesture you'll often see when someone feels uncomfortable while delivering a lie or deceit. Bear in mind that this behavior also indicates the feeling of anger or frustration.

Evaluative Gestures

Evaluative gestures are often shown by a closed hand resting on the chin or cheek, often with the index finger pointing upward. Sometimes you'll see the head cocked to one side as the person is listening. In poker, when someone is engaging in an evaluative gesture, he'll often be deliberating on the best course of action. The evaluative gesture is normally the first behavior that someone will engage in, followed by clusters of behaviors associated with how the person feels at that given moment.

You'll see the more inexperienced players engage in evaluative gestures for longer periods as they decide on the most effective play.

Pay particular attention to the behaviors that follow the evaluative gesture, as these are very important.

Watch for biting of the lip, which may indicate insecurity, uncertainty, or concern. In this image, the player is engaging in an evaluative gesture (hand supporting and stroking the chin), which indicates a low level of confidence.

Good hands don't require a lot of evaluation from a strong player.

How To Practice

The most effective way at improving your skills at identifying body language and deceptive cues and signals in poker is to study televised tournaments. The advantage of watching a televised tournament is that you can see what cards the players are actually holding. Studying these television shows gives you the added advantage of directing all your attention to picking up tells on your opponents without having to play. If you observe carefully and take notes, you can probably identify tells in key opponents that you can use in the future.

Galileo had it right when he said, "All truths are easy to understand once they are discovered. The point is to discover them." Watch, observe, listen, and benchmark your opponent's behavior at all times, then look for deviations from their normative behavior. Even identifying only a couple of your opponent's behaviors will make you a better player.

Online Tells

Online, you're not looking for a hand that shakes, crossed arms, or furtive glances, but there are still some patterns to observe. The most common one is how long an opponent takes to respond. Of course, we don't know if the baby just turned breakfast over, or the doorbell is ringing, or the curtains are on fire ... but in most cases *a long pause adds emphasis to the action being taken.* If a player thinks a long time, then checks, he likely has a weak hand and wants to see another card, hoping that you think he's considering betting. He's looking for a "free card." Don't accommodate him. Bet!

If a player "goes into the tank," activating his time extension, then bets ... look out! Often, he's got a huge hand and is just pretending to need an eternity to think. He might be thinking about how big a bet you'll call. The most likely scenario, though, is that he's just "hollywooding," acting up a storm in the hopes you'll think he's weak. This is one of the situations where it's most useful to take notes. You might be unsure the first or second time you observe this pattern, but by the third time, you've likely picked up an important tell.

A famous online player whose name will go unmentioned routinely stalls when he has a monster, making sure his time clock has been activated prior to putting in a substantial raise. In every instance, he's shown a big hand when called. Most amateurs act right away with both very strong and very weak hands, but they think about the hands they're unsure of.

Another timing factor to be aware of is when players act instantly. Some players are entirely honest with their instant actions and only do this when they're 100% confident in their play, likely meaning strength in the event of a bet or raise. Some clever professionals attempt to use this to their advantage, particularly when it comes to open shoving hands on a short stack, so it looks like it was a big hand and an obvious shove.

Professionals are harder to pigeonhole, but most generally try to take the same amount of time on each decision, à la Chris "Jesus" Ferguson. Against amateurs, though, they may try to sneak in a curve ball if they think it might work, by making either slower or quicker decisions, depending on the circumstances.

Keep several other things in mind. Of paramount importance is position. Would you have called with his hand from mid-position with four players yet to act? Would you have called a raise with his hand from that position?

One clue to a player's expertise is whether the math involved in a decision influences him. Did he even pause in calling a player where he's likely to be a 10-to-1 underdog and the pot is offering him only 4-to-1 odds? If not, *why* not? Most commonly, the reason is that he's oblivious to the odds, but is listening to his gut, his intuition. After all, every situation is 50-50 for him—either he'll win or lose. Make a note about these weak players.

Next, observe whether implied odds influence a player. Does he understand the concept and make decisions based on it? Does he call with a draw, getting the wrong price, when his opponent is all-in (no implied odds here)? If an opponent hits his draw and moves in, will he pay him off? These patterns and tendencies may win you a big pot later.

Frequency of play is important both online and in person. If your opponent is in 80% of the hands, then you're dealing with someone who's taking the flop with a lot of weak and vulnerable hands. You may be able to trap such a player for all his chips, especially if he overplays his hands on the flop and beyond. Pay particular attention to how this type of player plays draws and how to best exploit his tendencies.

Putting out a bet of an odd amount that looks visually imposing is another potential tell. An example of this is a bet of $99 (a stack of three $25 chips, four $5 chips, and four $1 chips). The theory is that most players are much more willing to call a smaller-looking bet than a more threatening-looking stack of chips—even though in actuality the $99 bet is less than a $100 bet. This is only a tell if they usually bet an even amount and suddenly bet an odd amount. For example, some players normally open-raise to 400 with blinds and antes of 75/150, but if they have a speculative hand or are on a blind steal, they might reduce this amount to 399, a much larger and more intimidating pile of chips. You can often exploit this by 3-betting them.

Near the bubble, some players stall, depleting their time bank, then folding in an attempt to sneak into the money. These players tend to be very tight and are easily exploited by attacking their blinds. Beware, however, if they decide to play a hand, since they'll often have a very narrow range, such as JJ+, AK.

Surprisingly, some players actually give away their emotional state in the chat box. Some blow up with swear words or gibberish after losing a big pot, or make cliché complaints in chat. If you suddenly notice that a player's actions are becoming congruent to his behavior, namely that he's becoming much more loose-aggressive after some form of chat blow-up, it's pretty safe to assume he's on tilt. Some people who talk trash in the chat often fancy their own flashy play; they're more likely to be bluffy or aggressive, though they might sometimes attempt to use that chat during a hand to portray that image and get you to call lighter.

Appendix II

Detailed Mathematical Hand Analysis

[The hand analyzed here is described on pages 64.]

Here's a detailed example that will show you how to use many of the concepts we've taught you, including estimating ranges and fold equity. The math here is more detailed than in other examples; this one has two villains, so there's no way you could figure all this out during a hand. I'll walk you through these calculations, so you can do a similar post-mortem on your own hands.

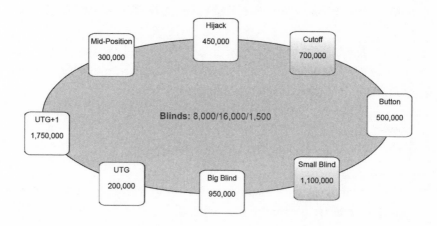

This is from the 2010 EPT in Deauville (covered in Chapter 5, Early-Stage Play). We've passed the money bubble and around 30 players remain. In this hand, a pro in the cutoff (Freddy Deeb) open-raises to 40,000 and an aggressive Romanian player on the button 3-bets to 110,000. ElkY holds pocket tens in the small blind and here we debate his correct action.

We'll make certain assumptions about the different players and evaluate the EV of each of our possible actions. I'll start by doing the calculations with "chip EV" to make the math a little easier, but we'll also talk about prize-payout considerations later.

Folding is certainly reasonable, facing a raise and a re-raise. Our EV is easy to determine. We lose our ante and small blind: -9.5k.

Flat-calling doesn't seem appropriate in this spot. The 3-bet is more than 10% of our stack and an even larger fraction of the raisers' stacks. We don't have the odds to set-mine, which is essentially what we're doing with a call. The opener can re-raise, putting us in an even tougher spot than we are now. Let's ignore this option.

Raising is our last option, and let's say we've decided on a raise to 250k. The EV of this is tough to figure out, but let's start by making a few assumptions.

- Opener will make his initial raise with 22+, A5o+, A2s+, KJo+, K9s+, QJo, Q9s+, J9s+, T8s+, 98s, 87s, 76s, 65s (top 25% of hands).
- The button will 3-bet with 99+, AQ+, ATs+, and KQs.
- If we raise, opener will shove KK+ and AK, plus QQ 75% of the time and JJ 50%, and will fold all other hands.
- If opener folds, the button will shove JJ+, AK, plus AQs 75% of the time and TT 75%, and will fold otherwise.
- If opener shoves, the button will call with KK+.

For simplicity, we'll assume the big blind won't play if we 4-bet. While in reality, he might play with KK+, the chances are small enough that it won't affect our EV much. Two other players seem to like their hands, possibly taking some aces and kings out of the deck, making the chances that the big blind has KK+ less often than normal.

To calculate our EV, we have to use this equation:

Raise EV =	chance everyone folds	x	EV of taking the blinds	+
	chance opener only pushes	x	EV against opener	+
	chance button only pushes	x	EV against button	+
	chance both push	x	EV against both	

What are the chances that the opener will push? The best way to figure this out is to count out all the different ways to make the various hands. For example, there are six different ways he could have pocket aces (A♠A♥, A♠A♦, A♠A♣, A♥A♦, A♥A♣, A♦A♣). Likewise, there are six ways to make KK, QQ, or JJ and 16 ways to make AK (four of them suited). However, if we weight QQ 75% and JJ 50%, that will total 35.5 hands he'll push with. He has 307 different hands in his opening range, once you take our tens out of the deck. Therefore, the chances the opener will push are 35.5/307, or 12%.

If the opener folds, how often will the button push? We'll use the same logic. If you count them out and weight them appropriately, he'll shove with 43.75 hands. He only had 73 hands in his opening range, so he'll shove 60%[5]. If we multiply this by the chance that the opener doesn't push (88%), we get a 53% chance we'll be up against only the button.

To get the chance they both push, we have to multiply the chance that the opener pushes by the chance that the button has KK+. We can't just assume it's 12 hands out of 73, because when the opener shoves, he almost always holds kings or aces. Usually, that cuts the number of ways we can make AA or KK in half, but it also takes a big chunk out of the 73 hands he could have. It would take many steps to figure out the exact answer, so I'll do some hand-waving and say we should discount it to 10 hands out of 73, which is pretty close to the exact answer. So, 10/73 = 14%, and

---

[5] In this step and some future steps, we ignore the fact that the opener folded or pushed, since his action actually changes the chances of the button having various hands. This analysis is complicated enough as it is; we don't want to go down that road ...

multiplying this by the chance the opener pushes (12%) gives us a 1.6% chance we're up against two pushes. We're up against only the opener 12% x (100% - 14%) = 10% of the time.

The chance everyone folds is 88% x (100% - 60%) = 35%.

Therefore, we'll see the following actions behind us if we raise to 250k:

Action	Probability
Everyone folds	35%
Opener pushes	10%
Button pushes	53%
Both push	1.6%

Adding all the probabilities together (after a little rounding) gives us 100%, which is a nice double-check that we didn't make a math error. The next step is to figure out the EV of each situation.

If everyone folds, we take the whole pot and net 16k + (7 x 1.5k) + 40k + 110k = +176.5k.

If anyone pushes and we fold, we lose the 250k bet and 1.5k ante or -251.5k, plus the damage to our image and our stack. Let's remember this for now and compare it to the EV of calling each bet so we can pick the better option. Here are all of our situations:

Situation	EV
Everyone folds	+176.5k
We raise and fold	-251.5k
We win against opener	+835k
We lose against opener	-700k
We win against button	+565k
We lose against button	-500k
We win against both	+1,222k
We win side pot in 3-way all-in	-300k

If we call the opener's push, we have to calculate our winning percentage against his range of hands. There are many free hand calculators on the web today that can help you with this step. Using a calculator program such as *PokerStove* allows you to put in hand ranges for different players. For example, we can put in TT for the range of one player and KK+, AKo, AKs for the other and it will tell us that TT has 40.3% equity in the pot. Our example is a little complicated, since we have to weigh a few of the hands differently. But if we take each range individually, we can do a weighted average of the whole thing.

Range	Equity	Combinations	Weight		Weighted Combinations
KK+, AK	40.3%	28	100%		28
QQ	18.4%	6	75%		4.5
JJ	18.0%	6	50%		3
Total	35.6%				35.5

The total equity is determined by multiplying each range's equity by the weighted combinations and adding them up, then dividing by the total number of weighted combinations.

$$\text{Equity} = [(40.3\% \times 28) + (18.4\% \times 4.5) + (18.0\% \times 3)] / 35.5 = 35.6\%$$

So facing a shove from the opener, calling would have an EV of (+835k x 35.6%) + (-700k x 64.4%) = -153k. This is better than -250k for raising then folding, so we would call the opener's shove.

We'll do the same thing when it's only the button pushing:

Range	Equity	Combinations	Weight		Weighted Combinations
JJ+, AK	33.7%	40	100%		40
AQs, TT	53.3%	5	75%		3.75
Total	35.3%				43.75

Calling the button's shove would have an EV of (+565k x 35.3%) + (-500k x 64.7%) = -124k. So we would also call a shove from the button.

Now we'll use a little trick to estimate our equity when both players push. In addition to specifying a hand like JJ, *PokerStove* allows you to specify individual hands like J♥J♣. Since JJ is getting 50% weight from opener, if we use three of the six ways to make JJ and combine them with all of the KK+ and AK, it's like weighting the JJ to 50%! This should work fine as long as we randomly pick the suits and don't specify the suits of our own TT. Unfortunately, we can't get exactly 75% of the six ways to make QQ, so we'll have to make do with four or five of them. Putting those in, I got the following equities for the three-way race:

Player	Range	Equity
ElkY	TT	17.4%
Opener	KK+, Q♣Q♦, Q♣Q♥, Q♣Q♠, Q♦Q♠, J♣J♦, J♦J♥, J♥J♠, AKs, AKo	24.7%
Button	KK+	57.9%

The three-way EV is a little more complicated, since we could win a side pot. What's the chance of this happening? We'll approximate it by taking the ratio of our equities. So for the 57.9% of the time that the button wins, we'll win the side pot in a 17.4-to-24.7 ratio. That means our EV of calling a three-way all-in is:

Situation	Probability	EV
We win	17.4%	+1,222k
Opener wins	24.7%	-700k
Button wins, we win side	23.9%	-300k
Button wins, we lose side	34.0%	-700k
Total		-270k

Calling the three-way all-in has a lower EV than raising and folding, so if both players push, we should fold.

Now it's just a matter of matching all of our EV assumptions with the probabilities that each will happen:

Situation	Probability	EV
Everyone folds	35%	+176.5k
Opener pushes	10%	-153k
Button pushes	53%	-124k
Both push	1.6%	-251.5k
Total		-22k

So that was a lot of work, but finally we have an answer that raising to 250k is slightly worse from a chip-EV perspective than folding our small blind. The main reason that raising isn't correct is because we don't have enough fold equity. The button is calling too often and when he does, we're often a big dog.

In the beginning, we decided to do this exercise using chip EV instead of prize EV. We could repeat this exercise using prize EV instead and in your own calculations, you should always use prize

358 • Raiser's Edge

EV. If this were a final table, we could put all the chip stacks into an ICM calculator[6] and determine our prize EV for each one of the situations above. Then you just use those EVs instead of the chip EVs.

Unfortunately, we can't use this for a 30-player situation, because the ICM calculations would literally take years and years, even on a fast computer! One easy thing we can say right off the bat is that folding would also be correct with prize EV. *Losing chips always hurts more in a tournament than in a cash game, so any choice that involves risking chips will always be worse than chip EV suggests.*

You can do a crude approximation of prize-EV decisions if you're familiar with the bubble-factor concept from *Kill Everyone*. Again, we can't figure out our bubble factor exactly, but we can take a guess. It's probably in the range of 1.3 to 1.5, since we're in the money and we're a slightly large stack going up against medium stacks. Our crude approximation would be to multiply each of our losses by the bubble factor, while keeping our winnings unchanged.

I won't go through all the calculations again, but if you did, I'm sure you'd find that folding JJ would also be correct in this situation.

At the table in Deauville, ElkY didn't have the benefit of equity calculators or a computer spreadsheet to keep track of all the EV possibilities. Even so, he correctly folded his pocket tens. He reasoned it was a -EV situation, plus he wanted to maintain his healthy stack. Since he had an above-average stack of almost 70 BB, he wanted to maintain the extra flexibility this stack size gave, rather than taking a chance of being reduced to 25 BB. Growing his stack to more than 100 BB wouldn't give him that much additional advantage over 70 BB. This is a core part of the bubble factor.

---

[6] Chillin411.com has a simple, free, ICM calculator; SnG Power Tools and SitNGo Wizard are more sophisticated and powerful, but must be purchased.

Glossary

3-betting: Making a re-raise over an original raiser, often done pre-flop.

4-betting: Making a re-raise after there's already been a raise and re-raise, often done pre-flop.

Air: A hand that completely misses the flop and has virtually no showdown or drawing equity.

Balanced range: Having a range that has the exact correct amount of hands in it to create maximum deception, depending on the situation.

BB: Abbreviation for the term "big blind."

Bricks out: When the board is dealt out in such a way that a hand, often a draw, misses its outs.

Button: The player who's dealt to last and is last to act in the hand, and the best position to have in hold 'em.

C-bet: A continuation bet, mostly made on the flop after raising pre-flop.

Check-call: To check a street of action, then call a bet made by an opponent.

Check-fold: To check a street of action, then fold to a bet made by an opponent.

Check-raise: To check a street of action, then raise a bet made by an opponent.

Check-shove: To check a street of action, then raise all-in over a bet made by an opponent.

CO: The position of being on the cutoff.

Cold 4-betting: To make a 4-bet when you have no serious chips committed to the pot, such as when there's a raise and a 3-bet before the action gets to you pre-flop.

Cold-calling: To make a call when you have no chips committed to the pot and there have been a raise and a re-raise, or a bet and a raise, in front of you.

Connected flop: A flop where the texture is such that the cards are in close rank or with shared suits, such as J♥-9♥-8♠ or 6♦-7♦-8♣.

Come over the top: To make a raise over someone's bet or raise.

Cutoff: The position one to the right of the button, second last to act in the hand.

Donk bet: To begin the action on a street by betting into a player whose bet or raise you called out of position on the previous street.

Donk lead: To begin the action on a street by betting into a player whose bet or raise you called out of position on the previous street.

Dry flop: A flop that's uncoordinated and without probable draws, such as K♥-7♦-2♣ or J♦-6♥-3♠.

Early position [EP]: Being in a position that's one of the first to act in the hand, generally considered the first three positions to the left of the big blind.

Effective stack size: The smaller stack in a heads-up-pot situation, as no larger number of chips is capable of being wagered once the shorter stack is all-in.

Fear equity: The advantage gained by having your opponents afraid to play with you.

Flat-call: To call a bet from an opponent, as opposed to raising or folding (synonymous with smooth-call).

Flatting: To call a bet from an opponent, as opposed to raising or folding. Often used as a slang term for "flat-call."

Floating: To call an opponent's bet with a weak or mediocre holding, with the intention of attempting some kind of bluff on a future street of action.

Flop texture: A way of describing the type of cards that have come down on the flop.

Fold equity: The advantage gained by having the potential that an opponent will fold a better hand to your bet or raise.

Getting it in: To get the entirety of your stack or an opponent's stack into the pot.

Gutshot: A straight draw that involves a singular card to complete the straight, normally meaning you have four outs. For example, holding AT on a board of K-Q-5.

Heads-Up (HU): Playing against a single opponent.

Hijack: The position two to the right of the button, third to the last to act in the hand.

In position (IP): To be the player in the hand who acts after the opponent.

Jam: To push all-in.

Late position (LP): To be in one of the positions that is last to act, generally considered to be the last three players to act in a hand on a nine-handed table.

Light: Taking an action with a wide range or hand that likely doesn't want to be called.

Limp: To call the BB pre-flop, as opposed to raising.

Mid-position (MP): To be in one of the positions that act between early and late position, often considered the seats between three and five players right of the dealer.

Mid-stage: Often considered the levels of a tournament in which antes are in play, but the bubble hasn't yet been approached.

Monster: A very big or strong hand.

Nuts: The best possible hand.

Out of position (OOP): To be the player who has to act first in the hand. For example, the player in the small blind always acts out of position.

Over the top: To make a raise over another player's bet or raise.

Position: The order of players to act. The player first to act is "out of position," the player last to act is "in position."

Post-flop: The play of a hand on all streets after the flop has been dealt.

Pot odds: The odds a player is receiving based on how much money is in the pot and how much more it is for him to a call a bet or raise.

Pre-flop (PF): The action in the hand prior to the flop being dealt out.

Push: To make an all-in bet.

Rainbow: A flop texture of all different suits, such as K♥-T♦-6♣.

Raise-fold: To make a raise and then fold to an opponent's ensuing re-raise.

Re-shoving: To move all-in over a player who has already moved all-in.

SB: Abbreviation for the term "small blind."

Smooth-call: When a player makes a bet, gets raised, and elects to call instead of re-raise or fold.

Streets of value: A street being one street of action, value being a bet made hoping to get called for the potential of gaining chips.

Under the gun (UTG): The first player to act pre-flop.

UTG+1: The player next to act after the player under the gun.

Variance: The swings or unpredictability created by randomness.

About the Authors

Bernard "ElkY" Grospellier is a 30-year-old French tournament-poker phenomenon. Starting out as one of the world's top-ranked pro StarCraft gamers, he switched to poker and has been climbing the money ladder ever since. ElkY was the first player ever to reach ever to reach "Supernova" and "Supernova Elite" status on PokerStars. In 2008, he won the European Poker Tour's Caribbean Poker Adventure and the World Poker Tour's Festa al Lago Tournament at Bellagio. In 2009, he won the 2009 Caribbean Poker Adventure's $25,000-buy-in High Roller side event and was named World Poker Tour Player of the Year. Recently, at the European Poker Tour Grand Final in Madrid in May 2011, ElkY won both the $10,000-buy-in High Roller Turbo, $25,000-buy-in High-Roller event, and $25,000-buy-in SCOOP Heads-Up tournament, cashing more than a US$1 million. As of that date, his total live tournament winnings exceeded $7,500,000.

♠ ♠ ♠

New Zealander **Lee "Final Table" Nelson** has been playing tournament poker for 14 years, with live-tournament wins well in excess of US$2,000,000. His nickname was given to him by a tour-

nament director who claimed that Lee made the final table so frequently, he was like "final-table furniture." Nelson won the 2006
Aussie Millions, taking down US$1,000,000 (A$1,300,000), along
with the Party Poker World Open in 2005 (US$400,000). He is
the lead author of the tournament poker classic *Kill Everyone* and

he co-authored the highly acclaimed
poker book, *Kill Phil*. Nelson has hosted
celebrity pokerTV shows in Australia
and New Zealand, and had a prominent
role aside Joe Hachem in the hit reality
TV poker show The Poker Star. Lee is
a founding member of the Australian
Poker Hall of Fame and is the only New
Zealander to achieve this honor. He's the
Ambassador for poker at Sky City Ca-
sino in Auckland and a member of Team Poker Stars.

♠ ♠ ♠

Tysen Streib has been playing poker since 1998, both online
and in live play. He specializes in the mathematical aspects of tournament structures, game theory, and optimal plays. He wrote a majority of the advanced quantitative analy-
sis for the highly popular poker book *Kill
Everyone*. His recent projects include
new game design as well as developing
artificial intelligences for computer players in both poker and other card/strategy
games. He holds an engineering degree,
as well as an MBA.

♠ ♠ ♠

Tony Dunst is a professional live and online tournament poker  player and hosts the World Poker Tour's latest addition, "The Raw Deal." Tony cashed 6 times in the 2010 World Series of Poker for a total of $199,962, including a 50ᵗʰ place finish in the WSOP Main Event worth $168,556. Dunst has conducted seminars with Lee Nelson, Tysen Streib, and Joe Hachem, and is a highly respected articulate poker writer, speaker, and analyst.

Color Charts

The charts in this section come from the body of the book, where they are displayed in black and white. Here they are produced in full color. Each chart is tagged (in parentheses in the upper left-hand corner) with the page number of its corresponding black-and-white chart in the book.

(Pg. 156)   Equilibrium Solutions for 3- and 4-Betting

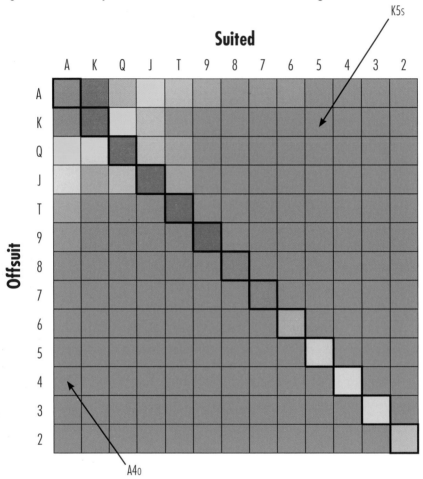

Suited

Offsuit

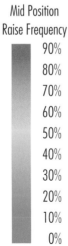

Mid Position
Raise Frequency

90%
80%
70%
60%
50%
40%
30%
20%
10%
0%

(Pg. 157) Defending Your Big Blind Against a Mid-Position Raiser
(10,000 Stacks, Blinds 100/200/25, Raise to 500)

Suited

Offsuit	A	K	Q	J	T	9	8	7	6	5	4	3	2
A	P70J	P	P90J	p	p	F60p	F	F	F	F70J	F	F	F
K	J70P	P	C	p70C	C	C	C	C	C	C	C	C	C
Q	p	C	P60J	C	p60C	C	C	C	C	C	C	C	F
J	C	C	C	p	C90p	C	C	C	C	C	C	C	F
T	F	C	C	C	P	C	C	C	C	C	C	C	F
9	F	C	C	C	C	C	C	C	C	C	C	C	F
8	F	C	F	C	C	C	C	C	C	C	C	F	F
7	F	C	F	F	F	C	C	C	C	C	C	C	F
6	F	F	F	F	F	F	F	C	C	C	C	C	F
5	F	F	F	F	F	F	F	F	F	C	C	C	C
4	F	F	F	F	F	F	F	F	F	F	C	C	C
3	F	F	F	F	F	F	F	F	F	F	F	C	C
2	F	F	F	F	F	F	F	F	F	F	F	F	C

F	Fold
C	Call
P	Make pot-sized 3-bet and be willing to get it all in
p	Pot 3-bet but fold to 4-bet
J	Jam

X#Y	means do the first action #%
	For example:
p70b	= p 70% and b 30%

The key below refers to the charts on the following pages.

F	Fold
C	Call
S	Make small (0.5x pot) 4-bet and be willing to get it all in
s	Small 4-bet but fold to 5-bet
P	Make pot-sized 4-bet and be willing to get it all in
p	Pot 4-bet but fold to 5-bet
J	Jam

(Pg. 162)

4-Betting Over Various 3-Bets
(10,000 Stacks, Blinds 100/200/25)

10,000 Stacks

Hand	His 3-Bet Size			
	Small	Pot	Big	Jam
AA	J60 S20 P20	J	J	C
KK	C	C70 J20 S10	C50J	C
QQ	C	C	C80J	C
JJ	C	C	C	C80F
TT	C	C	C	C90F
99	C	C	C70F	F
88	C	C	F80 C10 J10	F
77	C90J	C50F	F70J	F
66	C	C50 J40 F10	F60J	F
AKs	C	C	C	C
AQs	C	C	C70J	F
AJs	C	F50J	F	F
A8s	F60 J30 p10	F	F	F
A7s	J60 F20 p20	F	F	F
A6s	F70 J20 p10	F	F	F
A5s	J90p	J	F60J	F
A4s	J80 p10 F10	F70J	F80J	F
A3s	J70 p20 F10	F	F90J	F
A2s	J50 F30 p20	F	F	F
AKo	C	C	C	F60C
AQo	C	F90J	F	F
KQs	C	C	F80J	F
KJs	C	C50 J40 s10	F	F
KTs	C70 F20 s10	F80J	F	F
KQo	C	F70C	F	F
KJo	C60 F20 s20	F	F	F
QJs	C	F50C	F	F
76s	F80C	F	F	F
Other calling hands	22+, ATs, JTs, 65s, 54s	none	none	none

(Pg. 166)

Equilibrium 3-Bets With a Variety of Stacks, Raises, and Antes

10,000 Stacks

Hand	100/200/25 Open to 500	100/200/25 Open to 600	100/200 Open to 600
AA	P70J	P80J	P60 J30 B10
KK	P	P	P
QQ	P60J	P60J	P70 B20 J10
JJ	p	p	p
TT	P	p90C	p80C
AKs	P	P	P
AQs	P90J	P	P70J
AJs	p	p90C	C80p
ATs	p	p	p80F
A9s	F60p	F	F
A5s	F70J	F90J	F
A4s	F	F	F
A3s	F	F	F
AKo	J70P	J70P	p50 J40 b10
AQo	p	p	p90b
AJo	C	F	F
KJs	p70C	C90p	C70p
K2s	C	F	F
KJo	C	C80p	C
QTs	p60C	p	C70 p20 b10
QJo	C	C	C
JTs	C90p	C50p	C70p
JTo	C	C	C
Other calling hands	22+, K2s+, K7o+, Q3s+, Q9o+, J3s+, J8o+, T3s+, T8o+, 93s+, 97o+, 84s+, 87o, 73s+, 76o, 63s+, 52s+, 42s+, 32s	22+, K3s+, K9o+, Q5s+, QTo+, J6s+, JTo, T6s+, 95s+, 85s+, 74s+, 64s+, 53s+, 43s	22+, K3s+, K9o+, Q5s+, QTo+, J6s+, JTo, T6s+, 95s+, 85s+, 74s+, 64s+, 53s+, 43s

(Pg. 167) ## Equilibrium 3-Bets With a Variety of Stacks, Raises, and Antes

6,000 Stacks

	100/200/25	100/200/25	100/200
Hand	Open to 500	Open to 600	Open to 600
AA	J50 P30 S20	J80S	P50 S30 J20
KK	J60 P30 S10	J90S	P50S
QQ	J	J	J90P
JJ	J	J	P90S
TT	S50P	J60S	s
AKs	P70S	J	S60 P40
AQs	J60 P30 S10	J70S	P80S
AJs	J	J	J
ATs	J	J	J90s
A9s	s50 p30 J20	J	F
A5s	J	J	F90J
A4s	J90F	J	F
A3s	F	F80J	F
AKo	J	J	J80P
AQo	J70 s20 p10	J	p60s
AJo	C	C80s	C
KJs	C	C	C
K2s	C80p	F	F
KJo	C	C	C90p
QTs	C	C	C
QJo	C	C	C70p
JTs	C	C	C70p
JTo	C80p	F	F
Other calling hands	22+, K2s+, K9o+, Q4s+, Q9o+, J5s+, JTo, T6s+, T9o, 95s+, 85s+, 74s+, 64s+, 53s+, 43s	22+, K5s+, KTo+, Q8s+, QJo, J8s+, T7s+, 96s+, 86s+, 75s+, 65s, 54s	22+, K5s+, KTo+, Q8s+, J8s+, T7s+, 96s+, 86s+, 75s+, 65s, 54s

(Pg. 172) **Responding to a 3-Bet**

(100/200/25 Blinds, Opening Raise to 500)

10,000 Stacks

Hand	\multicolumn{4}{c}{His 3-Bet Size}

Hand	Small	Pot	Big	Jam
AA	J60 S20 P20	J	J	C
KK	C	C70 J20 S10	C50J	C
QQ	C	C	C80J	C
JJ	C	C	C	C80F
TT	C	C	C	C90F
99	C	C	C70F	F
88	C	C	F80 C10 J10	F
77	C90J	C50F	F70J	F
66	C	C50 J40 F10	F60J	F
AKs	C	C	C	C
AQs	C	C	C70J	F
AJs	C	F50J	F	F
A8s	F60 J30 p10	F	F	F
A7s	J60 F20 p20	F	F	F
A6s	F70 J20 p10	F	F	F
A5s	J90p	J	F60J	F
A4s	J80 p10 F10	F70J	F80J	F
A3s	J70 p20 F10	F	F90J	F
A2s	J50 F30 p20	F	F	F
AKo	C	C	C	F60C
AQo	C	F90J	F	F
KQs	C	C	F80J	F
KJs	C	C50 J40 s10	F	F
KTs	C70 F20 s10	F80J	F	F
KQo	C	F70C	F	F
KJo	C60 F20 s20	F	F	F
QJs	C	F50C	F	F
76s	F80C	F	F	F
Other calling hands	22+, ATs, JTs, 65s, 54s	none	none	none

(Pg. 173)

Responding to a 3-Bet
(100/200/25 Blinds, Opening Raise to 500)

6,000 Stacks

Hand	His 3-Bet Size			
	Small	Pot	Big	Jam
AA	J90S	J	J	C
KK	C	J90C	J90C	C
QQ	C	C50J	J	C
JJ	J90S	J	J	C
TT	C	C60J	J70C	C
99	C	C60F	F60 C30 J10	C70F
88	C	C40 F40 J20	F60 C30 J10	F60C
77	C	F70J	F70 C20 J10	F
66	C	F50J	F70 C20 J10	F
AKs	C	C	J80C	C
AQs	C	C	C	C
AJs	C70J	C	F90C	F
A8s	F	F	F	F
A7s	F	F	F	F
A6s	F	F	F	F
A5s	F90J	F	F	F
A4s	F	F	F	F
A3s	F	F	F	F
A2s	F	F	F	F
AKo	C60 J30 S10	J60C	J90C	C
AQo	C60J	C40 F30 J30	F70J	F90C
KQs	C	F90C	F	F
KJs	C50J	F80C	F	F
KTs	F	F	F	F
KQo	C	F	F	F
KJo	F70 J20 s10	F	F	F
QJs	C	F	F	F
76s	F	F	F	F
Other calling hands	44+	none	none	none

F	Fold	C	Call	J	Jam

(Pg. 176)   Equilibrium 3-Bets Depending on Opener's Position
and Tournament Pressures
(10,000 Stacks, Blinds 100/200/25)

Facing a Mid-Position Raise

Hand	No Pressure	Medium Pressure	High Pressure
AA	P70J	P	P90B
KK	P	P	P
QQ	P60J	P	P
JJ	p	P	P
TT	P	p50C	C60p
99	C	C	C
88	C	C	C
77	C	C	C
66	C	C	C
55	C	C	C
44	C	C	C
33	C	C	p70F
22	C	C80p	F
AKs	P	P	p
AQs	P90J	p	p
AJs	p	p	p90b
ATs	p	p80F	p60F
A9s	F60p	F	F
A8s	F	F	F
A7s	F	F	F
A6s	F	F	F
A5s	F70J	F	F
A4s	F	F	F
A3s	F	F	F
A2s	F	F	F
AKo	J70P	P	p90B
AQo	p	p	p
AJo	C	F	F
ATo	F	F	F
A9o	F	F	F

Equilibrium 3-Bets Depending on Opener's Position and Tournament Pressures (cont.)
(10,000 Stacks, Blinds 100/200/25)

Facing a Mid-Position Raise

Hand	No Pressure	Medium Pressure	High Pressure
A8o	F	F	F
A7o	F	F	F
A6o	F	F	F
A5o	F	F	F
A4o	F	F	F
A3o	F	F	F
A2o	F	F	F
KQs	C	C	C
KJs	p70C	C	p90b
K8s	C	C	c90p
K7s	C	C	F70 p20 b10
K6s	C	C	F60p
K5s	C	C	F80p
KQo	C	C	C
KJo	C	p80C	F90p
K2o	F	F	F
QJs	C	C	C
QTs	p60C	p	p
QJo	C	F90p	F
JTs	C90p	p	p
J9s	C	C	F80p
JTo	C	F	F
J6o	F	F	F
J5o	F	F	F
T9s	C	C	p80F
T2s	F	F	F
T9o	C	F	F
T6o	F	F	F
T5o	F	F	F
92s	F	F	F

Equilibrium 3-Bets Depending on Opener's Position
and Tournament Pressures (cont.)
(10,000 Stacks, Blinds 100/200/25)

Facing a Mid-Position Raise

Hand	No Pressure	Medium Pressure	High Pressure
98o	C	F	F
82s	F	F	F
87o	C	F	F
73s	C	F	F
72s	F	F	F
76o	C	F	F
75o	F	F	F
63s	C	F	F
62s	F	F	F
52s	C	F	F
Other calling hands	K2s+, K7o+, Q3s+, Q9o+, J8o+, T3s+, T8o+, 93s+, 97o+, 84s+, 87o, 73s+, 76o, 63s+, 52s+, 42s+, 32s	K5s+, KTo+, Q7s+, J7s+, T7s+, 96s+, 86s+, 75s+, 65s, 54s	K8s+, KQo, Q9s+

The key below refers to the "Equilibrium 3-Bets Depending on Opener's Position and Tournament Pressures" charts.

F	Fold
C	Call
S	Make small (0.5x pot) 4-bet and be willing to get it all in
s	Small 4-bet but fold to 5-bet
P	Make pot-sized 4-bet and be willing to get it all in
p	Pot 4-bet but fold to 5-bet
J	Jam

(Pg. 179) **Equilibrium 3-Bets Depending on Opener's Position and Tournament Pressures**
(10,000 Stacks, Blinds 100/200/25)

Facing an Aggressive Button Raise

Hand	No Pressure	Medium Pressure	High Pressure
AA	P	P	P
KK	P	P	P
QQ	P80B	P90B	P70B
JJ	P70B	B90P	P
TT	B80P	B	P50 S40 B10
99	J	B90P	s50 p40 b10
88	J	P70B	p70s
77	J	P70B	p80 s10 b10
66	J60 P30 B10	C50 P40 B10	p80s
55	B60 P20 C20	C	C70p
44	C	C	C
33	C80J	C	C
22	J90C	C	C70s
AKs	P	P	S90P
AQs	B90P	P	P70S
AJs	P	P	P
ATs	P	P	p70S
A9s	P	P	s50 p40 B10
A8s	P	p	p80s
A7s	P80B	B70p	p60 s30 B10
A6s	J80B	B50p	s80p
A5s	B80J	B	s50 p40 B10
A4s	J80B	B	s70p
A3s	J	b	s80p
A2s	J	p90b	s60p
AKo	P90B	P90B	P70S
AQo	J90B	B	P40 S40 B20
AJo	P70 B20 J10	B50P	P80S
ATo	P90B	p90B	S
A9o	p	p	s

Equilibrium 3-Bets Depending on Opener's Position
and Tournament Pressures (cont.)
(10,000 Stacks, Blinds 100/200/25)

Facing an Aggressive Button Raise

Hand	No Pressure	Medium Pressure	High Pressure
A8o	p	p90b	p80s
A7o	p90C	p70b	p70s
A6o	p90b	p60b	p60s
A5o	p	b50p	s80p
A4o	p60b	b70p	s50p
A3o	b50p	p70b	s80p
A2o	p90b	p90b	p80b
KQs	C	C90P	S
KJs	P	P	S90p
K8s	C	C	C
K7s	C	C	C
K6s	C	C	C
K5s	C	C	C
KQo	C	C	C50S
KJo	C90J	C	p70C
K2o	C	C	C90s
QJs	C	C	C
QTs	C90J	C	s80C
QJo	C	C	C
JTs	J90C	C	s60C
J9s	C	C	C
JTo	C	C70 p20 b10	p50 C40 b10
J6o	C	C	p50C
J5o	C	C	F90p
T9s	C90J	C	C
T2s	C	C	s50 p30 C20
T9o	C	C50 b30 p20	p90b
T6o	C	C	F90p
T5o	C	F90b	F
92s	C	C70p	F

Equilibrium 3-Bets Depending on Opener's Position
and Tournament Pressures (cont.)
(10,000 Stacks, Blinds 100/200/25)

Facing an Aggressive Button Raise

Hand	No Pressure	Medium Pressure	High Pressure
98o	C	p	p90b
82s	C	C60p	F
87o	C	p70C	p90F
73s	C	C	F60 s30 p10
72s	C	p	F
76o	C	C	p50F
75o	C	C90p	F
63s	C	C	C90s
62s	C	p50C	F
52s	C	C	F50 s40 p10
Other calling hands	any suited, K2o+, Q2o+, J2o+, T4o+, 95o+, 85o+, 75o+, 64o+, 53o+	any suited, K2o+, Q2o+, J4o+, T6o+, 96o+, 86o+, 75o+, 65o, 54o	K2+, Q2s+, Q4o+, J2s+, J6o+, T2s+, T7o+, 93s+, 97o+, 84s+, 74s+, 63s+, 53s+, 43s

(Pg. 185)   ## Responding to a 3-Bet Under High Pressure
(100/200/25 Blinds, Opening Raise to 500)

Mid-Position

Hand	His 3-Bet Size			
	Small	Pot	Big	Jam
AA	S60 P30 C10	C80S	C90J	C
KK	C	C	C	C
QQ	C90S	C80S	C90J	F90C
JJ	C90S	C	C80F	F90C
TT	C	C	C50F	F90C
99	C80F	C60F	F50 C40 J10	F
88	C80F	F60S	F50 C40 J10	F
77	C70F	F90s	F90J	F
66	F70C	F90s	F90J	F
55	F70C	F90s	F90J	F
44	F70C	F	F	F
33	F80C	F	F	F
22	F80C	F	F	F
AKs	C	C	C	C
AQs	C	C	F60 C30 J10	F
AJs	C80 s10 p10	F80s	F	F
ATs	C50 s30 F10 p10	F	F	F
A9s	C60F	F	F	F
A8s	C50 F30 s20	F	F	F
A7s	C60 F20 s10 b10	F	F	F
A6s	C60 F20 s10 b10	F	F	F
A5s	C60 s20 F10 b10	F	F	F
A4s	C60 s20 F10 b10	F	F	F
A3s	C60 s20 F20	F	F	F
A2s	C60 F20 s20	F	F	F
AKo	C	C	C	F
AQo	F50s	F	F	F
AJo	F90s	F	F	F
ATo	C50 s30 F10 p10	F	F	F
A9o	F	F	F	F
A8o	F90s	F	F	F

Responding to a 3-Bet Under High Pressure (cont.')
(100/200/25 Blinds, Opening Raise to 500)
Mid-Position

Hand	His 3-Bet Size			
	Small	Pot	Big	Jam
A7o	F90s	F	F	F
A6o	F90s	F	F	F
A5o	F90s	F	F	F
A4o				
A3o		N/A		
A2o				
KQs	C	C	F	F
KJs	C	F70s	F	F
KTs	C40 F40 s10 p10	F	F	F
K9s	C50F	F	F	F
K8s	F90s	F	F	F
K7s				
K6s				
K5s				
K4s		N/A		
K3s				
K2s				
KQo	C	F50C	F	F
KJo	F90C	F	F	F
KTo	C40 F40 s10 p10	F	F	F
QJs	C	F	F	F
QTs	C50F	F	F	F
Q9s	F90C	F	F	F
Q8s	F	F	F	F
Q7s				
Q6s				
Q5s				
Q4s		N/A		
Q3s				
Q2s				
QJo	F90s	F	F	F

Responding to a 3-Bet Under High Pressure (cont.')
(100/200/25 Blinds, Opening Raise to 500)

Mid-Position

Hand	Small	Pot	Big	Jam
	His 3-Bet Size			
QTo	F	F	F	F
JTs	C50 F50 s10	F	F	F
J9s	F	F	F	F
J8s	F	F	F	F
J7s	N/A			
T9s	F	F	F	F
T8s	F	F	F	F
T7s / T9o	N/A			
98s	F	F	F	F
97s / 86s	N/A			
65s	F	F	F	F
54s / 43s	N/A			
Other calling hands	none	none	none	none

(Pg. 189)

Responding to a 3-Bet Under High Pressure
(100/200/25 Blinds, Opening Raise to 500)

Button

Hand	His 3-Bet Size			
	Small	Pot	Big	Jam
AA	S	S50 C40 J10	C90J	C
KK	S	C90S	J	C
QQ	S	S70J	J	C
JJ	S	S	J80C	C
TT	S	S70C	C50J	C
99	S	C50S	J	C
88	S	S70C	J60C	C
77	C80S	C80S	C40J	F60C
66	C90S	C	C80 J10 F10	F
55	C	C80s	C50 J40 F10	F
44	C	C70s	J60 F20 C20	F
33	C	s50C	J50F	F
22	C	s70F	F90J	F
AKs	C80S	C	C	C
AQs	C	C90S	C	C
AJs	C50S	C60S	C	C
ATs	C	C	C	F
A9s	C	C	C	F
A8s	C	C	C	F
A7s	C	C	C	F
A6s	C	C	C70F	F
A5s	C	C	C60F	F
A4s	C	C	F	F
A3s	C	C	F	F
A2s	C	C90F	F	F
AKo	S	S90J	J	C
AQo	S	S70J	J	C
AJo	S	S	J80 C10 F10	F
ATo	S80C	S60C	F60 J30 C10	F
A9o	C	F	F	F
A8o	C	F60C	F	F

Responding to a 3-Bet Under High Pressure (cont.')
(100/200/25 Blinds, Opening Raise to 500)
Button

Hand	His 3-Bet Size			
	Small	Pot	Big	Jam
A7o	F80s	F	F	F
A6o	F	F	F	F
A5o	F60s	F	F	F
A4o	s60F	F	F	F
A3o	F60s	F	F	F
A2o	F80s	F	F	F
KQs	C	C	C70J	F
KJs	C	C60s	J90C	F
KTs	s90C	J50s	J	F
K9s	s	s60J	J90F	F
K8s	F60s	s80F	F70J	F
K7s	s70F	F50s	F80J	F
K6s	s50 C40 F10	F90s	F90J	F
K5s	F80s	F80s	F	F
K4s	F70s	F	F	F
K3s	F60s	F	F	F
K2s	F90s	F	F	F
KQo	C	C90s	C50J	F
KJo	s	s	F60J	F
KTo	F60s	F70 s20 J10	F90J	F
QJs	C	C	C80J	F
QTs	C	s50J	J	F
Q9s	s	s70J	J80F	F
Q8s	s80F	s80F	F70J	F
Q7s	F60s	F	F	F
Q6s	s60F	F	F	F
Q5s	F80s	F	F	F
Q4s	F60s	F	F	F
Q3s	F60s	F	F	F
Q2s	F90s	F	F	F
QJo	C	s60 F20 J10 C10	J70F	F

Responding to a 3-Bet Under High Pressure (cont.')
(100/200/25 Blinds, Opening Raise to 500)
Button

	His 3-Bet Size			
Hand	Small	Pot	Big	Jam
QTo	C50s	F70s	F90J	F
JTs	C	C60s	F60J	F
J9s	C	F70s	F90J	F
J8s	s50 C40 F10	F	F	F
J7s	F60s	F	F	F
T9s	C	s70F	F90J	F
T8s	C80s	F	F	F
T7s	s90F	F	F	F
T9o	F90s	F	F	F
98s	C	F	F90J	F
97s	C90s	F	F	F
86s	F50 C40 s10	F	F	F
65s	C90s	F	F	F
54s	s50F	F	F	F
43s	F90s	F	F	F
Other calling hands	JTo, 87s, 76s	none	none	none

(Pg. 195) **How Blind Defense Changes Based on Opener's Range**
(3-to-1 Pot Odds and SPR of Six)

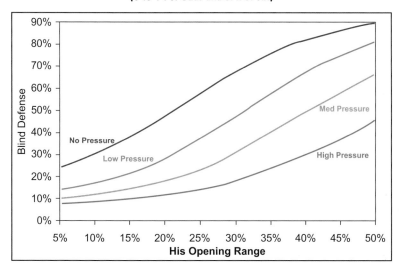

(Pg. 196) **How Blind Defense Changes Based on SPR**
(3-to-1 Pot Odds and Opener Raises 10%)

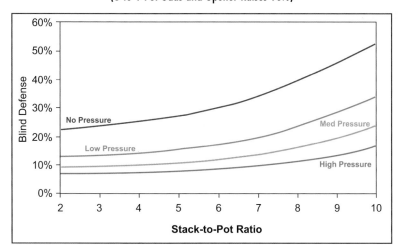

(Pg. 197) How Blind Defense Changes Based on Pot Odds
(SPR of Six and Opener Raises 10%)

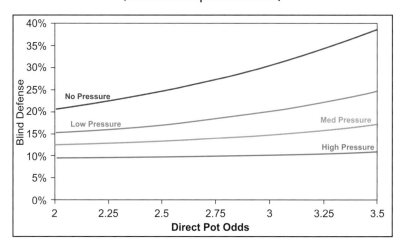

(Pg. 198) Implied Odds Needed to Call from Big Blind
with 76s and Light Tournament Pressure

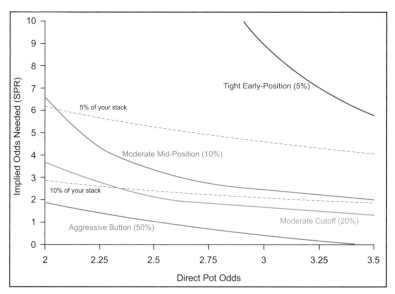

(Pg. 199) Implied Odds Needed to Call from Big Blind
Against a Mid-Position Raise with Various Hands
and Light Tournament Pressure

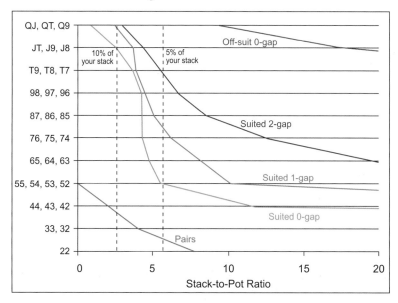

(Pg. 202) ## Comparison of Equilibrium vs. Exploitive Play
(Light Tournament Pressure)

Hand	Equilibrium	Exploitive
AA	P80B	B
KK	P	B
QQ	B70P	B
JJ	P60B	S
TT	P90B	S
99	p	S
88	C	S
77	C	S
66	C	S
55	C	S
44	C	p
33	C	p
22	C	p
AKs	P	B
AQs	p	B
AJs	p	p
ATs	p80C	p
A9s	p	p
A8s	p	p
A7s	p90b	p
A6s	F70b	p
A5s	b60p	p
A4s	F80b	p
A3s	F	p
A2s	F	p
AKo	P60B	B
AQo	p80b	p
AJo	C80p	p
ATo	C	p
KJo	C70p	p
QTs	C60 b30 p10	p
QJo	C60b	p

Comparison of Equilibrium vs. Exploitive Play (cont.')
(Light Tournament Pressure)

Hand	Equilibrium	Exploitive
JTs	p	p
J2s	C	p
JTo	C	p
T9s	p70C	p
98o	C	p
87o	C	p
Other calling hands	any suited (except 92s, 83s, 82s, 72s, 62s), K4o+, Q6o+, J7o+, T7o+, 97o+, 86o+, 76o	none
Other pot (bluff) hands	none	any suited, A2o+, K2o+, Q2o+, J2o+, T6o+, 96o+, 85o+, 75o+, 64o+, 54o

(Pg. 204)

A More Balanced Exploitive Play
(Light Tournament Pressure)

Hand	Equilibrium	Exploitive	Balanced
AA	P80B	B	P70 B20 S10
KK	P	B	P80 B10 S10
QQ	B70P	B	P60B
JJ	P60B	S	P50B
TT	P90B	S	P70 B20 S10
99	p	S	P40 C40 s20
88	C	S	C
77	C	S	C
66	C	S	C
55	C	S	C
44	C	p	C
33	C	p	C
22	C	p	C
AKs	P	B	S50P
AQs	p	B	P80 B10 S10
AJs	p	p	s40 p40 C20
ATs	p80C	p	p60C
A9s	p	p	p
A8s	p	p	p
A7s	p90b	p	p90b
A6s	F70b	p	p70b
A5s	b60p	p	p60 b30 s10
A4s	F80b	p	p60b
A3s	F	p	b40 p30 F30
A2s	F	p	F70b
AKo	P60B	B	P70B
AQo	p80b	p	p90b
AJo	C80p	p	C60 p30 s10
ATo	C	p	C70 s20 p10
KJo	C70p	p	C70p
QTs	C60 b30 p10	p	C80p
QJo	C60b	p	p40 C40 b20

A More Balanced Exploitive Play (cont.')
(Light Tournament Pressure)

Hand	Equilibrium	Exploitive	Balanced
JTs	p	p	C50p
J2s	C	p	C90b
JTo	C	p	C60 p30 s10
T9s	p70C	p	C90p
98o	C	p	C90s
87o	C	p	C90s
Other calling hands	any suited (except 92s, 83s, 82s, 72s, 62s), K4o+, Q6o+, J7o+, T7o+, 97o+, 86o+, 76o	none	any suited (except 92s, 83s, 82s, 72s, 62s), K4o+, Q6o+, J7o+, T7o+, 97o+, 86o+, 76o
Other pot (bluff) hands	none	any suited, A2o+, K2o+, Q2o+, J2o+, T6o+, 96o+, 85o+, 75o+, 64o+, 54o	none

(Pg. 264)

Button's Initial Strategy (20 BB stacks)

Suited (columns) / **Offsuit** (rows)

	A	K	Q	J	T	9	8	7	6	5	4	3	2
A	S	S	S70C	C	C	C	S	C	C	C	S	S	S60C
K	C90S	S	S	C60S	C	C	C	C80S	S	S	S	S	C
Q	C	S	C	S	S50C	C	C	C	S	S	C60S	C	C
J	C	C	C	C	S	S70C	C	C	C	S	S	C	C
T	C	C	C	C80S	C	C70S	C	C	C	C	C	C	C
9	C90J	C	C	C	C	C60S	C	C	C	C	C	C	C
8	C	C	C	C	C	C	C80S	C	C	C	C	C	C
7	C	C	C	C	C	C	C	C	C	C	C	C	C
6	C	S	S90C	C	C	C	C	C	C	C	C	C	C
5	C	S	S	C	C	C	C	C	C	C70S	C	C	C
4	C	S	C	C	C	C	C	C	C	C	C90S	C	C
3	C	C	C	C	C	C	C	F	F	F	F	C80S	C90F
2	C	C	C	C	C	C	C	F	F	F	F	F	C70J

F	Fold
C	Call
S	Make a small (2BB) raise, then use a later table for follow-ups
J	Jam

(Pg. 266) Button: You limp, he makes it 2 BB (20 BB stacks)

Suited

Offsuit \ Suited	A	K	Q	J	T	9	8	7	6	5	4	3	2
A	-	-	P	P	P	P	-	C	C	C	-	-	C
K	P	-	-	C	P	P90J	C80p	C	-	-	-	-	C
Q	P	-	P	-	C	C	C	C	-	-	C	C	C
J	J	P70J	C	P	-	C	C	C	C	-	-	C	C
T	J	p	C	C	P	J	J	J70C	J70C	C	C	C	C
9	J	C90p	C	C	C	P	C90J	C	C	C	C	C	C
8	P	C	C	C	C	C	P50C	C	C	C	C	C	C
7	p70J	C	C	C	C	C	C	C	C	C	C	C	C
6	J50p	-	C	C	C	C	C	C	C	C	C	C	C
5	J	-	-	C	C80p	C	C	C	C	C	C	C	C
4	J80p	-	C	C	C	C	C	C	C	C	C	C	C
3	J	C	C	C	C	C	C	-	-	-	-	C	C
2	J70p	C	C	C	p80C	C70p	C	-	-	-	-	-	C

F	Fold
C	Call
P	Make a pot-sized raise, and be willing to get it all in
p	Make a pot-sized raise, but fold to a re-raise
J	Jam
–	Not limped

(Pg. 267) Button: You limp, he makes it 3 BB (20 BB stacks)

Suited

Offsuit	A	K	Q	J	T	9	8	7	6	5	4	3	2
A	-	-	C90S	J90S	S90J	C90J	-	C	C	C	-	-	C
K	S	-	-	C	C80S	C	C	C	-	-	-	-	C
Q	J	-	S60J	-	C70J	J70C	C	C	-	-	C	C	C70s
J	J	C80 J10 S10	J50C	J	-	J90C	C90J	C	C	-	-	F90C	F80 s10 C10
T	J	C	C	C	J90S	C90J	C	C	C60F	F	F	F	F
9	J	C	C	C	C	J	J90C	C90J	C	F90C	F	F	F
8	J80s	C	C	C80F	F	C90F	J80 S10 C10	J80C	C60J	C	F	F	F
7	C	C	C80F	F	F	F	C	C90S	C	C	F80C	F	F
6	C	-	F60C	F	F	F	F	C	C	C90J	C	F90C	F
5	J80C	-	-	F	F	F	F	F	C	C	C80J	C	C
4	C	-	F	F	F	F	F	F	F	F	C	C80F	F
3	C50 s30 J20	C	F	F	F	F	F	-	-	-	-	J90C	F
2	J80s	C	F	F	F	F	F	-	-	-	-	-	J

F	Fold
C	Call
S	Make a small (0.5x pot) raise, and be willing to get it all in
s	Make a small (0.5x pot) raise, but fold to a re-raise
J	Jam
-	Not limped

(Pg. 268) Button: You limp, he makes it 4 BB (20 BB stacks)

Suited (columns) / Offsuit (rows)

	A	K	Q	J	T	9	8	7	6	5	4	3	2
A	-	-	J	J	J	J	-	C	C	C	-	-	C
K	J	-	-	C70J	J	J	J80C	C	-	-	-	-	F
Q	J	-	J	-	J		C	C	-	-	C	F	F
J	J	J	C	J	-	J80C	C90J	C60F	F	-	-	F	F
T	J	C60J	C	C	J	J	J	J90F	F	F	F	F	F
9	J	C	C	F50C	F	J	J	C	F	F	F	F	F
8	C60J	F	F	F	F	F	J	C90J	F90C	F	F	F	F
7	C	F	F	F	F	F	F	J	C	F	F	F	F
6	C	-	F	F	F	F	F	F	C70J	F90C	F	F	F
5	C	-	-	F	F	F	F	F	F	J90C	J90C	F	F
4	C	-	F	F	F	F	F	F	F	F	J	F	F
3	C	F	F	F	F	F	F	-	-	-	-	J	F
2	F40 C40 J20	F	F	F	F	F	F	-	-	-	-	-	J

F	Fold
C	Call
J	Jam
-	Not limped

(Pg. 269)   **Button: You limp, he jams (20 BB stacks)**

Suited

Offsuit	A	K	Q	J	T	9	8	7	6	5	4	3	2
A	–	–	C	C	C	C	–	C	C	C	–	–	F
K	C	–	–	C	C	C	F	F	–	–	–	–	F
Q	C	–	C	–	C	F	F	F	–	–	F	F	F
J	C	C	F80C	C	–	F	F	F	F	–	–	F	F
T	C	C90F	F	F	C	F	F	F	F	F	F	F	F
9	C	F	F	F	F	C	F	F	F	F	F	F	F
8	C	F	F	F	F	F	C	F	F	F	F	F	F
7	C	F	F	F	F	F	F	C	F	F	F	F	F
6	F	–	F	F	F	F	F	F	C	F	F	F	F
5	F	–	–	F	F	F	F	F	F	C	F	F	F
4	F	–	F	F	F	F	F	F	F	F	C	F	F
3	F	F	F	F	F	F	F	–	–	–	–	C	F
2	F	F	F	F	F	F	F	–	–	–	–	–	F

F	Fold
C	Call
–	Not limped

(Pg. 270)

Button: You make it 2 BB, he makes it 4 BB (20 BB stacks)

Suited

	A	K	Q	J	T	9	8	7	6	5	4	3	2
A	J	C	C	–	–	–	C90J	–	–	–	C	C	J90C
K	C60J	C80J	C	C80J	–	–	–	J	C90J	C70J	C70J	C90J	–
Q	–	C	–	C	C	–	–	–	C90F	C	C	–	–
J	–	–	–	–	C	C70J	–	–	–	C	C90F	–	–
T	–	–	–	C	–	J80C	–	–	–	–	–	–	–
9	J	–	–	–	–	C70J	–	–	–	–	–	–	–
8	–	–	–	–	–	–	J60C	–	–	–	–	–	–
7	–	–	–	–	–	–	–	–	–	–	–	–	–
6	–	F	F	–	–	–	–	–	–	–	–	–	–
5	–	F80C	F	–	–	–	–	–	–	C	–	–	–
4	–	F	–	–	–	–	–	–	–	–	C	–	–
3	–	–	–	–	–	–	–	–	–	–	–	C	F
2	–	–	–	–	–	–	–	–	–	–	–	–	F80C

Offsuit (row labels)

F	Fold
C	Call
J	Jam
–	Not 2-bet

(Pg. 271)   **Button: You make it 2 BB,**
                    he makes it 6 BB (20 BB stacks)

Suited

	A	K	Q	J	T	9	8	7	6	5	4	3	2
A	J	J	C	–	–	–	C	–	–	–	C	C50F	F
K	J	J60C	C	C	–	–	–	F	F	F60J	F	F	–
Q	–	C	–	C	C60J	–	–	–	F	F	F	–	–
J	–	–	–	–	J50C	J50C	–	–	–	F	F	–	–
T	–	–	–	C	–	J80C	–	–	–	–	–	–	–
9	C90F	–	–	–	–	C80J	–	–	–	–	–	–	–
8	–	–	–	–	–	–	J90C	–	–	–	–	–	–
7	–	–	–	–	–	–	–	–	–	–	–	–	–
6	–	F	F	–	–	–	–	–	–	–	–	–	–
5	–	F	F	–	–	–	–	–	–	J50C	–	–	–
4	–	F	–	–	–	–	–	–	–	–	C60J	–	–
3	–	–	–	–	–	–	–	–	–	–	–	J50C	F
2	–	–	–	–	–	–	–	–	–	–	–	–	J

Offsuit (row label, left side)

F	Fold
C	Call
J	Jam
–	Not 2-bet

(Pg. 272)

**Button: You make it 2 BB,
he jams (20 BB stacks)**

Suited

	A	K	Q	J	T	9	8	7	6	5	4	3	2
A	C	C	C	–	–	–	C	–	–	–	F	F	F
K	C	C	C	C	–	–	–	F	F	F	F	F	–
Q	–	F	–	C	C	–	–	F	F	F	–	–	–
J	–	–	–	–	C	F	–	–	–	F	F	–	–
T	–	–	–	F	–	F	–	–	–	–	–	–	–
9	C	–	–	–	–	C	–	–	–	–	–	–	–
8	–	–	–	–	–	–	C	–	–	–	–	–	–
7	–	–	–	–	–	–	–	–	–	–	–	–	–
6	–	F	F	–	–	–	–	–	–	–	–	–	–
5	–	F	F	–	–	–	–	–	–	C	–	–	–
4	–	F	–	–	–	–	–	–	–	–	C	–	–
3	–	–	–	–	–	–	–	–	–	–	–	C	F
2	–	–	–	–	–	–	–	–	–	–	–	–	C

Offsuit

F	Fold
C	Call
–	Not 2-bet

(Pg. 273) # Big Blind: He limps (20 BB stacks)

Suited

	A	K	Q	J	T	9	8	7	6	5	4	3	2
A	S	S	P70B	B	B	B	B	B	B80J	J	J	J	J
K	P70S	S	S	B	S80P	S*	s*	s*	K60s*	s*	p*60s*	p	K
Q	J	S*60B	P	S	P60S	S	S*	S*	S*	S*	S*	s*	s*80 p10 K10
J	J70B	J	J90B	S90B	J	S	S*	S*	s*	s*	s*	K	K
T	J70B	P	J90p*	J	B70S	J	S*	s*	s*80 K10 p*10	K90p*	K	K	K
9	J	p	s*	s*	K	S70P	J	K	K	K	K	K	K
8	J	K80p	s*	s*	K	K	B30 S30 P20 J20	K	K	K	K	K	K
7	J	K	s*	s*90K	K	K	K	J	K	K	K	K	K
6	b70p	K	s*	K60s*	K	K	K	K	J80S	K	K	K	K
5	J	K	s*	b50 K30 p20	K	K	K	K	K	S60J	K	K	K
4	J	K	p90s*	K90b	K	K	K	K	K	K	J90P	K	K
3	b80J	K	b60K	K	K	K	K	K	K	K	K	J	K
2	b	K	K	K	K	K	K	K	K	K	K	K	J

Offsuit

K	Check
S	Make a small (2 BB) raise, and be willing to get it all in
S*	Make a small (2 BB) 2-bet, then call up to a pot-sized 3-bet
s*	Make a small (2 BB) 2-bet, then call up to a 4 BB 3-bet
P	Make it 3 BB, and be willing to get it all in
p*	Make it 3 BB, then call up to a 6 BB 3-bet
p	Make it 3 BB, but fold to 3-bet
B	Make it 4 BB, and be willing to get it all in
b	Make it 4 BB, but fold to 3-bet
J	Jam

(Pg. 275)   ## Big Blind: He makes it 2 BB (20 BB stacks)

Suited

	A	K	Q	J	T	9	8	7	6	5	4	3	2
A	P90S	P	P	J90P	J90P	P70J	J	P90J	J	J	J	J	J
K	P	P70S	C	C	C	C	C	C	C	C	C	C	C
Q	P80J	C	J70P	C	C	C	C	C	C	C	C	C	C
J	J	C90J	C90J	J	J	C80s	C	C	C	C	C	C	C
T	J	C	C	J	J	J	C	C	C	C	C	C	C
9	J70P	C	C	C	J50C	J	C90J	C	C	C	C	C	C
8	J	C	C	C	C	C	J	C	C	C	C	C	C
7	P80J	C	C	C	C	C	C	J70S	C	C	C	C	C
6	J50 p40 s10	C	C	C	C	C	C	C	C	C	C	C	C
5	J	C	C	C	C	C	C	C	C	C	C	C	C
4	J	C	C	C	C	C	C	C	C	C	C90J	C	C
3	J90p	C	C	C	C90p	C	C	C	C	C	C	p50 C20 s20 J10	C
2	p60J	C	C	C	C70p	C90p	C	C	C	C	C	C	p70C

Offsuit

C	Call
P	Make a pot-sized 3-bet, and be willing to go all in
p	Make a pot-sized 3-bet, but fold to 4-bet
S	Make a small (0.5x pot) 3-bet, and be willing to go all in
s	Make a small (0.5x pot) 3-bet, but fold to 4-bet
J	Jam

(Pg. 276)   **Big Blind: He makes it 2.5 BB (20 BB stacks)**

Suited

Offsuit	A	K	Q	J	T	9	8	7	6	5	4	3	2
A	J	J	J	J	J	J	J	J	J	J	J	J	J
K	J	J	C	C90J	C	C	C	C	C	C	C	C	C
Q	J	C	J	C50J	J	C	C	C	C	C	C	C	C
J	J	C90J	J	J	J	J60C	C	C	C	C	C	C	C
T	J	C	J	J	J	J	J60C	C	C	C	C	C	C
9	J	C	C	C	J60C	J	J	C	C	C	C	C	C
8	J80C	C	C	C	C	F90C	J	C	C	C	C	F90C	F
7	J70C	C	C70F	C	C70F	F90C	F	J	C	C	C	C	F
6	J80C	C90F	C	F90C	F	F	F	F	J	C	C	C	C
5	J	F80C	F60C	F70C	F	F	F	F	C	J90C	C	C	C
4	J	F	F	F	F	F	F	F	F	C	J90C	C	C
3	J	F	F	F	F	F	F	F	F	F	F	J50C	C
2	J	F	F	F	F	F	F	F	F	F	F	F	C70J

F	Fold
C	Call
J	Jam

(Pg. 277)   ## Big Blind: He makes it 3 BB (20 BB stacks)

Suited

	A	K	Q	J	T	9	8	7	6	5	4	3	2
A	J	J	J	J	J	J	J	J	J	J	J	J	J
K	J	J	C	J	C	C	C	C	C	C	C	C	C
Q	J	C	J	C	J	C	C	C	C	C	C	C	C
J	J	J	J90C	J	J	C	C	C	C	C	C	C	C
T	J	C	J80C	J80C	J	J	C	C	C	C	C	C	F
9	J	C	C	C	J60C	J	C	C	C	C	C	C	F
8	J	C	C90F	C	C	F	J	C	C	C	C70F	F	F
7	C	C	F70C	C90F	F	F	F	J	C	C	C	F	F
6	C	F	F	F	F	F	F	F	J	C	C	C	F
5	J	F	F	F	F	F	F	F	F	J	C	C	F
4	J	F	F	F	F	F	F	F	F	F	J	C	F
3	J	F	F	F	F	F	F	F	F	F	F	J	F
2	J80F	F	F	F	F	F	F	F	F	F	F	F	J

Offsuit (row axis label)

F	Fold
C	Call
J	Jam

(Pg. 278)   **Big Blind: He open jams (20 BB stacks)**

Suited

	A	K	Q	J	T	9	8	7	6	5	4	3	2
A	C	C	C	C	C	C	C	C	C	C	C	C	F
K	C	C	C	C	C	F	F	F	F	F	F	F	F
Q	C	C	C	C	C	F	F	F	F	F	F	F	F
J	C	C	F50C	C	C	F70C	F80C	F	F	F	F	F	F
T	C	F60C	C70F	F60C	C	C	C90F	F	F	F	F	F	F
9	C	F	F	F	F	C	F70C	F	F	F	F	F	F
8	C	F	F	F	F	F	C	C70F	F	F	F	F	F
7	F50C	F	F	F	F	F	F	C	F60C	F	F	F	F
6	F	F	F	F	F	F	F	F	C	F	F	F	F
5	F	F	F	F	F	F	F	F	F	C	F	F	F
4	F	F	F	F	F	F	F	F	F	F	C	F	F
3	F	F	F	F	F	F	F	F	F	F	F	C	F
2	F	F	F	F	F	F	F	F	F	F	F	F	C

Offsuit (row labels)

F	Fold
C	Call

(Pg. 279)

Button's Inital Strategy (15 BB stacks)

Suited (columns) / **Offsuit** (rows)

	A	K	Q	J	T	9	8	7	6	5	4	3	2
A	C	C70S	C	C	C	C	C	C	C	C	C	C	C
K	C	C50S	S	C	C	C	J	J	C80S	C	C	C	C
Q	J	C	C	C90S	C90S	S40 C40 J20	C70S	C	S	C	C	C	C
J	J	J	C	C	C90S	J	C80J	C	C	C80S	C	C	C
T	J80C	C90J	C70J	C90S	C	J	J	C	C	C	C	C	C
9	J	C80S	C	C	C	C90S	J	J	C	C	C	C	C
8	C	C	C	C	C	C	C	J	J	C	C	C	C
7	C	S90C	C	C	C	C	C	C90S	J	J	C	C	C
6	J	C	C70S	C	C	C	C	C	C80S	J	C70J	C90F	F
5	J	C	C	C	C	C	C	C	C	C	J	C	F
4	J	C	C	C	C	C	F	F	F	F	C	C	F
3	C60J	C	C	C	C	C	F	F	F	F	F	J90C	F
2	C	C	C	C	C	C	F	F	F	F	F	F	J

F	Fold
C	Call
S	Make a small (2BB) raise, then use a later table for follow-ups
J	Jam

(Pg. 280) Button: You limp, he makes it 2 BB (15 BB stacks)

Suited

	A	K	Q	J	T	9	8	7	6	5	4	3	2
A	P	P	P	P80J	J70P	P	P	C80P	P	P	P	P	P
K	P	P	–	C70P	P	P	–	–	C	C	C	C	C
Q	–	C	P	C	P90C	C	C	C	–	C	C	C	C
J	–	–	C90J	P	P60J	–	C	C	C	C	C	C	C60p
T	J	P	C	C90p	P	–	–	p50C	C60p	p60C	C	C	p80C
9	–	C50p	C	C	C	P	–	–	C	C	C	C	C
8	P	C	C	C	C	C	C	–	–	C	C	C	C
7	P	C	C	C	C	C	C	C	–	–	C	C	C
6	–	C	C	C	C	C	C	C	C	–	C	C	–
5	–	C	C	C	C	C	C	C	C	C	–	C	–
4	–	C	C	C	C	C	–	–	–	–	C60p	C	–
3	J	C	C	C	C80p	C	–	–	–	–	–	p	–
2	J70p	C	C	C90p	p	C90F	–	–	–	–	–	–	–

*(Left axis label: **Offsuit**)*

F	Fold
C	Call
P	Make a pot-sized raise, and be willing to get it all in
p	Make a pot-sized raise, but fold to a re-raise
J	Jam
–	Not limped

(Pg. 281) Button: You limp, he makes it 2.5 BB (15 BB stacks)

Suited

	A	K	Q	J	T	9	8	7	6	5	4	3	2
A	S90J	C60S	C80S	J90S	J70S	S60 C20 J20	C80S	C	C	C	C	C	C90S
K	S60J	S80J	–	C	C	C	–	–	C	C	C	C	C
Q	–	C	J	C	S70J	C50 J40 S10	C60 J20 S20	C60 J20 S20	–	C90J	F	J40 F30 C20 S10	J50 C20 F20 S10
J	–	–	C70 J20 S10	J	C80 S10 J10	–	C	C	F	C80F	F	F	F
T	J	C	C	C	S60J	–	–	C50 J30 S20	F60 C20 J20	F	F	F	F
9	–	C	C	C90F	C	S80J	–	–	C90J	C80F	F	F	F
8	J60S	C	C70F	F80C	F	C	C50 S40 J10	–	–	C80J	F	F	F
7	C60 J30 S10	C	F90C	F	F	F	C	C70 S20 J10	–	–	F	F	F
6	–	C	F90C	F	F	F	F	C80F	C90S	–	F	F	–
5	–	C	F80C	F	F	F	F	F	C50F	C70 S20 J10	–	J50 S40 C10	–
4	–	C	F	F	F	F	–	–	–	–	C	F	–
3	J40 C40 S20	C70F	F	F	F	F	–	–	–	–	–	J80S	–
2	J60 S30 C10	F60C	F	F	F	F	–	–	–	–	–	–	–

Offsuit (row label, left side)

F	Fold	
C	Call	
S	Make a small (0.5x pot) raise, and be willing to get it all in	
s	Make a small (0.5x pot) raise, but fold to a re-raise	
J	Jam	
–	Not limped	

(Pg. 282)   Button: You limp, he makes it 3 BB (15 BB stacks)

Suited

	A	K	Q	J	T	9	8	7	6	5	4	3	2
A	J	J	J	J	J	J	J	C90J	C	C	C	C	C
K	J	J	–	C60J	C	C	–	–	C	C	C	C	C90F
Q	–	C	J	C	J	C80J	C90J	C	–	C60F	F	F	F
J	–	–	J70C	J	J70C	–	J80C	F80C	F	F	F	F	F
T	J	C	C90J	C	J	–	–	C50 F40 J10	F	F	F	F	F
9	–	C	C90F	F	F60C	J	–	–	F	F	F	F	F
8	J	C	F	F	F	F70C	J	–	–	F	F	F	F
7	J90C	C	F	F	F	F	F	J	–	–	F	F	F
6	–	C	F	F	F	F	F	F	C60J	–	F	F	–
5	–	C70F	F	F	F	F	F	F	F	J90C	–	F	–
4	–	F	F	F	F	F	–	–	–	–	J70C	F	–
3	J	F	F	F	F	F	–	–	–	–	–	J	–
2	J80C	F	F	F	F	F	–	–	–	–	–	–	–

Offsuit (row labels)

F	Fold
C	Call
J	Jam
–	Not limped

(Pg. 283)   Button: You limp, he jams (15 BB stacks)

Suited

	A	K	Q	J	T	9	8	7	6	5	4	3	2
A	C	C	C	C	C	C	C	C	C	C	C	C	F80C
K	C	C	-	C	C	C	-	-	F	F	F	F	F
Q	-	C	C	C	C	C	F	F	-	F	F	F	F
J	-	-	C	C	C	-	F	F	F	F	F	F	F
T	C	C	C	F	C	-	-	F	F	F	F	F	F
9	-	F	F	F	F	C	-	-	F	F	F	F	F
8	C	F	F	F	F	F	C	-	-	F	F	F	F
7	C	F	F	F	F	F	F	C	-	-	F	F	F
6	-	F	F	F	F	F	F	F	C	-	F	F	-
5	-	F	F	F	F	F	F	F	F	C	-	F	-
4	-	F	F	F	F	F	-	-	-	-	C	F	-
3	F	F	F	F	F	F	-	-	-	-	-	C	-
2	F	F	F	F	F	F	-	-	-	-	-	-	-

*(Row labels A–2 along the left are marked **Offsuit**.)*

F	Fold
C	Call
−	Not limped

(Pg. 284)

Button: You make it 2 BB,
he makes it 4 BB (15 BB stacks)

Suited

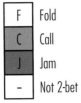

Offsuit	A	K	Q	J	T	9	8	7	6	5	4	3	2
A	–	J	–	–	–	–	–	–	–	–	–	–	–
K	–	J60C	C	–	–	–	–	–	C	–	–	–	–
Q	–	–	–	C	C	C50J	C	–	C70 F20 J10	–	–	–	–
J	–	–	–	–	C	–	–	–	–	–	–	–	–
T	–	–	–	–	–	–	–	–	–	–	–	–	–
9	–	C	–	–	–	J	–	–	–	–	–	–	–
8	–	–	–	–	–	–	–	–	–	–	–	–	–
7	–	–	–	–	–	–	–	C50J	–	–	–	–	–
6	–	–	–	–	–	–	–	–	C90J	–	–	–	–
5	–	–	–	–	–	–	–	–	–	–	–	–	–
4	–	–	–	–	–	–	–	–	–	–	–	–	–
3	–	–	–	–	–	–	–	–	–	–	–	–	–
2	–	–	–	–	–	–	–	–	–	–	–	–	–

F	Fold
C	Call
J	Jam
–	Not 2-bet

(Pg. 285)

Button: You make it 2 BB, he makes it 6 BB (15 BB stacks)

Suited

Offsuit \ Suited	A	K	Q	J	T	9	8	7	6	5	4	3	2
A	–	J	–	–	–	–	–	–	–	–	–	–	–
K	–	J90C	C	–	–	–	–	–	C	–	–	–	–
Q	–	–	–	C	C80J	C60J	J70C	–	F	–	–	–	–
J	–	–	–	–	C90J	–	–	–	–	–	–	–	–
T	–	–	–	–	–	–	–	–	–	–	–	–	–
9	–	C70F	–	–	–	C90J	–	–	–	–	–	–	–
8	–	–	–	–	–	–	–	–	–	–	–	–	–
7	–	–	–	–	–	–	–	C60J	–	–	–	–	–
6	–	–	–	–	–	–	–	–	C80J	–	–	–	–
5	–	–	–	–	–	–	–	–	–	–	–	–	–
4	–	–	–	–	–	–	–	–	–	–	–	–	–
3	–	–	–	–	–	–	–	–	–	–	–	–	–
2	–	–	–	–	–	–	–	–	–	–	–	–	–

Key	
F	Fold
C	Call
J	Jam
–	Not 2-bet

(Pg. 286) Button: You make it 2 BB, he jams (15 BB stacks)

Suited

	A	K	Q	J	T	9	8	7	6	5	4	3	2
A	–	C	–	–	–	–	–	–	–	–	–	–	–
K	–	C	C	–	–	–	–	–	F	–	–	–	–
Q	–	–	–	C	C	C	F	–	F	–	–	–	–
J	–	–	–	–	C	–	–	–	–	–	–	–	–
T	–	–	–	–	–	–	–	–	–	–	–	–	–
9	–	F	–	–	–	C	–	–	–	–	–	–	–
8	–	–	–	–	–	–	–	–	–	–	–	–	–
7	–	–	–	–	–	–	–	C	–	–	–	–	–
6	–	–	–	–	–	–	–	–	C	–	–	–	–
5	–	–	–	–	–	–	–	–	–	–	–	–	–
4	–	–	–	–	–	–	–	–	–	–	–	–	–
3	–	–	–	–	–	–	–	–	–	–	–	–	–
2	–	–	–	–	–	–	–	–	–	–	–	–	–

Offsuit

F	Fold
C	Call
–	Not 2-bet

(Pg. 287)   **Big Blind: He limps (15 BB stacks)**
Suited

	A	K	Q	J	T	9	8	7	6	5	4	3	2
A	S	S	J60B	B	B60J	B	J70B	J	J	J	J	J	J
K	P60B	S	S	P60 B30 S10	S	S	s*	S*	S*	S*	s*	s*90p*	J90K
Q	J	S	S70P	S	S	S	S	s*	S	S*	s*	s*	K
J	J	B70J	J	S	S	S	S*	s*	s*	K90s*	K	K	K
T	J	B80P	J50 B40 P10	J	S80P	J	K80J	J70K	K90J	K	K	K	K
9	J90B	K90p*	s*	J90s*	J	S80 P10 B10	J	J90K	J70K	K	K	K	K
8	J	K	s*	s*90K	K	K90J	B	J	K90J	K	K	K	K
7	J	s*80K	s*	s*90K	K	K	K	K80B	J	K	K	K	K
6	J	s*90K	s*	K70 b20 p10	K	K	K	b70 K20 J10	J60B	K	K	K	K
5	J	s*90K	s*	K	K	K	K	K	K	J	K	K	K
4	J	p80 K10 b10	K70 b20 p10	K	K	K	K	K	K	K	J	K	K
3	J	K60b	K90b	K	K	K	K	K	K	K	K	J	K
2	J	b80K	K80b	K	K	K	K	K	K	K	K	K	J

Offsuit *(row labels, left margin)*

K	Check
S	Make a small (2 BB) raise, and be willing to get it all in
S*	Make a small (2 BB) 2-bet, then call up to a pot-sized 3-bet
s*	Make a small (2 BB) 2-bet, then call up to a 4 BB 3-bet
P	Make it 3 BB, and be willing to get it all in
p*	Make it 3 BB, then call up to a 6 BB 3-bet
p	Make it 3BB, but fold to 3-bet
B	Make it 4 BB, and be willing to get it all in
b	Make it 4 BB, but fold to 3-bet
J	Jam

(Pg. 289) **Big Blind: He makes it 2 BB (15 BB stacks)**

Suited

	A	K	Q	J	T	9	8	7	6	5	4	3	2
A	S70P	P	J	J	J	J	J	J	J90P	J	J	J	J
K	J80P	S	C	S	S	C	C	C	C	C	C90J	C60 J20 s20	C40 s30 J30
Q	J	C70S	J50P	C	S70P	C	C	C	C	C	C	C	C
J	J	S	J60 C20 s10 P10	P60J	J	C	C	C	C	C	C	C	C
T	J	S70C	C70s	J90p	P50 J40 S10	J	C	C	C	C	C	C	C
9	J90P	C	C	C	C70 J20 s10	S60J	J	C	C	C	C	C	C
8	J	C	C	C	C	J40 C30 s30	J	C80J	C	C	C	C	C
7	J	C	C	C	C	C	C	J80S	C	C	C	C	C
6	J80P	C	C	F	F	C	C	C	C50 J30 P10 S10	C	C	C	C
5	J	C	C	C80F	F	C	C	C	C	J80P	C	C	C
4	J	C	C	F50 C40 p10	C50 p30 F20	F	C	F80C	C	C	J90P	C	C
3	J	C90s	C50F	F	F	F	F	F	F	C	C	J	C
2	J	C50 s30 p20	F90C	F	F	F	F	F	F	F	F80C	F	J90S

Offsuit

F	Fold
C	Call
S	Make a small (0.5x pot) 3-bet, and be willing to go all in
s	Make a small (0.5x pot) 3-bet, but fold to 4-bet
p	Make a pot-sized 3-bet, and be willing to go all in
p	Make a pot-sized 3-bet, but fold to 4-bet
J	Jam

(Pg. 290) **Big Blind: He makes it 2.5 BB (15 BB stacks)**

Suited

Offsuit \	A	K	Q	J	T	9	8	7	6	5	4	3	2
A	J	J	J	J	J	J	J	J	J	J	J	J	J
K	J	J	C90S	J	J80 S10 C10	C	C	C	C	C	C	C	C
Q	J	J	J	J	J	C	C	C	C	C	C	C	C
J	J	J	J	J	J	C80 S10 J10	C	C	C	C	C	C	C
T	J	J80C	J	J90C	J	J	C80J	C90J	C	C	C	C	C
9	J	C	C	C	C90J	J	J90C	C90J	C	C	C	C	C
8	J	C	C	C	C	F90C	J	J90C	C	C	C	F	F
7	J	C	F	F	F90C	C	F	J	J90C	C	C	C	F
6	J	C	F90C	F	F	F	F	F90J	J	C	C	C	C
5	J	C90F	F	F	F	F	F	F	F80C	J	C	C	C
4	J	C90F	F	F	F	F	F	F	F	F	J	C	C
3	J	C90F	F	F	F	F	F	F	F	F	F	J	C
2	J	C80F	F	F	F	F	F	F	F	F	F	F	J

F	Fold
C	Call
S	Make a small (0.5x pot) 3-bet, and be willing to go all in
J	Jam

(Pg. 291)   ## Big Blind: He makes it 3 BB (15 BB stacks)

Suited

	A	K	Q	J	T	9	8	7	6	5	4	3	2
A	J	J	J	J	J	J	J	J	J	J	J	J	J
K	J	J	C90J	J	C90J	C	C	C	C90J	C	C90J	C	C
Q	J	J80C	J	J	J	C90J	C	C	C	C	C	C	C
J	J	J	J	J	J	C90J	C	C	C	C	C	C	F
T	J	C	J	J90C	J	J90C	C	C	C	C	C	C	F
9	J	C	C	C	C	J	C	C	C	C	F	F	F
8	J	C	F	F	F	F	J	C	C	C	F	F	F
7	J	F	F	F	F	F	F	J	C	C	F	F	F
6	J	C	F	F	F	F	F	F	J	C	C	C	F
5	J	F80C	F	F	F	F	F	F	F	J	C	C	C
4	J	F	F	F	F	F	F	F	F	F	J	C	C
3	J	F	F	F	F	F	F	F	F	F	F	J	F
2	J	F	F	F	F	F	F	F	F	F	F	F	J

Offsuit (row axis label)

F	Fold
C	Call
J	Jam

(Pg. 292)   **Big Blind: He open jams (15 BB stacks)**

Suited

	A	K	Q	J	T	9	8	7	6	5	4	3	2
A	C	C	C	C	C	C	C	C	C	C	C	C	C
K	C	C	C	C	C	C	C	C	F	F	F	F	F
Q	C	C	C	C	C	C	C	F	F	F	F	F	F
J	C	C	C80F	C	C	C	F70C	F	F	F	F	F	F
T	C	C	C70F	C50F	C	C	F60C	F	F	F	F	F	F
9	C	F	F	F	F	C	F	F	F	F	F	F	F
8	C	F	F	F	F	F	C	F	F	F	F	F	F
7	C	F	F	F	F	F	F	C	F	F	F	F	F
6	C	F	F	F	F	F	F	F	C	F	F	F	F
5	C	F	F	F	F	F	F	F	F	C	F	F	F
4	F60C	F	F	F	F	F	F	F	F	F	C	F	F
3	F	F	F	F	F	F	F	F	F	F	F	C	F
2	F	F	F	F	F	F	F	F	F	F	F	F	C

Offsuit (row axis)

| F | Fold |
| C | Call |

About Huntington Press

Huntington Press is a specialty publisher of Las Vegas- and gambling-related books and periodicals, including the award-winning consumer newsletter, *Anthony Curtis' Las Vegas Advisor*.

Huntington Press
3665 Procyon Street
Las Vegas, Nevada 89103

Find more world-class poker products at ShopLVA.com.
Find more poker news and discussion at LVAPoker.com.